SEASONS IN HELL

SEASONS IN HELL

With Billy Martin, Whitey Herzog and
"The Worst Baseball Teams in History"—
The 1973–1975 Texas Rangers

MIKE SHROPSHIRE

Donald I. Fine Books
New York

DONALD I. FINE BOOKS
Published by the Penguin Group
Penguin Books USA Inc., 375 Hudson Street,
New York, New York 10014, U.S.A.
Penguin Books Ltd, 27 Wrights Lane,
London W8 5TZ, England
Penguin Books Australia Ltd, Ringwood,
Victoria, Australia
Penguin Books Canada Ltd, 10 Alcorn Avenue,
Toronto, Ontario, Canada M4V 3B2
Penguin Books (N.Z.) Ltd, 182–190 Wairau Road,
Auckland 10, New Zealand

Penguin Books Ltd, Registered Offices:
Harmondsworth, Middlesex, England

Published in 1996 by Donald I. Fine Books
an imprint of Penguin Books USA Inc.

1 3 5 7 9 10 8 6 4 2

Library of Congress Cataloging-in-Publication Data
Shropshire, Mike.
Seasons in hell : with Billy Martin, Whitey Herzog,
and "the worst baseball teams in history," the
1973–76 Texas Rangers / Mike Shropshire.
    p.   cm.
Includes index.
ISBN 1-55611-495-8
1. Texas Rangers (Baseball team)—History.
2. Martin, Billy. 1928– . 3. Herzog, Whitey.
    I. Title.
GV875.T4S56   1996   96-6129
                                        CIP

All interior photos courtesy of Linda Kaye

This book is printed on acid-free paper.
∞
Printed in the United States of America

WHY THIS BOOK?

LIKE MANY, I watched Ken Burns' baseball documentary on PBS in the fall of 1994 and found it, forgive me, just a trifle sappy.

What qualifies me to offer that appraisal? For one thing, I doubt that Ken Burns ever experienced hours four and five of a cross-country charter with the Texas Rangers baseball team, when the back of that plane took on the carnival air of Field Day at Attica.

Nor, I suspect, did he devote perhaps 1,000 semester hours to face-to-face encounters with the two greatest baseball strategists of all time, Whitey Herzog and Billy Martin—lecture sessions that were fortified with the sustenance that comes from corn and barley.

For me, the most satisfying and worthwhile aspect of this experience was not the who and what, but the when. My exposure to the major leagues happened during that greatest of decades, the Seventies, when the nation was gripped by a mood of nothing in particular. There was that one crisis, when people in my part of the country slowed from 105 mph to 85, in the spirit of energy conservation. Other than that, no limits were imposed on one's key personal objectives.

I can happily report that I lived the Seventies like Audie Murphy lived the Forties and Fatty Arbuckle experienced the Twenties. That's what this book is about and I thought it important to write it now, before the film archives of my memory and mind incur the ravages of smoke damage and theft.

AUTHOR'S NOTE

MORE THAN A few people have commented that I appear to have what they call "total recall." Certainly, all of the twenty-plus-year-old events that are detailed in this book stand out as vivid personal recollections, although no extraordinary feats of memory were involved in that. I remember these experiences with the same crystal clarity that someone might remember being shot in the kneecap at Shiloh or having his luggage stolen on his honeymoon.

When it comes to the concept of total recall, nobody can compete with the powers of retention stored upon the microfilm reproductions of newspapers and periodicals on file at the Dallas and Fort Worth public libraries. Names and numbers in major-league box scores are never embellished by the rapid passage of time.

The large majority of facts and many of the word-for-word quotes appearing in this book were extracted from my actual daily accounts of the adventures of the Texas Rangers that appeared in the Fort Worth *Star-Telegram*.

Other material covering events not associated with the Rangers was extracted from wire-service stories and newspaper accounts. Additionally, quite a few of the scenarios recounted here, on and off the field, have been verified and fortified by recent interviews with many of the individuals depicted in the book.

Some passages of dialogue have been reproduced from several dozen pages of typewritten notes compiled at the time

(1973–1975), in the remote hope that I might someday sell them to anybody peculiar enough to want to write a book about the early days of the Texas Rangers baseball franchise.

Additionally, I want to offer thanks to my wife, Karen, for her ongoing encouragement and support. I can confirm that this book would not have been possible without her, in a very literal sense, because the project was entirely her idea.

—MIKE SHROPSHIRE
November 23, 1995

SEASONS IN HELL

CHAPTER

———

1

Pompano Stadium, ordained according to the billboard in the parking lot as the Spring Home of the Texas Rangers, could be identified as one of those architectural curiosities that sometimes evoke sonnets and elegies from the disillusioned ranks of American journalism.

Minor-league baseball parks, the old ones at least, inspire wistful reminiscences and an elusive kind of longing that gnaws into unexplored regions of the male psyche. The core of the thing involves a little boy's relationship with his father that can never again be restored . . . the Dad that we all knew and treasured before he decided to move in with his secretary.

Somebody even produced a book about various selected baseball fields, most of them ancient and abandoned but still standing, and called it *Green Cathedrals*.

My initial impression of Pompano Stadium, as I opened the chain-link gate for my first day on the job in the big leagues, was that there was nothing cathedral-like about the facility. It reminded me, if anything, of the Yello-Belly drag strip in Grand Prairie, Texas. This Pompano Stadium, which was in fact a stadium in the sense that Ponca City, Oklahoma, is a city, obviously had a past, but had not aged gracefully. The grandstand consisted of two sets of bleachers, covered by a corrugated metal roof that extended along both foul lines only as far as first and third bases. The pressbox perched on the top row consisted of a peculiar white frame structure that looked like the sort of place the Japanese would put prisoners of war if they misbehaved. Atop the pressbox on this particular morning was the nation's future. Three kids from the high school across the street were up there passing around a joint. The palm trees behind the leftfield fence were sort of bent over at mid-trunk, suffering from a mangy looking plant fungus that coated them. Adjacent to this was a smaller practice diamond that the ballplayers called Iwo Jima.

Of the perhaps 1,000 or so baseball fields like this one scattered throughout the land, Pompano Stadium absolutely had to stand out as the only one void of character and charm. Actually the stadium pretty fairly represented the town of Pompano Beach itself, a community that served as the wrong side of the tracks for both Fort Lauderdale just to the south and Deerfield Beach in the other direction.

Surveying the premises, I had to remind myself of what I was doing here. My job was to produce articles for the Fort Worth *Star-Telegram* and chronicle the spring training exploits of an American League baseball team, the Rangers. There had been a couple of reasons for accepting, with reluctance, this assignment, and those entailed first-rate travel accommodations to some of the finer urban venues of our land (I'd never been to Cleveland or Milwaukee, for instance). Also, I was to be fortified with a constant cash flow source from a generous expense account. And I was to receive baseball's off-season as an extended paid vacation.

In return, the lone requirement was simply to file some reasonably accurate accounts of the activities of this peculiar baseball team. As I approached Day One of spring training 1973, however, it became apparent that this task would not be so easy.

I'd already missed the first workout, having spent most of the morning at the American Express office on Atlantic Avenue, getting due reimbursement for $1,300 worth of traveler's checks that had somehow disappeared the night before. (I should note that, in those days, I was what is known in some quarters as a drinking man.)

Most of the players were already gone, along with most of my newspaper competition, so I headed down to the little lunchroom that was stuck at the end of the bleachers on the leftfield side. Inside was Bob Short, the fascinating character who owned the Rangers. I was relieved to see Short in there, because I desperately needed some good quotes from a key source for my world premiere article as the baseball writer for the *Star-Telegram*.

Short lived in Minneapolis, where he owned a trucking line and some hotels, and it was his proud distinction also to serve as Hubert Humphrey's bagman. His association with the Happy Warrior had been gratifying. While moonlighting as the national treasurer of the Democratic Party, Short had concocted a grand scheme in which he would buy the congenitally threadbare Washington Senators, wait a couple of years, then shift the franchise to some prosperous Sun Belt locale—it didn't matter where—and then sell the team at a substantial profit to some ego-crazed locals who were fair busting at the seams with ready cash.

Bob Short's plan was running perfectly according to schedule with the Senators relocated in North Texas, but on this particular morning in the Pompano Stadium lunchroom, his private universe was etched with concern. Short, a tall, stoop-shouldered man who favored pastel sports jackets, was addressing Captain Jack, a delightfully spry little character who couldn't have been a day under eighty-five. Captain Jack's job was to cater the free lunchroom for the ballplayers and assorted other people like me.

"Uh . . . Jack," Short was saying. "What happened to those frankfurters you had in here last year? These here . . . they're not the same."

"Well, Mr. Short, I have to order those out of a deli wholesaler down in Miami and it's a three-hour round trip. With the traffic and all I just didn't have time to get down there this morning."

Short nodded, then said, "Jack, you worthless old fart, I want you to get your ass down there and get those frankfurters . . . NOW!" Then Short marched out of the lunchroom, slammed the screen door and was gone.

Jack, a treasure of a human being endowed with a bottomless lagoon of wisdom that he mostly chose to keep to himself, gazed for a moment at the spot where Short had been standing, lit up a Newport menthol cigarette and said, "Cocksucker."

It occurred to me then that transcribing this vignette into my bright and breezy Ranger Notes column might prove challenging, so I ventured over to Whitey Herzog's office and dressing room next door in search of hard news.

Like me, Herzog was on his first day at work on a new job; in his case, as manager of the Texas Rangers. As farm director of the New York Mets, Herzog had produced the likes of Nolan Ryan and Tom Seaver. But that had been in the National League, and now Herzog was observing the talents of his Rangers personnel for the first time. I was eager to gather some of his first-day insight, but was less than happy to see David Fink already in his office.

Fink, who covered the Rangers for the Dallas *Times Herald,* employed an interviewing technique that was stylistically consistent with the good people who conduct audits for the IRS. He would peer over his horn-rimmed glasses in a practiced, prosecutorial manner and submit questions in tones that were etched with skepticism. "And I suppose you can provide receipts for these co-called business expenses? Ha!"

Herzog sat naked at his desk, stroking a cold, sixteen-ounce can of Busch Bavarian, smoking a cigar and gazing at David Fink with the sort of expression a man might muster after discovering that somebody had spray-painted "Eat Me" across the side of his new car.

Fink had his notebook open. "How about some first-day evaluations, Whitey . . . *ahem* . . . any surprises?"

Herzog leaned back, gazed at the ceiling, and finally said, "Yeah. I was surprised to see that Bill Madlock is black. Mostly, blacks don't go by Bill, you know. They call themselves Willie."

Fink, never known to his working associates as David or Dave or El Finko or the Finkster but always and simply as Fink, scribbled those comments into his notebook and waddled out, presumably to phone his paper with instructions to stop the presses.

That left me alone with Herzog, who gave me a more in-depth evaluation of the talent pool, beginning with the backbone of the franchise, the starting pitchers. "They didn't tell me that Mike Paul and Rich Hand were a couple of shitballers," Herzog offered cheerfully. "Or that Pete Broberg was a big cunt."

And, as I was leaving . . . "Oh. And I noticed that one of my outfielders looks kind of, uh, tentative out there, but he told me not to worry. He said his epilepsy medication makes him feel sluggish sometimes."

Understand that Herzog's immediate predecessor in this Rangers managerial assignment had been Ted Williams. Yes, *that* Ted Williams, the man often described by the most knowledgeable critics of the game as—even though modifiers like "arguably" and "many insist" are employed as preambles—the most talented hitter in the century-and-a-half-old history of the North American version of the sport. The immortal Teddy Ball Game had not, despite the rumors, been driven babbling into voluntary confinement at the nearest madhouse by the habitual flair of the Rangers for less than mediocre public display. More than anything, Williams had quit because of a personal malediction to the thermal excesses of the Texas summer. Now it was Whitey Herzog's turn in the barrel, and the early chapters of the initiation process had left the skipper on edge.

On the way out of Pompano Stadium, I recognized one of the new players, Bill McNulty, refining his game in the outfield. His golf game. McNulty was lining seven-iron shots over the fence

and into the mosquito-infested field of swamp grass that ad-
joined the stadium.

McNulty would be my first player interview. I knew nothing
about him, other than he had been traded over from the Oakland A's in the off-season. But like virtually every candidate for
the Texas Rangers roster, McNulty was in Pompano Beach for a
reason.

"Yeah, Oakland called me up from AAA at the end of the
season," said McNulty. "I got messed up on one of the flights
and spilled my drink all over [manager] Dick Williams. Not all
over him, actually. But some of it got on him . . . enough to
punch my ticket to Texas." McNulty laughed heartily.

Back at the team-and-media-housing compound, a glorified
flophouse known as the Surf Rider Resort, I initiated a ritual
that would be repeated countless times for the next four years.
First, I bought a six-pack of Löwenbräu (remember, this was no
Pabst Blue Ribbon expense account), and then I retreated to
my room to practice my craft. At the time, articles were composed on a portable standard Smith-Corona typewriter and
transmitted back to the paper on a Xerox telecopier, a device
more commonly known now as a fax.

Forty-five minutes later, half of the Löwenbräu was gone and
the paper in the typewriter remained blank. Back in Texas, the
Star-Telegram was about to be distributed to a quarter-million
households and there was an empty hole at the top of the front
page of the sports section.

I began to type. I wrote about Whitey Herzog and how he saw
some things in rookie Bill Madlock that made him stand out
from the crowd. I wrote that Whitey, after only a day, had already established a keen feel for the strengths and weaknesses
of his pitching staff. I wrote that slugging outfielder Bill Mc-
Nulty carried himself with the confidence and poise that came
from his experience with the reigning champion Oakland A's. I
wrote about three and a half pages of that crap and proceeded
directly to the Surf Rider's Banyan Room Lounge to celebrate

the completion of my first day in the big leagues. The Banyan poured the hard stuff until four A.M., and that morning a manager, three coaches, perhaps a dozen players and a handful of sober and cerebral professional sports journalists were there to shut it down.

In the immediate days ahead, I actually began researching the talent pool around the American League and from that attempted to produce some radical thesis leading to the astounding proposition that the Rangers might not finish last. What I learned was that virtually every team the Rangers would face that year in the American League employed some personnel that would either wind up in the Hall of Fame in Cooperstown or in the nearby outskirts.

Oakland had won the World Series the previous season, would win it again this season and the season after that. Why not, with the likes of Catfish Hunter, Blue Moon Odom, Reggie Jackson, Rollie Fingers, Vida Blue, Sal Bando and Joe Rudi?

The White Sox offered personalities such as slugging Dick Allen (formerly known as Richie when he was the home-run terror of the National League). Minnesota came to the table with Harmon Killebrew, Tony Oliva, Rod Carew and the best "young curve ball pitcher in the game" (according to Herzog), Bert Blyleven.

Kansas City seemed eager to show off the skills of rookie third baseman George Brett, and the California Angels had a pitcher about to experience the best year of his career—Nolan Ryan—who threw two no-hitters and struck out 383 batters in 1973.

The Baltimore Orioles would win the Eastern Division again, with Brooks Robinson, Jim Palmer, Dave McNally and company. Carl Yastrzemski and Carlton Fisk anchored the Red Sox. Al Kaline, Mickey Lolich and Bill Freehan were some of the names that adorned the Detroit roster. Even Cleveland, a team thought capable of perhaps challenging the Rangers in the loss column, offered names such as Gaylord Perry and Frank Robinson to attract paying fans through the turnstiles.

And the Rangers? Well, they had an infield candidate whose name now tragically eludes me who claimed to have been born with two spleens. As a teenager, he told me, he had appeared, appropriately, as a guest on "I've Got a Secret."

CHAPTER

▬

2

As A CONNOISSEUR of essentially unhistoric details of modern Americana, I would rate 1973 as a year of outstanding vintage. Vietnam was winding down and Watergate was heating up. The national attitude that the media now falsely associates with the era known as the Sixties did not reach fruition until the early and mid-Seventies. Look up the Class of 1968 in every high school or college annual and you'll see that all the boys have haircuts like Forrest Gump's.

The so-called hippie attitude was reaching its zenith in 1973 and, although the lens on my retrospective processes might be a trifle blurred, it seemed then that almost everyone tended to agree that life was too short and therefore should be enjoyed to the maximum extent. Not like the sober Nineties, when—because of the economy and AIDS—everybody's getting laid off and nobody's getting laid. Not like now, when wellness is next to godliness.

Plus, back in glorious 1973, a person could experience an active evening amid the neon on a twenty-dollar bill and there was no better place to attempt to accomplish that than in March along what they call the Sun Coast. The armored divisions from the college spring break set—a largely obnoxious group of children—were flocking down to South Florida in multitudes, but they were jamming the beaches down in Fort Lauderdale.

Pompano Beach, safely situated maybe six miles up the road, served as the domain of the Canuck. Mostly female, they arrived in droves, twice a week, in tour groups from Toronto and were headquartered right there in the good old Surf Rider Resort and getting blasted nightly in the Banyan Lounge. The Canucks were a hell of a lot more approachable than the stuffy Kappas and Thetas from places like Bowling Green, some of whom had not yet learned about the adverse effect that too much saturated fat in their diets was imposing upon the backs of their thighs.

Canucks, on the other hand, maintained more of an open-door policy and they were in Florida not so much to experience the sun and sand as they were to enjoy a reprieve from their Canadian boyfriends who, at least according to the Canucks, were as dreary as the weather back home.

Don't get me wrong. It was not my mission in Florida to go chasing after a bunch of nineteen-year-old blood technicians from Kitchener and Niagara Falls, but they were pleasant to talk to (at least until the evil specter of David Fink would arrive at the table, at which time the girls would shriek and disperse in wild panic).

Even more appalling than Fink was the entertainment in the Banyan, consisting of the amazing Wayne Carmichael, who performed one of those lounge acts that comedians are always lampooning on "Saturday Night Live." Wayne bore a rather striking resemblance to Mr. Joyboy, the undertaker in the late and lamented Terry Southern's *The Loved One*.

Carmichael despised the Texans, who were inclined to shout insults across the room while he was putting on his show. Sometimes I'd feel kind of sorry for Carmichael when that happened, but then he'd launch into his patently tortured and off-key rendition of "Tie a Yellow Ribbon Around the Old Oak Tree" and I would only feel sorry for myself. Wayne, I heard, quit the business after a Banyan patron finally couldn't take it any longer, snapped, and sprayed the old trooper with a fire extinguisher.

Other than that petty annoyance, I was rapidly coming to appreciate life as a baseball writer. After that first week, it seemed that I was fitting in nicely with the players and media.

And why not? I was not only the consummate professional, but witty and urbane and had a large grocery bag full of premium grade marijuana under my bed. I never indulged in the stuff personally but didn't see anything wrong with giving it away. Besides, the Texas legislature had just passed a law that essentially decriminalized possession of up to four ounces of goofy bush for white folks. Several candidates for the Rangers ball club were clearly elated when I presented them with that news.

Contrary to the general public assumption, though, the baseball players of that era couldn't really qualify as big dopers. The extent of their participation in the mind alteration league certainly ranked as feeble when compared to their brethren in the dignified sport of football, both college and pro. A well-known player for the Dallas Cowboys once told me that he and most of his teammates played every game of his senior season at a Southeastern Conference school loaded on LSD.

The drug of choice in baseball of the Seventies, other than staggering quantities of CC and Seven, was greenies, mild amphetamines that the players referred to as "ability pills."

But according to what I was hearing from Whitey Herzog, no miracle of the pharmacological sciences could produce an ability pill potent enough to propel this assembly of Rangers talent out of the basement in the American League West. "Here's a team that won 54 games last year and lost 100, and then, over the winter, Shortie [Bob Short] goes and trades off the only two decent pitchers on the team," Herzog claimed. "And for what? The Beeg Boy!"

The Beeg Boy of note was Rico Carty, the affable Rico Carty, whose bat had been every bit as lethal as Hank Aaron's in the Braves lineup. Emphasize the word *had*. The ravages of age had caught up with Carty rather prematurely, which made him all too typical of the cast that Herzog was assembling in Pompano.

Some of the players had a commendable past and some would have a future (except for the pitchers who had neither) but none of the players who would do battle for Herzog that season were experiencing what might be described as their natural prime.

The legs go first, they say, and in Carty's case, Herzog told me that the team doctor had said "he'd seen better knees on a camel." This was the man signed up to act as the power supply, the horse hired to pull the wagon of the Rangers out of the ditch. "When Rico runs from homeplate to first, you could time him with a sundial," said Herzog. He also voiced an additional concern. "I think the guy [Carty] must be practicing voodoo or something. Check out his eyes. Rico's crazier than a peach orchard sow. This team is two players away from being a contender—Sandy Koufax and Babe Ruth."

Herzog offered this keen assessment in the bar of the Yard Arm Restaurant, where he was consuming containers of scotch and soda at a pace that I could not begin to approach—me, the bronze medalist from the Mexico City games back when scotch drinking was an Olympic event. The skipper assured me that the Rangers had the potential to put a cruel new twist on the baseball concept of the Long Season.

After about ten days of "conditioning" and intrasquad games at Pompano Stadium, the Rangers finally embarked on their exhibition schedule. For someone in search of the narcotic ingredients that leave so many baseball enthusiasts hooked for life, Florida is where they should go. When the vast legion of baseball existentialists congregate to sing their anthems of rejoicing about the serene rhythms and mystic qualities of the game that they find so hypnotic, the exhibition season offers the ultimate theatre.

One can feel reasonably safe in the presumption that most major-league baseball players cannot be presented as paragon examples of culture and refinement after they've drained two quarts of Old Swamp Rat. But they are graceful creatures in that enchanted realm between the white lines of the ball field, performing some difficult feats of athleticism with a nonchalance and economy of motion that defies the accepted ordinances of physical kinetics. In these exhibition games, their skills are showcased in modest pavilions like the one at Pompano Beach, suitable for a county fair, and since the outcome of the game doesn't count, the competition unfolds with the competitive intensity of a sack race at an office picnic.

The mainstream regulars and stars of the league put in about three innings. Then they depart for the golf course, yielding the podium to youngsters who had demonstrated some unrefined potential last year with the Discouraging Word, South Dakota Sandblasters in the Class A Saltpeter League.

Even in such an informal framework, Herzog, who was not only a virtuoso in the fine art of spotting baseball talent but also the absence of same, was offering dire prognostications. In his judgment, the entire pitching staff was afflicted with some rare phobic dysfunction when it came to confronting the strike zone. "It's like they're afraid they might get the clap or something if they throw strikes," Herzog sputtered.

The only comforting aspect of this discouraging scenario was that while I might have to create new adjectives to adequately describe the Rangers' standards of performance, I would at least be equipped with suitable companionship to share the horrors of the ride.

The aforementioned Harold McKinney would cover the team for the morning edition of the Fort Worth *Star-Telegram,* and in the category of hedonist pursuit, this man would be unsurpassed. McKinney had curly blond hair that he wore halfway down his back and a Fu Manchu mustache and could have been reasonably cast in a motion picture depicting the life story of George Armstrong Custer.

McKinney was a major asset for my spring training situation. For every dollar of company money that I was to spend in Florida, Harold was spending three to five, meaning that I would be totally protected when it came time to submit the expense forms. Plus, in my immodest opinion, the stories that McKinney was sending back to Texas made my stuff look like, say, John Steinbeck. McKinney established his own rules of professional conduct and one of those was never to devote more than ten minutes or so to the composition of a news story on the topic of baseball. Dick Risenhoover, who did the radio play-by-play for the team, once suggested that Harold devote more effort to his trade. "Harold, if you wrote like you talked, you'd be the greatest sports writer of all time," Risenhoover said.

"Good writing," McKinney countered, "is too goddamned much trouble." He was right, of course. McKinney had enough trouble in his life as it was, involving turbulent simultaneous relationships with the various women he had stashed across the continent. Women, I can't figure why, were attracted to McKinney.

My most poignant image of Harold goes back to a football trip to Indiana. I encountered a scene in a hotel hallway in which McKinney was stretched out on the floor with his head in the lap of a woman who claimed to be Hoagy Carmichael's daughter. She was stroking McKinney's hair and consoling him because he claimed to have an upset stomach.

Another member of the writing crew, Randy Galloway from the Dallas *Morning News,* had spent most of his life in the suburb of Grand Prairie, home of an aircraft assembly plant and a community that has produced some of the nation's leading paint sniffers. Galloway's only quest in life that spring was to attain a permanent suntan, and for five weeks he dressed in only a tattered pair of cutoffs and some fungus-lined tennis shoes.

I told Galloway that was a sorry strategy and shabby way to treat any human being. Later that summer, I would apologize to Galloway for having made those remarks.

Even though I once had to restrain Harold McKinney from attacking Galloway with a knife because he was sick of hearing "Dead Skunk in the Middle of the Road" on Randy's car stereo, this group of writers was largely compatible.

The big story of spring training that year didn't involve the

Rangers, naturally, but the Yankees, who were training in Fort Lauderdale. Two Yankees pitchers, Fritz Peterson and Mike Kekich, actually conducted a press conference to announce a trade. They were trading wives—and kids. It was entirely fitting that both Peterson and Kekich would eventually find their way onto the Rangers' roster, because the wife-swapping stunt was obviously not conducive to longevity on a team that wears pinstriped uniforms.

So when the Rangers played the Yankees in an exhibition game down at their lavish facility in Fort Lauderdale (unlike Pompano, the palm trees at the Yankees' park seemed free of disease), the Texas press corps condescended to attend the game.

Rather than exchange unpleasantries with the newspaper geeks who covered the Yankees, we climbed onto the roof of the pressbox so that Galloway could "absorb some rays." In the third inning, a security guard appeared on the rooftop. He must have presumed from the attire and demeanor of the trio lounging there that they could not possibly be representing the esteemed fourth estate but had more probably arrived in Fort Lauderdale for spring break via freight train some years earlier and chosen to stay on.

"Listen, the city commissioner says you guys can't stay here. You'll have to leave," said the security guy. He was trying to be polite. Galloway (who was even then preparing himself for his future as the top-rated radio talk show host in Texas) was deeply disturbed by the mandate to vacate the rooftop. "Well, I have a message for the city commissioner. Can you deliver it for me?" said Galloway.

"What's that?"

"Tell the city commissioner that he can kiss my dick."

After the game, we were confronted by the commissioner himself. "I got your message," he told Galloway. "I checked and found out that you guys are who you claim to be. But you don't look like any sportswriters I've ever seen before."

Harold McKinney, now blissful from the contents of the bag beneath my bed back at the Surf Rider, looked at the commissioner and said, "Sir, that's the finest compliment I've received in my life."

CHAPTER

———

3

IT IS WITH some regret that I must report that based upon the thoughts, philosophies and deeds of those associated with the Texas Rangers baseball organization, the essential points of the current militant feminist manifesto can be deemed correct.

A spring training conversation with Harold McKinney in 1973 illustrates this point. McKinney was perplexed. Separated from his wife, McKinney had been seeing, so to speak, a woman in Fort Worth whom he had promised to fly to Florida for a week's holiday.

Harold was also enjoying cordial interchange with a trio of Canucks named, coincidentally, Debbie, Debbie and Debbie. He was having serious second thoughts about making good on his invitation to bring the woman in Fort Worth—call her Debbie, too—to Pompano.

"She's been calling twice a day, wanting to know where in the hell the plane ticket is," McKinney said. "I think I'll just tell her that I'm working too hard down here and that she can't come." He rationalized this decision with the announcement that "she [the Fort Worth friend] is so screwed up she's been taking shock treatments for depression. She says the treatments are supposed to erase all this traumatic stuff from her brain. So now they've zapped her about ten times and she still remembers all the bad stuff but can't remember her own name. The problem with getting laid these days is that you have to deal with all those goddamn women."

He was telling this saga not only to me but also to two elderly French Canadian couples who were sharing our table at a Benihana restaurant on Sunrise Boulevard and the Intracoastal Canal in Fort Lauderdale. They listened to Harold rave on, nodding sympathetically while obviously making a mental note that, henceforth, the Benihana would be a place to avoid.

McKinney here defined the root cause of the Great American Neurosis. Men, at least most of the ones under the age of fifty, have but one purpose in mind when it comes to establishing relationships with the other gender. Women like to articulate their hopes, fears, frustrations, inner joys and deeper aspirations, and the men simply don't care. Oh, there does exist a limited percentage who might be attentive to some aspect of the female persona other than the size of her tits. The ones in this category generally also have a major crush on Julio Iglesias.

The hormone testosterone sustains man's obsession with all things sociopathic. Testosterone not only compels men to abuse women, emotionally and otherwise, but also serves as the diabolical ingredient that causes the male species to drive recklessly, join patriot militia clans, talk baseball and shoot deer.

Card-carrying members of the Rangers American League fraternity would naturally dabble in these types of pursuits. Happily, they were so preoccupied with the "talking baseball" category that not much time was available for the other stuff that often causes bloodshed.

Whitey Herzog was sure talking a lot of baseball during the course of that lovely azure South Florida spring of 1973, but not with a great deal of relish. Of all the public personalities that I have encountered during a "career" in journalism, I never dealt with anybody who was as unafraid of telling the truth as Whitey Herzog.

The whole purpose of spring training, other than to get the players' livers in shape for the extended season to come, traditionally has been to inflate the media with artificially optimistic hype and outrageous propaganda regarding the prospects of the hometown team. "Now that old Spud Jones had that cataract surgery, I wouldn't be surprised if he hit .450." That's the kind of spring training rhetoric that sells those season ticket packages back home. Under more conventional circumstances, Herzog might have been willing to do that. But this season he apparently felt that it was his obligation as a responsible citizen to alert the public back in North Texas that something dreadful was about to happen. Poor Whitey was trying to cry out a warning, like somebody shouting to the captain of the Hindenburg to turn on the "No Smoking" sign.

As a player, Whitey experienced considerable exposure to teams of the Rangers' ilk. He'd spent time with the old Kansas City A's, a team that consistently lingered near the rear of the pack. It was with KC that Herzog proudly claimed to be "the first and only player to hit into an all-Cuban triple play—Camilo Pascual to Jose Valdivelso to Julio Becquer." Herzog additionally served time with the original Washington Senators. But he had also briefly savored the bouquet of life as a utility player with the New York Yankees—the Yankees of Casey Stengel's empire of gold. Herzog, the most accomplished storyteller that I ever encountered in the entire spectrum of sport and second only to John Forsythe in all categories of public life, offered a ceaseless barrage of tales from another time. Typical was his recollection of a road trip with the Yankees when general manager George Weiss got on an elevator and encountered relief pitcher Ryne Duren, a lover of the grape, barely able to stand. According to Herzog, Weiss stiffened and said, "Drunk again." To which Duren grinned a crooked grin, slapped Weiss on the back and said, "Oh yeah? Me too."

Sadly for Whitey, the thrilling days of yesterday had been replaced by the unfunnier realities of the day. His first baseman, Mike Epstein, hit a grand-slam homerun in an exhibition game against the Orioles. Herzog's response: "That'll look great in the box scores you guys send back to Texas. But tell the readers that in this rinky-dink little Pompano ballpark, the wind blows every lousy pop up over the rightfield fence. Back in Texas, that ball Epstein hit wouldn't have carried past the pitcher's mound.''

The manager's direst concerns involved the pitching staff and he offered these evaluations: The "ace" of the group, Dick Bosman, now in the twilight of a mediocre career, was capable of producing seven decent innings every other start. Of the remaining four, Pete Broberg and Don Stanhouse had good arms but didn't know how to pitch. The other two, Mike Paul and Rich Hand, knew how to pitch but had arms like worn-out rubber bands. Paul told me that he so loved the great American game "that when they finally run me out of the major leagues, I'll go pitch in the Mexican League." One year later, Paul did just that.

Herzog's everyday lineup included talent that might not have offered first-division potential. They were, however, entirely qualified to hold their own in conversations on topics like bass fishing and provide welcome company at cocktail parties of almost any social strata. The test of time would demonstrate over and over that the Rangers ballplayers were far more entertaining in person than they were on the field.

Epstein, the first baseman, had a World Series ring from the previous season but now agreed with Oakland's director of player personnel who had determined that his job skills were better suited to a team like the Rangers. Life in baseball, Epstein told me, was cluttered with too much "inconsequential bullshit" and he had devoted more of spring training to securing his pilot's license than attempting to regain his timing in the batting cage.

Even before the start of spring training, Herzog had said, "If Rich Billings is the starting catcher again, we're in deep trouble." When that evaluation was passed along to Billings, he simply nodded and said, "Whitey, obviously, has seen me play." But Whitey, obviously, had not seen the other candidates for that position play, and now Billings was again pencilled in as the starting catcher.

Third baseman Joe Lovitto came endowed with what all the scouts insist are the four essentials necessary for major-league stardom. Lovitto could run, throw, hit and hit with power. The problem was that while he could do all of these things, Lovitto seldom did. Lovitto told me of an encounter he'd had with Ted Williams the season before. "We were on the road somewhere and Ted called me into his hotel room," Lovitto said. "He told me that I had my head up my ass and that I was wasting my talent."

How, I inquired, had Lovitto responded to a critique like that from such a man as Ted Williams? Lovitto seemed astounded that I would even ask the question. "Well, what would you do?" he demanded. "I told him to go fuck himself and slammed the door in his face."

Meanwhile, the manager was gaining a sharper focus of what he anticipated from this season's team. "Defensively," said Herzog, a man of keen intuitions about the game, "these guys are really substandard, but with our pitching, it really doesn't matter."

Herzog had three players he did like. He correctly predicted that outfielder Jeff Burroughs and shortstop Toby Harrah would be future all-stars. And of Bill Madlock, the player Herzog was surprised to discover was black: "That kid can flat play. But he's not quite ready yet and I'm going to send him back to AAA because I don't want Madlock to pick up too many bad habits from the guys I'm going to keep." It was Bill Madlock's destiny to become a four-time batting champion of the National League. Madlock owes Herzog a round of drinks, at least, because almost all of the twenty-five players who did break camp in Rangers uniforms had hitched a ride on an express train to baseball's scrap heap.

How was it that those responsible for orchestrating the lyrics and melody of the franchise could produce such a blueprint for failure? Well, remember that this team until now had been the

Washington Senators, which for the preceding seven or eight decades had gone to war carrying the banner emblazoned: "Washington—First in War, First in Peace and Last in the American League."

Read the Rules of Baseball. It's right there in Article VI, Paragraph 14, etched in boilerplate. "Three strikes and you're out, four balls take your base and if the New York Yankees don't finish first and if the Washington Senators don't finish last in the American League, then call the attorney general because the fix is in."

This was the team that had been the topic of a hit Broadway musical, *Damn Yankees,* in which a fan sold his soul to the devil so the Senators could win a pennant. When Bob Short bought the team, he wasn't about to mortgage his hereafter for such a happening, but what he did do was sell off whatever marginal talent was available in order to pay the rent at Robert F. Kennedy Stadium.

Short was also amenable to any ploy that might sell tickets or, as he put it, "put butts in seats." That was why he authorized a trade that sent a couple of rookies to the Detroit Tigers for pitcher Denny McLain, who in 1968 had been the first (and the last) pitcher since Dizzy Dean to win thirty games in a season. By the time McLain joined the Senators, his arm was dead and gone and he would eventually wind up a convict in the federal pen. The two players that Short ceded in that trade, Ed Brinkman and Aurelio Rodriguez, acted as the cornerstones for an outstanding Tigers infield that remained intact for the next ten years. Such was the Texas Rangers legacy.

In a move that reflected his desperation, Herzog agreed to a player transaction that brought another outfielder, Alex Johnson, into the Rangers' nest. Since this was the same Alex Johnson who had led the American League in hitting two seasons earlier, one might wonder why a player with such reasonably up-to-date credentials might now be pressed into the ranks of the vagabonds and grifters who wore Rangers blue. The explanation was to be found in more recent events. Johnson had apparently agreed with Mike Epstein's equation of baseball with inconsequential bullshit to the extent that the latter entailed catching routine fly balls and running toward first base after hitting the ball. These had become chores that Alex Johnson, in his last days with the California Angels, had for unexplained reasons refused to perform. "I dunno," conceded Herzog. "A guy like that can poison a ball club. But how do you poison *this* club?"

According to reports from California, Alex Johnson also was not inclined to invite members of the media over to his house for sweet rolls and hot chocolate. That crossed my mind when, by accident, I encountered Johnson as he stepped out of a rental car around midnight at the Surf Rider. He had just hit town. Johnson struck me as having the torso of a rhinoceros and apparently the personality to match. I introduced myself and asked him what he thought about being traded to the Rangers.

"Work is work. It don't matter where," said Johnson, and then promptly concluded what would become the most extensive interview he would conduct in a season and half with the Rangers.

MARCH TURNED INTO April. Spring training was ending and I didn't want to leave. Neither, probably, did Whitey Herzog or anybody else associated with the club except Harold McKinney. He'd plowed his rental car into a parked car on the lot in front of the Banyan Room and vaguely recalled having then abandoned the scene. For days, the car he'd clobbered remained there in the lot with its left side caved in. "I wish they'd tow the goddamn thing. It makes me nervous every time I look at it," said McKinney, apprehensive that a witness might still emerge and that he would be led off in chains. McKinney was also marginally concerned about the expense report he would eventually file back at the paper, highlighted by a bar tab at the Banyan that exceeded three grand.

With the Rangers poised to load the wagons and roll back to Texas, I made my last visit to the Banyan for a final pop or two.

The sign outside said "Happy Hour" but, inside, two players were staging a wake. Herzog had posted his final roster and Bill McNulty, the outfielder who had been sent over for soiling his manager's suit in Oakland, and a right-handed candidate for the bullpen weren't on it. "I guess," reasoned McNulty, "that when you've been released by the Rangers, that's God's way of telling you to look into a new career field. But goddamn, ball-players live this dream of making the big league. Most of them get weeded out in Class A and they figure what the hell and go on with whatever it was they were going to do in the first place. But when you make it to the fringes of the big leagues, close enough to taste it . . . I guess I'll always wonder what might have happened if I'd had a chance to take that last step."

Amid the deafening clatter of icecubes, the pitcher was intro-spective. "I have a wife back in Denver who'll be more disap-pointed over this than I am," Henninger said, and I figured he was going to reach in his billfold and produce a snapshot. "She was going to hit me with the divorce papers last winter, but her lawyer told her to hold off, waiting to see if I made the majors and the big money. Knowing them, they'll probably encourage me to try to catch on somewhere in AAA and then try again next year."

The next day was getaway day and the Rangers' entourage prepared to depart the Surf Rider. While Canucks wept and Wayne Carmichael pondered his comeback, I stood on the bed to admire my deep and radiant suntan in the bathroom mirror. I looked like the UN ambassador from Sumatra. Randy Galloway presented more of the dirt-floor Nicaraguan effect often associ-ated with the back streets of his native Grand Prairie. But on the charter flight back to Texas, one of the pitchers, Rich Hand, put matters into a harsh perspective. "It's nuts to get a tan like that because now you just get to watch it fade. I don't think you'll be walking the beach much in Cleveland and Detroit."

A deep thinker.

CHAPTER

![black bar]

4

TAVERN LIFE IS eternal in Fort Worth, Texas, a historic place that's chin-deep in trail-dust heritage. After the Civil War the city based its economy around the prostitution industry and met with prosperity. Even when some Bible-thumping zealots managed to weasel their way into the state legislature in 1896 and enact a reform measure that raised the legal age of consent in Texas from ten to twelve, the people of Fort Worth rallied together in a show of support for the innkeepers. A protective guild was organized and, bolstered by the wholehearted endorsement of local law enforcement, the Fort Worth brothel trade became an entity that was truly greater than the sum of its parts. If anybody thinks I am exaggerating, an article written by a professor, Richard F. Selcer, in a 1992 issue of the Southwestern Historical Quarterly will back me up. When the Chamber of Commerce brags about Fort Worth being home of the "world's oldest indoor rodeo," they're technically correct but the events I'm thinking of don't include bronco bustin' and calf ropin'.

In the city "where the west begins," the natural laws of commerce came into play as well, and inevitably cottage industries like cattle and oil materialized in and around Fort Worth, utilizing the mercantile strength of the hooker trade as a life-support mechanism.

Those whorehouses—and they proliferated around the city at least as long as I lived there through the mid-1970s—are the reason the stockyards were founded on the North Side. The town's population of what Professor Selcer termed "soiled doves, daughters of joy, bawds, painted women, sluts, tarts, floozies, chippies and street walkers," brought the huge Swift and Armor meatpacking plants to town, not vice versa. The same goes for American Airlines, the Santa Fe Railroad and, I am privately convinced, it's the same reason Texas Christian University moved from Waco to Fort Worth. Why do you suppose General Dynamics put a huge factory in Old Cowtown? Because of the school system? Why would Cap Cities Communications buy a newspaper like the Fort Worth *Star-Telegram?* Why else would the National Association of Fire Chiefs stage its annual convention in Fort Worth year after year? And this particular civic attraction in my view is the only rational reason why Bob Short would transfer the Washington Senators franchise to Arlington Stadium, just a seven-minute drive along the Interstate from the East Fort Worth city limits. Pompano Stadium was meager in comparison to the other spring training ballyards in Florida, true enough, but the aesthetic gap that separated Arlington Stadium from the other eleven American League performance venues was even more pronounced.

The park had initially been constructed to house the Dallas-Fort Worth entry in the Texas League, a team called the Spurs, and was adequate for that function. When the opportunity came along in the form of Bob Short, the park added on 18,000 outfield seats to up the seating capacity of the place to 35,000. What resulted was an open-bowl effect, perfectly suitable for a stock car race in South Carolina but hardly what baseball patrons of the big-league genre would reasonably hope to expect. Civic boosters liked to think of the place as "intimate" and it was—intimate like a drunk tank in the Bronx on New Year's Eve. With no roof or protective overhang to offer shade, the arrival of summer meant that inside that stadium it was hotter than First Baptist Hell.

I wrote a column that first season pointing out that Arlington Stadium lacked the amenities that fans can expect in other American League ball armories. There were no rats in the restrooms, like they have in Chicago. No iron pillars to block the view, like they have in Detroit. No pack of teenage thugs roving the stands, looking for organ donors, like the ones you can encounter in the House that Ruth Built. Tom Vandergriff, the mayor of Arlington, wrote me a letter thanking me for that column. Unfortunately, none of those features adequately compensated for the fact that Arlington Stadium bestowed about as much big league magic as a Wal-Mart store.

As such, this arena was indeed a proper domain for the team offering the talent base and high-loss quotient of the Texas Rangers. Season ticket sales indicated that the fandom remained largely unconcerned about the Rangers' on-the-field plight. Marketing projections showed that ticket buyers intended once again to avoid the park in record numbers. Bob Short's only consolation might have been the immortal observation of Yogi Berra: "If the people aren't going to come, there's nothing you can do to stop them."

Late in spring training, when Rico Carty's exhibition batting average rested at .zero-something, he assured the fans back home via me, the oracle, that "when the bell rings, the Beeg Boy will heet."

"When the bell rings" is the term that ballplayers who are having a lousy spring use for the start of the regular season. Everything will fall into place and the cogs and gears will mesh "when the bell rings." John Donne referred to this when he wrote his baseball poem. Now, according to the schedule distributed by the main office from the American League, the Chicago White Sox would be on the field for a game that actually counted in the standings, so the Gong Show in Arlington Stadium would now begin.

* * *

SOMETHING ODD HAPPENED on what was supposed to have been Opening Day, 1973—a harbinger of a procession of conspicuously odd things that the Rangers would encounter that year. Through some divine providence, the game was called off because of a mid-afternoon snowstorm. To Whitey Herzog, that amounted to a stay of execution. Well into August, Herzog could be seen in his office before games, still praying for snow.

The White Sox won the opener when it was played the next night, Saturday, 3–1, before a paid gathering of 22,000. I could list the Rangers' 1973 opening night lineup here, for the benefit of baseball trivia enthusiasts, but I will not. Show me a trivia nut who can recite that lineup from memory and I will show you a person so anal retentive that he should be institutionalized immediately.

Oh, what the hell: Rich Billings was the catcher, Mike Epstein was at first, Dave Nelson (who appeared in the all-star game that season for the simple reason that every team had to be represented by at least one player) started at second base, Toby Harrah was the shortstop and Joe Lovitto was at third. The outfield consisted of Rico Carty, Elliot Maddox (who would go on to sue the City of New York after he claimed that he messed up his knee when he fell over a sprinkler pipe at Shea Stadium) and Jeff Burroughs. Alex Johnson was the designated hitter. The bench included Larry Biittner, famous around the majors for the spelling of his name, and Tom Grieve, who played twelve years in the majors and then became general manager of the Rangers. On the day that Grieve's son Ben graduated from high school in Arlington in 1994, he signed a contract with Oakland that included a bonus worth more money than his old man earned during his twelve seasons in the majors combined.

Dick Bosman was the starter in that 1973 opener and he pitched heroically for the Rangers that night until he yielded a key home run to Dick Allen that seemed to be still traveling on an upward trajectory when it passed over the centerfield fence.

Yes . . . Allen had been the American League's MVP the season before, but one or two Dick Allens would lurk in the batting order of every team on the Rangers' schedule. Meanwhile, Wilbur Wood, the Sox's big knuckleballer, limited the Rangers to four anemic singles in the opener.

Wilbur Wood, by the way, was typical of most of the upper-tier pitchers in the American League of that era in that he would deceive the hitter rather than overpower him. Poor Rico Carty. He was totally baffled by Wood's dip-and-dive knuckleball pitches and swung the bat like a man attempting to fight off a swarm of killer bees.

Up in the pressbox I was availing myself of the one amenity Arlington Stadium did provide that was as good as any in the major leagues. Baseball has its share of traditions, God knows, and the whole structure of the art form is based around these. But the custom I found most delightful was the one calling for the host team to provide free food and booze to the sportswriters. Standards of hospitality varied drastically from ballpark to ballpark. The most feeble spread was a dead heat between Oakland, naturally (if the legendary miser Charles Finley was notoriously renowned for his pinchpenny approach to paying players, one can only imagine the nature of the largest Charlie O. might extend to the unpressed gentlemen of the press) and Yankee Stadium, where the fare was one step up from jail food—processed cheese and stale bread, served with some anonymous brand of tap beer that always gave me the runs. Milwaukee's County Stadium was well known for its greasy beef spareribs that were prepared in a fashion guaranteed to offer gastronomic upheaval, but at least they never ran out.

On the other side of the ledger, standing tall, were the four-star operations (and these recommendations came from the findings of a league-wide poll and are not merely one man's opinion): Fenway Park (Oysters Rockefeller), Memorial Stadium in Baltimore (crab cakes and cherry vanilla ice cream) and Metropolitan Stadium in Minneapolis-St. Paul (Bloody Marys). And, surprisingly, Arlington Stadium. The barbecue buffet, featuring a rare beef-brisket, always drew raves from visiting writers and broadcasters. But the feature that extracted the raves from the likes of Harold McKinney and Randy Galloway happened to be of a procedural nature.

At most ballparks, the media lounge remained open for an hour and a half before and after the game and was closed while the game was actually in progress. But in Arlington, the bar not only never closed, a couple of college kids (Jeff and Eddie—why is it I remember their names to this day?) remained on call in the pressbox to fetch drinks.

Jeff and Eddie and I learned to work well together. We were a team. With the slightest gesture, a subtle wave of my right index finger, like a countess signalling the auctioneer during a sale at the Tate Gallery, Jeff or Eddie would be there instantaneously with my drink. The drink, by the by, consisted of José Cuervo, on the rocks, in a twelve-ounce plastic cup, a concoction locally known as a Fort Worth Air Conditioner.

Usually, I would require at least four of these to overcome a chronic condition known as writer's block and usually, by around the top of the eighth inning, I would at last muster the confidence to describe the latest Rangers defeat with the depth and grandeur that the event deserved. So when Dick Allen hit his homerun, that was not just another garden variety, pissant homer but perhaps "a celestial comet, streaking across the night prairie sky while earthlings in the cheap seats quivered with reverence and awe."

I suspect that there were occasions when readers and perhaps my superiors at the newspaper might have perused this type of material, paused and wondered to themselves: "What was that fucker on when he wrote *that?*" And to them, I hereby extend an honest answer. Usually, I was on straight tequila. Not that I was concerned about critiques from my superiors at the paper. The *Star-Telegram*, after all, was the newspaper that somehow managed to print "Championship Game . . . Madison Square Garden Fuck You Classic" in the basketball scores. That appeared in 300,000 papers and when a reader called to complain,

Bob Lindley, the sports editor, told him, "You should have seen what was in there before we cleaned it up."

I should also add here that I was not the only person in that pressbox to eventually receive honorable mention for the Betty Ford Hall of Fame. I saw guys being hauled out of there on stretchers. Some team official of the Rangers once told me what the liquor bill in the Arlington Stadium press lounge totalled for the entire season (although this was after Brad Corbett had bought the team and ordered in an additional enormous supply of red wine), and the number was so unbelievable that I erased it from my mind.

THE SUNDAY CONTEST against the White Sox was rained out. But this was probably the last time that the crass deity that administrates the elements during a baseball season would offer any benevolent gestures on behalf of the woebegone Rangers.

Monday, I was aboard the Ranger charter, destination Kansas City, about to be indoctrinated to the coast-to-coast stag party otherwise known as baseball travel, Rangers-style. Herzog, like most managers, sanctioned an open bottle policy on team flights. The presumption was that these ballplayers were adults and well-to-do professionals and if they wanted to drink their careers into early oblivion, then that was their absolute privilege.

Several players were in the process of doing exactly that, including one utility man with a conventional Rangers transcript . . . his job skills had eroded to the extent that he was no longer of use to his previous organization in the National League but were still servicable enough to perform for Texas. He stood in the back of the plane chatting with a flight attendant and suggesting that the two of them might participate in a carnal act that would also include a seesaw and a German shepherd. In our current society, the flight attendant would have filed suit against the player, the Rangers, the American League, the airline, probably the FAA and the air traffic controllers union, claiming sexual harassment. But that never happened back then and the flight attendant simply informed the player, "I don't get paid enough to put up with shit like that from dickheads like you."

The player was only mildly chagrined. "She took it all wrong," he complained. "I wasn't talking about getting it on with a dog. I meant a real German shepherd, this fat guy I know named Fritz."

I was sitting next to one of the players who was listed among the "bright hopes" of the organization in the Rangers pre-season promotional literature. He ignored his teammate's encounter with the flight attendant. The "bright hope" was reading Playboy and was disturbed by the contents. "Look at these women," he said, pointing at Miss April. "They don't look like real women. These models look like . . . plastic.

"The ones that I think are more attractive are the ones in that section they print in Oui, where the readers send in pictures of themselves and the caption always reads that the photo was taken by their boyfriends or their husbands. A lot of them are from New Jersey. You see some pretty strange looking bodies, with these saggy little monkey tits. But I'd a hell of a lot rather look at that stuff than at Miss April." Go figure that.

From there, the "bright hope" moved on to one of his favorite topics, that being himself, and recalled the events of his past that led him into pro ball. To the fans, the player usually offered a grim and brooding countenance but the player I was coming to know here was a sentimental cuss, at least when it came to his childhood years. "Me and some other guys would go over to each other's houses," he fondly recalled, "raid the parents' medicine cabinets and take every pill that was in there. And then," he said, "we'd each drink a six-pack."

Since this "bright hope" did eventually move on to enjoy a reasonably long and often productive career in the major leagues, I have often been given cause to think of the slogan "Breakfast of Champions" in a whole new context.

CHAPTER

━━━━━━

5

AFTER ABOUT ONE month's exposure to the nomadic nocturnal adventures of the Texas Rangers, a strong suspicion had begun to grow that I had somehow become a living character in a television script written by Rod Serling. Racked with chronic jet lag, I could not now help but sense that my late-night experiences more and more had taken on a rather surreal quality.

In Minneapolis one cheerless Friday night, I found that the hotel lobby and bar had been commandeered by a state convention of the Teamsters. They tried to ignore Don Stanhouse, the Rangers pitcher, as he cruised the lobby shouting, "Paging Mr. Gozinya! Mr. Peter Gozinya!" The Teamsters had also spilled into our usual haunt across the street, the Blue Ox, obliterating the oxygen supply in there with their Dutch Masters. These guys all knew where Jimmy Hoffa was buried and he wasn't even dead yet. Their collective brotherhood offered such an unmitigated sinister posture that Galloway, Billings the catcher and Bones Merritt, a lefthanded relief pitcher, and I were forced into the cold outdoors.

If people around the country think that Texans talk funny, they might listen to some native Minnesotans next time. Their twang is a hell of a lot more nasal than anything I ever heard in rural Texas, and I think the reason is that, in the winter, their sinuses actually freeze and rupture. The stoic Scandinavians maintain the plurality in that region and these people could not be reasonably depicted as passionate fools or hopeless romantics. This was in evidence at a topless bar. While the girls wiggled and danced, the customers, most of whom looked like the illustration on the label of a sardine can, just sat there, expressionless, as if they were attending a lecture on eighteenth-century Lutheran theology. With one of our group standing on his chair shouting, "Yaahhh, Baby! Shake it! Shake it!" I must say that I felt a little bit out of place.

Three hours later we decided to top off still another festive evening on the road at an all-night dive. Galloway ordered his usual Grand Prairie Special—fried eggs, fried potatoes, a bottle of Tabasco and a JB and soda. In the next booth, an old man with extremities and a neck of enlarged circumference suddenly pitched on his back and had a seizure. Apparently he'd overheard Galloway's selections from the menu. The poor guy was writhing and twisting, producing whoops and gurgles. Finally, Rich Billings sprang to his aid and offered the old-timer a cigarette.

The events of that evening were in no way atypical of the various small dramas that took place night after night after night, and usually late at night at that, since there was frequently a ball game to get out of the way before the serious explorations of the urban underworld could begin. The cumulative effects, I discovered, tended to make one rather nuts. At the time I was reading Dan Jenkins' (who, like me, had started writing at the Fort Worth *Press)* novel *Semi-Tough* and realized that the apocryphal madness he described in that book seemed genteel when compared to some of my recent experiences.

In mid-May the Rangers were enjoying a weekend in Detroit and, as usual, congregated at the Lindell AC, the nation's first and certainly most authentic sports bar. Back then, all four Detroit pro teams—Lions, Tigers, Pistons and Red Wings—played downtown, either at Tiger Stadium, the Olympia or Cobo Hall, and personnel from visiting teams practically lived in Lindell's.

Consequently, a collateral population of groupies appeared there as well, making for colorful mating rituals. It was on the Friday night of my first visit to Detroit that I heard a Rangers player tell a young woman, "What do you mean you're not into one-night stands? Hell. We're in town until Sunday."

On Saturday, after a day game (Tigers win, 7–1), several of the Rangers troupe ventured to Joe's Chop House, fancier than it sounded and a rather famous restaurant. After the dinner an endless cavalcade of distilled beverages appeared at our table while Harold McKinney and Burt Hawkins became entangled in perhaps the bitterest of an ongoing series of acrimonious political discussions.

Burt Hawkins was the Rangers' traveling secretary, or in his case, zookeeper. It is the immense task of the traveling secretary to coordinate plane, bus and hotel arrangements for the players, management and media—about thirty-five people in all. As a person with a hair-trigger disinclination to take any crap off anybody, Hawkins sustained the total respect of all of his strange ensemble of eccentrics and malcontents. With a battalion of wayward caballeros like this outfit, it became Hawkins' additional duty to inform next of kin when one of our number became hospitalized or incarcerated. Hawkins held the same job with the Senators before being transferred to the simmering flatlands of Texas, and prior to that had covered baseball for the old Washington *Star*. Hawkins despised all those "liberal pansies" at the Washington *Post* and told me that whenever he heard Sousa's "Washington Post March" he would break out in hives.

Everyone called him Hawk, and politically he was exactly that. In his final years back in Washington, Hawkins had hired David Eisenhower to work as his assistant and statistician. Hawk liked the hell out of Ike's grandson and was obviously sympathetic with the policies of David's father-in-law. But the onset of summer 1973 was not the best of times for the then First Family. Spiro Agnew (the letters of whose name can be rearranged to spell Grow A Penis) was about to resign and the troops were assembling for the first bloodletting in the Battle of Watergate.

Harold McKinney, who had intense political convictions of his own and envied and admired the likes of the Black Panthers, was equipped with limitless pejorative resources when his blood alcohol content matched the Rangers team batting average, about .217. On this Saturday at Joe's Chop House, Harold's hissing diatribe against Richard Nixon reached such a crescendo—with Hawkins responding in perfect harmony—that I decided to evacuate the premises before the FBI showed up.

There's nothing like a prolonged solo stroll through the streets of Motown at midnight if a person wishes to display a disregard for his own well-being. So I was rather pleased with myself after making it back to the hotel room intact, a sensation that vanished after I couldn't get my key into the door. After several attempts, it occurred to me that my motor skills were not at blame here. It was the key's fault.

I returned to the lobby, approached the night manager and expressed my dissatisfaction with the faulty key in a short speech of fiery eloquence. The manager examined the key and, as a rather self-satisfied half-smile crossed his face, announced, "It appears, my man, that the problem isn't the key. The problem is that you seem to be in the wrong hotel. But don't look so glum. You only missed it by a block."

At the time I certainly did not regard the hotel episode as such a stupendously misguided excursion into the land of the absurd. If I had I certainly would have kept the incident to myself. After all, hotels, like most everything else in Detroit, all look the same. But when I casually recounted the event to someone the next night on the plane headed to Milwaukee, the story became quite the little knee-slapper.

On a day when Toby Harrah would play nine innings at shortstop with congealed vomit in his hair, here I was being held up as the village imbecile. For months—even years—later, I found myself being introduced to people as "this is the guy I've been telling you about—the schmuck who wound up in the wrong hotel.'' It wasn't until I started fighting back—"Yeah. Well, at least I didn't get arrested driving south in the northbound lane of the freeway like *some* people I know"—that the derision began to subside.

Actually, the Rangers were easily amused by the slightest off-the-field diversion because the on-the-field aspects of their act were deteriorating from mediocre to melancholy to sometimes macabre. In a game at Chicago, Dave Nelson, the second baseman and anything but a power hitter, cracked a two-run homer in the seventh inning and banged a three-run shot again in the ninth. Thanks to Nelson's rare explosive display, the Rangers only lost 10–5 instead of 10–0. The wire services were starting to carry scores like 17–2 (once against Oakland and a week later against Detroit).

An exhausting road swing that carried the Rangers from Anaheim to Spokane (which I thought was a hell of a place to spend my thirty-first birthday) for an exhibition game against Texas' AAA farm team, to Oakland and then all the way over to New York, had seen Texas lose so much ground that the taillights of the fifth-place Angels had vanished into the distance. And the Angels were hardly setting the league afire. The only Rangers player who was accomplishing anything on a consistent basis was Alex Johnson, the guy Herzog had feared might "poison" the ball club. AJ was hitting about .315, but his promising production was of little use to the Rangers media. Johnson restricted his post-game remarks to bizarre figures of speech that were so off-color that I couldn't begin to reproduce them in a "family" newspaper—hey, they couldn't have printed them in Screw magazine.

On an early afternoon in New York an event happened that nicely summarized Whitey Herzog's frustrations. After a rain-out at Yankee Stadium that completed the road swing, the team climbed aboard the bus to LaGuardia. While some equipment trunks were being loaded into the baggage bin, a kid of about twelve who was typical of the attitude and demeanor of the youth who prowl the badlands around the stadium, sneaked on

the bus. Standing in the aisle near the front, the youngster began a little tap dance, all the while yelling, "Rang-uhs fuck!
Rang-uhs suck! Rang-uhs eat shit!"

That routine continued for about forty seconds, to the combined amazement and amusement of everyone on the bus, until
Herzog himself issued a suggestion: "Hey, kid. Why don't you
go beat your meat!"

"Yeah," added the bus driver. "You gettin' ready to get a
shoe up you ass." With that, the driver grabbed the kid by his
shirt and heaved him through the door and onto the hard side-
walk. I was sitting close enough to Herzog to hear him mutter,
"The hell of it is, the kid's *right*." He paused, then laughed and
said, "And it hurts, too."

Whitey Herzog, who had joined the team to oversee what
amounted to a three-year neighborhood improvement project
with the Rangers and who fully realized that the initial phases
were going to be painful, was already at work planning radical
reconstructive cosmetic alterations to the face of the 1973 Rangers. He passed the word around the major leagues that he was
seeking, to paraphrase the Marine recruiting slogan, "a few
men." In this case, they didn't necessarily have to be "good."

Herzog had already traded his best pitcher, Dick Bosman, for
somebody he thought was a bit better, Sonny Siebert. Rich
Hand and Mike Epstein were gone by now, too, traded to the
California Angels. The manager had decided that the pitching
material he had inherited in spring training offered physical
tools more befitting the American Legion than the American
League. Within weeks, Herzog had replaced the entire five-man
starting rotation that opened the season. And he would replace
that five with another five before the year was out.

One casting upgrade was located in Memphis, languishing in
the Cardinals farm system. When righthander Jim Bibby joined
the Rangers he presented an immediate departure in that he at
least *looked* the part of a ballplayer. Most of the Rangers wore
straggly mustaches, generally appeared consumptive and, when
the team marched through an airport en route to the bar, could

have been easily mistaken for a bunch of ex-cons. Bibby, at six-foot-seven, had legs like oak trees. His brother Henry had been a key figure in UCLA's basketball dynasty and was now a star with the Knicks.

Jim Bibby, who for reasons known only to himself went by the "stage name" of Fontay O'Rooney, was by no means a complete major league pitcher. But he threw a vicious fastball—"serious heat . . . severe gas"—that would scare the bejesus out of most American League batters. Parenthetically, Bibby could also lay claim to owning the biggest apparatus of manhood in baseball—an appendage of near-equine proportions—and it was to Bob Short's eternal frustration that he could never harness that particular novelty into a gate attraction at Arlington Stadium.

Short's marketing scheme was entirely one-dimensional. Every night was Something Night at the ball park. Bat Night—they staged about five of those. Ball Night. Cap Night. T-shirt Night. Rangers Keychain Night. Rangers Calendar Night. Yes, and even Rangers Panty Hose (guaranteed to yield fewer runs than the home team) Night. Still on the drawing board was Insane Relative Night and Law Enforcement Appreciation Night, where Grand Prairie cops would stage a pre-game demonstration of interrogation techniques.

When I suggested to Short that he was processing junk merchandise, he puffed up and said, "Got any better ideas?" Whenever the turnstile count hit 10,000, it was a good night in Arlington. The solemn reality was that the Dallas–Fort Worth area was gaga over the Cowboys and the lame antics of a last-place baseball team were not inflaming fan response.

In short, Bob Short needed a miracle.

The Rangers could claim one asset. By virtue of their record from the season before, worst in the league, Texas received the top selection in the upcoming amateur draft. All of the scouts unanimously anointed a high school pitcher in Houston, a left-hander, as the best prospect in the country and perhaps the best of the previous ten years or the best since Bob Feller or even, according to some, as—aw, what the hell?—the best of all time.

Whitey Herzog, pragmatist and skeptic, had traveled to Austin to watch David Clyde pitch in the high school state championships and was now firing a twenty-one-gun salute too. According to the manager, Clyde clearly "had the gun" and the only missing ingredient was "developing a change-up and getting the fine tuning that separates the big leaguers from, well, the guys we've got now.

"Start him off in an all-rookie league, where he'll get used to being away from home with some guys his own age, then pull him all the way to AA or even AAA next year . . . and I think the kid will be primed for the majors by the time he's twenty. And after that," Whitey said (he'd just watched Secretariat win the Belmont Stakes by thirty-one lengths on TV), "we can bottle his sperm." Herzog was fostering visions of a time when managing the Rangers might not be the grotesque experience he was presently forced to endure.

That was Whitey's timetable. Bob "You Can Fool Some of the People Some of the Time and That's Good Enough for Me" Short was hatching a different and more accelerated schedule for David Clyde's professional advancement. This was showbiz, after all, and while there were plenty of big butts in North Texas, not nearly enough were located in the box seats at Arlington Stadium.

In David Clyde, Short figured he was blessed with the most promising overnight gate attraction since Jo-Jo the Lizard Boy hit the State Fair of Texas.

CHAPTER

6

ACCORDING TO A recent government study, it has been determined that ninety-seven percent of all present and former major-league baseball pitchers believe that the earth has been visited by extraterrestrial life-forms. It was also noted that seventy-one percent of these same pitchers, living or dead, at some point attempted to patent a perpetual motion machine.

Well, perhaps they didn't take that survey, but if they had, these figures would hold true and simply confirm one of baseball's oldest axioms: that good arms do not usually come equipped with sound or stable minds. Additionally, it has long been believed that elevated levels of eccentricity can be located in lefthanders and knuckleballers.

So Whitey Herzog deemed it only appropriate that his 1973 Rangers pitching staff should include that rarest of species, the lefthanded knuckleballer. This was Charlie Hudson, a versatile sort who was being utilized not only for long relief and short relief but also as a spot starter. Consistency was Charlie's forte and he maintained a 6.50 earned-run average in each of those capacities.

As mid-June approached, Charlie Hudson performed an act that at the time seemed entirely rational, given the guidelines that are conventionally extended to lefthanded knuckleballers.

He shot himself. He didn't stick the gun in his mouth and pull the trigger. Charlie, in the proud fraternal spirit of lefthanded knuckleballers everywhere, had accidentally shot himself in the middle finger of his pitching hand.

The mishap appeared all too Rangeresque on that day's installment of the latest entries to the American League disabled list distributed to the wire services.

Kansas City: Pitcher Steve Busby, torn rotator cuff.

Chicago: Third baseman Bill Melton, pulled hamstring.

Texas: Pitcher Charlie Hudson, gunshot wound.

"It was just one of those accidents that hunters and gun enthusiasts have from time to time," Charlie explained while showing off his bandage. "I was cleaning my .38 revolver and the thing went off." Nobody bothered to ask Charlie exactly what type creatures he liked to hunt with a .38 revolver just as nobody questioned the wisdom, whether intentional or not, of his accident.

Privately, most of Hudson's teammates were thinking, "Nice going, Charlie. Now you can take your Purple Heart and split. I wish I had your guts." Soon there were unconfirmed sightings of several Rangers players browsing the pawnshops in East Fort Worth. Shortly, though, a team doctor delivered the punch line. "Not so fast, Charlie," he said when the prognosis came down. "This isn't as bad as it looks. You can rejoin this circus in six weeks and then have a bone graft after the season."

Hudson now realized how Clyde Barrow must have felt when he chopped off a toe with an axe to avoid a chain-gang assignment at the Texas state penitentiary only to learn that he was scheduled for parole the following week.

Jim Bibby, the big righthander recently snatched from the bowels of the Cardinals farm system, would replace Charlie Hudson on the roster. With the pitching staff's in-transit format now a matter of daily routine, Herzog didn't know if he was managing a major league baseball team or a Mexican bus station. The unsettled nature of the Rangers mound ensemble was illustrated in the American League ERA listings.

Ken Holtzman of the A's topped the list in mid-June with a figure just under 2.20, followed by Bill Lee, Jim Colbert, Wilbur Wood, Dave McNally, Bert Blyleven, Jim Palmer, Paul Splittorff, Nolan Ryan, Doc Medich, Mickey Lolich, etc., etc. Anybody seeking to locate a Ranger on the list would count down past thirty-six names to finally discover Don Stanhouse at 4.23. And Herzog had already confirmed that Stanhouse was being sent down to Spokane as soon as the AAA affiliate could provide space on its roster. Three dozen names later, one could locate Mike Paul and Pete Broberg with twin ERAs of 5.70. Whitey was concocting travel plans for them, too. When the media asked Whitey about his rotation for an upcoming series against Boston, he replied that he would blindfold himself, pull some names out of a fishbowl and let us know.

On a late Saturday afternoon the team gathered in the clubhouse at Arlington Stadium just before taking the field for batting practice. Most of the players congregated around a TV set to watch the Belmont Stakes. What they saw was, in my view, the most impressive performance in televised sport as Secretariat won by thirty-one lengths. If that horse had had a rearview mirror, jockey Ron Turcotte would have witnessed the astronaut's view of the earth after blastoff.

The 1973 Belmont Stakes was oddly similar in reverse form to the 1973 pennant chase in the American League West at that point, with most of the field tightly bunched and another entry separated from the pack by a ridiculous margin. The White Sox led by a neck, at 32–25, shadowed by Oakland, Minnesota, Kansas City and California in fifth place at 30–30 and only three games back. Then, playing in their own league, came the Texas Rangers at 19–38 and 13 games down. One might note that while the Rangers occupied last place in the American League, the last place finisher in that 1973 Belmont Stakes was a horse named Sham.

Another Rangers home stand mercifully closed one day after that memorable horse race. The highlight of a ten-day stay in Arlington had come against the Yankees. Bob Short's director of special events, Oscar Molomont—a Danny DeVito clone whose credentials for the job amounted to his background as a book-keeper with Short's trucking line in Minnesota—had concocted a promotion known as Slurpee Night that attracted 10,000 to the park. Any five-figure attendance was always big news in Arlington.

Factors beyond the inept nature of the home team seemed to be repelling fans from the stadium. What marketing people might now call the "full-phase entertainment setting" at the ballpark was as much a turnoff as the won-lost record of the Rangers. The core of the problem was organ music. The ancient hard-liners insist that the organ ranks as an essential element to the overall ballpark package and I couldn't argue with that.

But between innings at Arlington Stadium, imagine this: The Rangers are getting beat 11–2 or whatever and the organist gives the fans a downbeat rendition of "Slow Boat to China." Or "Beautiful Dreamer." Or "Tennessee Waltz." Or "Ole Buttermilk Sky." Or "Miss Otis Regrets." And the instrument itself sounds in acute need of a big shot of nasal spray. The guy who goes to the game once a season sits there and thinks, "Good God. That music really sucks." Then he goes home and forgets about it. The guy such as myself who goes to the park every night soon finds that the organ music becomes one more item contributing to a personal list of growing neuroses.

I presumed that the organist himself was, indeed, the Phantom of the Opera. Eventually, I learned that my nightly torment was provided by either the son, grandson or nephew (I forget which) of Dr. Felix Gwodz. That didn't mean much to most Americans but everybody living in Fort Worth knew who Dr. Gwodz was—the county coroner. Not a single day passed for a quarter of a century when Dr. Gwodz's name did not appear in the local papers. "Tarrant County medical examiner Dr. Felix Gwodz ruled today that the cause of death was a shotgun blast to the face and not the fire that left the victim looking like, according to Dr. Gwodz, a 'toasted marshmallow.' " To the population of Fort Worth, Dr. Gwodz was like a member of the family. He was also well known for playing his accordion at polka festivals in the area. I finally went to the stadium management people and proposed that the organ be replaced by Dr. Gwodz and his accordion. My pitch was rejected at first. Later, they would begin to come around.

IN THE FINAL game against the Red Sox on Sunday night (as a footnote to history it should be pointed out that the Rangers were the first major league team to schedule its Sunday home games under the lights because it was too damn hot in Arlington to humanely consider anything in the afternoon), an assortment of spectators charitably estimated at 1,200 got to see a couple of future Hall of Famers at work. Carl Yastrzemski and Carlton Fisk each lined homers that landed in the abandoned cheap seats with such velocity that one could hear the thud all the way back up in the pressbox.

The Red Sox won that one, 12–1, and Whitey Herzog gathered his F troop and headed north.

First stop: Cleveland. This was my first visit to what at that time might have been the only U.S. city to rank beneath Dallas in national esteem. I don't know why. After devoting the better part of a young lifetime to confinement in North Texas, with its nondescript and horizontal landscape that turns brown by the Fourth of July and stays that way until the next April, Cleveland, the Mother City of the Rust Belt, exuded, I thought, a certain charm long before its present renaissance.

To a denizen of the prairie tribes, there is something near-mesmerizing about industrial decay. The fact that the Cuyahoga River once burst into flames was held out as a source of civic embarrassment, but I never detected so much as a puff of smoke on any of the lakes and streams on my visits to Cleveland.

Cleveland, of course, utilized the immense Municipal Stadium as the showcase for the hometown Indians, and if there is any such thing as an authentic burial ground haunted by lost spirits, this is the place.

The proud and regal 1954 Indians, winningest major league team in what is now the fifty seasons since the end of World War II, lost games three and four of the World Series at this arena, thus completing an upset sweep perpetrated by the New York Giants. For baseball purposes this park was seemingly cursed and abandoned forevermore. True, Arlington Stadium provided an unoccupied quality with its usual crowd of 6,000 or so. Like numbers in this immense structure on the shores of Lake Erie, designed to comfortably accommodate 80,000, presented a spectral effect.

The size of the crowds in those years had been largely ordained by the ineptness of the home team, which explained the reason why so many former Indians were now wearing Rangers Blue. Municipal Stadium in 1973 was nothing more than a glorified factory outlet mall for Stroh's beer.

Another unique aspect of the stadium setting on the lake front was the presence of two fans who situated themselves deep in the rightfield stands. They were equipped with kettle drums, and whenever the home team was at bat these guys pounded their drums in the traditional Western movie tom-tom cadence. *BOOM-boom-boom-boom. BOOM-boom-boom-boom.* Year in, year out. Every inning of every game. In the largely deserted ballpark, the echoes took on the quality of distant thunder. This place would be hell on earth for a man sporting a hangover and I quickly made a mental notation to arrange my late-night activities in Cleveland accordingly.

A mid-week afternoon game completed the Rangers' two-game visit to Cleveland and the drummers and beer vendors were literally the only living creatures in the stands to watch Whitey's Kids beat Gaylord Perry. Final: Texas 4–2.

After the game I approached Herzog with the usual stale questions about Perry and the alleged use of his notorious grease ball. Herzog was clearly delighted by the outcome. "The old greaser wasn't greasing so good today, was it?" Whitey said. "I understand that he gets that stuff off some doctor. Guess his prescription ran out."

Herzog was further exhilarated here because, just this once, the two "live young arms" of the staff, Broberg and Stanhouse, often characterized by Herzog as suffering from attention-deficit disorder, actually outpitched a Hall of Famer. Stanhouse, with elongated sideburns, was holding a Stroh's bottle in both hands and hoisting a personal toast to "my first save, ever, in organized ball. Sitting on the bench before the ninth inning I had a real strong feeling and I told myself that I was going to strike out the side." Stanhouse's trio of dead Indians included Jack Brohamer, Buddy Bell and John Lowenstein.

In a season that was by now just one-third old, the Rangers had adapted to a communal mind-set that enabled them to take the losses in stride. The occasional wins, then, provided the feeling of warmth and convivial fellowship that permeates, say, a New Year's Eve party at the Elks Club.

A minor fiasco involving travel arrangements did not dampen the mood. According to the mandates of the labor contract between the Major League Players Association and baseball ownership, when charter flights were not available the players would occupy all of the first-class seats on domestic flights. The remainder of the entourage would then be situated two to a row in the tourist section and afforded first-class food and beverage accommodations. The regular passengers were then crammed into the six or seven rows in the back of the plane.

But, when the Rangers arrived at the Cleveland airport for the flight to Baltimore, traveling secretary Burt Hawkins was horrified to learn that the gate agent had screwed up. The "civilian" ticket holders had already been allowed to board and were situated in seats throughout the plane. With takeoff in five minutes, it was too late to correct the situation. Hawkins expressed his dissatisfaction to the gate agent in most colorful language.

These ballplayers, when sprinkled among the general population and in a festive mood, offered potentially unwholesome catalytic potential for a ninety-minute flight. Sure enough, as the plane rolled down the runway to take off, I heard someone

shout, "HEY, STEWARDESS! BRING ON THE FUCKIN'
BOOZE."

Fortunately, that request was handled promptly enough to en-
sure reasonable tranquility on the flight. Stanhouse, still flush
from his resounding ninth inning back in Cleveland, prowled
the aisles, autographing paper napkins and stuffing them into
the shirt pockets of the various passengers who had no idea who
Stanhouse was or what convention he and his bizarre cronies
were headed to. I was fearful that Stanhouse would soon lapse
into his patented "Paging Mr. Gozinya . . . Mr. Peter Gozinya"
routine but for some reason he chose to refrain.

We were at the early developmental stages of the man who, six
years later, would be immortalized by his future manager Earl
Weaver as Stan the Man Unusual—or Fullpack, which is what
Weaver claimed he would smoke whenever Stanhouse pitched
for him with the game on the line.

Meanwhile, an anxiety-stricken middle-aged woman sat
wedged between me, on the aisle, and Rico Carty in the window
seat. Rico, halfway through the flight, was getting oiled and began a one-sided conversation with his seat companion. I got the
immediate impression this woman was not accustomed to being
placed in close proximity to enormous men with rich Caribbean
accents. Nor did she appear to be an avid follower of the Great
American Pastime.

"They call me the B-e-e-e-g Boy," he told her. "Ho-ho-ho.
They say the B-e-e-g Boy no longer h-e-e-t. And you know what I
say? Horse sh-e-e-t!" Now Carty was gripping an imaginary bat
and waving it in her face. "The B-e-e-g Boy," he assured this
woman, "will h-e-e-e-t!"

Since Rico Carty, customarily a gracious and adequately re-
strained individual when away from the ballpark, was apparently
succeeding in marginally traumatizing this woman, I was fearful
of what might be taking place elsewhere on the airplane.

Naturally, this peculiar trip, of all trips, would have to be one
of those that would encounter upper-air turbulence. Things
were beginning to go bump in the night. After several minutes I

heard a voice, unmistakably that of catcher Ken Suarez, yell, "WHO'S FLYING THIS THING? HELEN KELLER?"

At this point I halfway expected to see Leslie Nielsen emerge from the cockpit area wearing a parachute. Stanhouse, though strapped into his seat because the plane had apparently managed to fly into a hurricane, continued to make himself the center of attention.

He spotted my media colleague, David Fink, seated about eight rows behind him, and began yelling, "FINK! YOU ASSHOLE! YOU MISERABLE SON OF A BITCH! YOU HAD ME ALL READY TO GO TO SPOKANE! YOU PUT THAT IN YOUR GODDAMN NEWSPAPER BUT I SHOWED YOU! WAIT'LL WE GET ON THE GROUND . . . I'M GONNA KICK YOUR BALLS OFF!"

The plane, of course, eventually did land and amazingly "without further incident." I felt sorry, though, for the regular passengers—the non-baseball people, the normal ones.

CHAPTER

7

A TRUE-LIFE PASSION play presented through the miracle of television made me glad that I was wasting Friday afternoon in my room at the Lord Baltimore Hotel and not sitting where Maurice Stans was sitting, about thirty miles away in a U.S. Senate hearing.

Poor Stans. A year before, this man was a blissfully content non-celebrity working at a job that must have included good compensation and even better self-esteem—Nixon campaign committee finance chairman. Now, having already been indicted for obstruction of justice, he was having to endure some senator who wanted to know why the documentation of the whereabouts of $1.7 million in cash seemed to have disappeared just six days after the Watergate burglary.

"A pure and innocent coincidence," Stans told the senator. Ordinarily I would have been watching a replay of Ralph Edwards honoring John Foster Dulles on "This Is Your Life." The traveling baseball writer (at least the ones not terminally addicted to the Victoria's Secret catalogue) ordinary got to watch a great deal of nostalgia-oriented daytime TV. But this Watergate inquisition was too compelling to miss, and in order to be barroom-conversant in the summer of 1973, the informed citizen was required to remain up-to-date with the hearings. This

amazing public-affairs burlesque also offered a happy respite
from the monotony of filing daily updates on the death march
of the Texas Rangers.

Baltimore, with its quaint personality of other-worldliness, at
least presented the visitor with a few extras that I found lacking
in Minneapolis, Anaheim, Detroit, Oakland and Milwaukee.
Within walking distance of the hotel was a tourist-friendly three-
block area that included nothing but tattoo parlors, porn shops,
strip joints, and fascinating little boutiques with a limitless selection of French ticklers and Benwah balls. There were also assorted dives that permeated a suffocating aroma of Lysol that
reminded me of my youth back in good ol' Cowtown and some
additional hole-in-the-wall operations so sinister that the front
doors bore signs reading "Off Limits To U.S. Navy Personnel."
It was fortunate that Randy Galloway of the Dallas *Morning News*
had chosen not to make the trip to Baltimore. Mother Nature
had endowed Galloway with a kind of AWOL ambiance and he
was the only member of the Rangers traveling party frequently
harassed by the Shore Patrol.

I also soon learned that Baltimore served as home office of
the ultimate novelty—the sportswriter groupie. God knows, the
world is equipped with an endless supply of the groupie genre.
Jock groupies. Rock-star groupies. Politician groupies. Chiro-
practor groupies. Undertaker groupies. But in Baltimore, the
world's only living sportswriter groupie stationed herself right
there in the lobby of the Lord Baltimore Hotel. Fittingly, the
world's only sportswriter groupie was more mature than the
girls customarily found lurking in the lobbies. This woman, in
fact, appeared to have been born sometime during the James K.
Polk administration.

What she did was have the various reporters sign their names
and newspaper affiliations on a baseball that she carried with
her. We all laughed about this old lady although, knowing the
true psyche of the membership of the Baseball Writers Association of America, I suspected that Baltimore Blanche often re-

ceived three A.M. phone calls from at least half of them requesting her to join them back in the hotel room for a nightcap.

Actually, it made sense that if such an animal as a sportswriter groupie did indeed exist, one would have to travel to Baltimore to find her. Here, to my knowledge, is the only major league city where baseball is usually viewed with what amounts to spiritual intensity.

The word "fan" apparently is derived from another word, "fanatic," and that can be aptly applied in Baltimore. Certain fans who frequent certain parks in certain cities bring a distinctive personality to the game. The American League champions of my "fan personality profile" was a dead heat—Baltimore and Boston. In these cities baseball was regarded as theatre. Fenway Park provided better seats, but the Oriole fans of the early seventies were getting to see what most critics would agree were better plays.

It should be remembered that Babe Ruth grew up as a pitcher in a Catholic reform school in Baltimore and didn't become a full-time slugger until he moved to New York, via Boston. The Baltimore baseball ethic historically has been based around pitching and defense and the Rangers would see those concepts exemplified on a grand scale while they were getting their tails kicked in this three-game weekend series against the Orioles.

Paul Blair, the best centerfielder that the big leagues would see in a decade, was flanked by Al Bumbry and Rich Coggins—a trio of antelopes that could not only flag down anything hit between the foul lines but was also particularly artful at snatching away homerun balls two or three feet over the fence.

With Mark Belanger and Brooks Robinson, the left side of the Baltimore infield was airtight, and Bobby Grich and Boog Powell were formidable at second and first, respectively. The Orioles did not have a solid defensive catcher. No. They had three: Earl Williams, Andy Etchebarren and Elrod Hendricks. Surveying the Orioles' lineup, it was beyond debate that the Rangers did not have a single player who could start for Baltimore.

The three starting pitchers that the Rangers would face in this series were Mike Cuellar, a future underwear model named Jim Palmer, and finally, lefthander Dave McNally, who, at that point, had won fifteen consecutive starts against the Texas-Washington franchise. Defense and pitching. Even the Baltimore PA announcer, Rex Barney, had been a star relief pitcher at Ebbets Field.

In his office before the Friday night opener, Whitey Herzog pondered the Orioles' lineup card and said, "I'm thinking about flying Charlie Hudson up here for the weekend so we can play a little Russian roulette." Herzog looked at his brain trust and added, "This is liable to get ugly."

The brain trust, by the way, included first-base coach Chuck Hiller and pitching coach Chuck Estrada. Hiller owned a proud spot in American trivia. He was the first National Leaguer to hit a grand slam homer in a World Series game. Amazingly, nobody had done that until Hiller did it with the Giants in 1962. Now Hiller's mission was to stand in the box by first base and yell "get back! . . . get back! . . . get back!" to any Rangers base runners who reached first. With what Herzog termed his "Punch and Judy" offense, not many Rangers ever reached first safely, so when they did, Hiller was to make damn certain that nobody got picked off.

Estrada, also known as Cha-Cha and Teen Angel because he looked like Frankie Avalon with his Fifties-style "a little dab'll do ya" Brylcreme look, was stuck with a task even more confounding than Hiller's. A former pitching star with the Orioles, Teen Angel understood the mechanics and theology of the craft of pitching. But attempting to function as pitching coach of the 1973 Rangers was like teaching a night course in calculus at Attica prison.

He lasted the better part of that one season. Since then, Estrada's name has never surfaced in any job capacity involving major-league baseball, but I am sure that he is productively occupied somewhere in the private sector. A lesser mortal would be located in blissful voluntary residence at some mental health-care facility working with modeling clay.

This Friday pre-game session in Herzog's little office at Memorial Stadium did involve something that Estrada would find uniquely challenging. In the best traditions of American business, Bob Short (the owner) had seen fit to overrule the better judgment of Whitey Herzog (the manager).

David Clyde, the high school pitching phee-nom and Number One choice in the amateur draft, would be pressed into immediate service as a starting pitcher in the major leagues.

True, Clyde's statistical credentials were overwhelming. In his last two seasons, against a level of high school competition that was perhaps as good as any in the country, he'd compiled a 35–2 record and was 18–0 as a senior with fourteen shutouts and five no-hitters. A Phillies scout, Lou Fitzgerald, had said, "I watched Clyde pitch three innings and left. Why waste time? We're picking second."

By drafting David Clyde, the Rangers bypassed two players who would probably wind up in Cooperstown—Dave Winfield and Robin Yount. Between them, they would collect over 6,000 major-league base hits.

Three other players taken in the first round of the 1973 draft, John Stearns, Lee Mazzilli and Gary Roenicke, went on to long and productive big-league careers. Interestingly, the Rangers' third round pick, Len Barker, emerged as a quality big-league starter (with the Indians) who would pitch a perfect game against Toronto in 1981.

At the time, no scout in baseball disputed that the Rangers did the right thing by claiming Clyde as their top pick, but the idea of bringing the prize stud directly into The Show left Herzog shaking his head. "This ain't high school. Up here, he'll find the strike zone shrinking fast and he won't find any 130-pound kids swinging at the high one.

"Another thing," Herzog cautioned, "in high school Clyde has been used to great success. In this league there will come the time when he can't get anybody out and that can really pull a kid down."

But Bob Short, in his fashion as showman, would have put a

gnome in the lineup to attract paying fans if Bill Veeck, the White Sox owner, hadn't thought of it first. Promotions like Cough Syrup Night were not filling seats in Arlington. The owner was getting desperate. Rumor had it that during the last home stand, someone had called the stadium ticket office asking what time the game started and was told, "What time can you be here?"

The deal was done. Clyde would join the team in Minnesota that coming Sunday and make his big-league debut at home the following week. Back in Texas, a press conference was held in the Rangers dugout to announce that Clyde had officially signed for what Short termed "a considerable amount . . . a very considerable amount." That amount, $150,000, was indeed deemed considerable for someone who had just turned eighteen in 1973. Clyde apparently had hired a Sunday-school teacher to script his comments for the press conference. "This fulfills a lifetime dream. It is wonderful to be the top draft choice." And so on. Significantly, as far as being tossed into the major-league shark tank for Bob Short Entertainment Enterprises, Clyde said that both he and his old man were all for it.

And, after what he would have to witness and withstand in his dugout in Baltimore over the next three days, Whitey Herzog was probably all for it, too. This team needed something and needed it bad. A fresh face. A transfusion. An iron lung. *Anything.*

In the first game of the series, the Rangers actually received what was their best pitching performance of the season so far. Sonny Siebert, the veteran that Herzog pirated away from the Red Sox, went the distance and held the Orioles to only one run. The Baltimore team at the plate was far less formidable than the Baltimore team on the mound and in the field.

Naturally, that one run was enough. Mike Cuellar regarded the Rangers batting order as a delight to behold. Rico Carty's impersonation of a cleanup hitter might have made a great skit on "Laugh-In," but beneath the harsh glare of ballpark lights the humor of the situation was wasted on Whitey Herzog. The

B-e-e-g Boy entered the game against Cuellar batting a cool
.194, which would sink a few more notches after another 0-for-4
showing against Cuellar.

Joe Lovitto, the player that Ted Williams had called the best
hitter in the Rangers organization, had been relegated to a limited role in the Texas attack. Herzog felt that made sound baseball sense inasmuch as Lovitto was 5 for 42.

Mike Cuellar's only problem Ranger on this night was Jim
Spencer, a decent first baseman Herzog had received when he
foisted off lost-cause Mike Epstein to California in late May.
Spencer belted a line drive directly off Cuellar's kneecap in the
third inning. After the game I approached Cuellar in the Oriole
clubhouse and, sure enough, his right knee, packed in ice, was
swollen the size of a volleyball. Cuellar grinned.

"Right leg hurt so much I forget about left leg," Cuellar said.
He'd been nursing a groin pull since spring training and under
normal circumstances might have left the game after being
nailed by Spencer's smash. But against this Rangers lineup, a
shutout just waiting to happen, Cuellar naturally had chosen to
stay on.

Since there would be no Watergate action on TV that next
day, a Saturday, I spent the following afternoon at the cinema
with Merle Heryford, another baseball writer from the Dallas
Morning News who was splitting the trips with Galloway that year.
Merle was an old-timer and like every old-timer I ever met on
the baseball beat, his heart and mind were welded to the past.
In his case, the past was exclusively immersed in the activities of
the long-extinct Dallas franchise in the Texas League. Merle had
covered that team through its metamorphoses as Rebels, Steers
and Eagles.

An amazing true story about Merle Heryford typified not only
the man himself but old baseball writers everywhere. In their
world, no current player could begin to measure up to the players of yesterday in terms of talent, grandeur or overall persona.
"Goddamn . . . I remember ol' Waffleface Watson. Sumbitch
could stand flat-footed and piss over a boxcar. Helluva guy.

Went 4-for-5 against Wichita Falls and died of smallpox the next day.''

In 1956 Merle was sitting at his desk at the paper, apparently engrossed in the minor-league reports in that week's edition of the *Sporting News* when a copyboy ran into the sports department and shouted, "Mr. Heryford! Mr. Heryford! The World Series game is in the sixth inning and Don Larson is pitching a perfect game!''

Merle smirked, bit down hard on his cigar and announced, "He'll never do it.''

Later, the copyboy appeared again, shouting, "Mr. Heryford! Mr. Heryford! He did it! Don Larson pitched a perfect game!''

Merle bit the cigar again and said, "Well, he'll never do it again.''

But Merle was a man who was impossible to dislike. That afternoon in Baltimore, Merle and I saw the first-run box office smash of that summer of 1973, *Walking Tall,* starring Joe Don Baker in his unforgettable real-life portrayal of Sheriff Buford "Big Stick" Pusser.

I would have to say that Big Stick Pusser was a helluva lot more entertaining than the piss-stick Texas Rangers. That night Herzog sent yet another "live young arm" to the mound. Steve Dunning had been a top draft choice by Cleveland a couple of years earlier and Herzog had secured his talents in the trade involving Dick Bosman. Dunning, who had graduated from Stanford, was known as Steve Stunning to his new teammates.

Steve Stunning, who later in the year would give up a homerun to the game's first batter in three consecutive starts, would last exactly two-thirds of an inning in this particular outing against the O's. His relief practitioner was still another "live young arm" recently imported from the Angels, Lloyd Allen. Herzog's quick evaluation: "Lloyd hasn't yet learned how to work the hitters with varied pitch selection and changing speeds. But even if he could, it wouldn't do much good because when he throws the ball Lloyd has absolutely no idea where it's going.''

After the Orioles had finished with Dunning and Allen, they led 9–0 after five innings. Meanwhile, Jim Palmer was fashioning what was looking more and more like a perfect game. That lasted two outs into the eighth inning and with the crowd entering an uproar mode, the Rangers' catcher, Ken Suarez, who stood all of five-foot-seven and choked up on the bat a good four inches, slapped a seeing-eye grounder up the middle past Mark Belanger for a single.

Afterward, Rico Carty told me that an inning earlier he had intentionally fouled off a pitch that he thought was ball four because he'd never been involved in a perfect game and didn't want to see it spoiled by a base on balls. When I happened to relay Carty's "disclosure" to Whitey, the manager rolled his eyes and said, "Oh. What a bunch of crap. Besides. If anybody throws a perfect game against this lineup, they oughtta slap an asterisk on it."

The Sunday afternoon finale of the series produced another excruciating excursion through purgatory. Against Dave McNally, the pitcher the Rangers hadn't beaten in seventeen straight starts, it was business as usual, with the Orioles on cruise control and leading 4–1. But the Rangers rallied in the eighth, chased McNally and tied the game when Alex Johnson doubled home two runs off reliever Eddie Watt.

Only the Rangers could prolong the agony like this. The game lasted sixteen innings. Then Merv Rettenmund (once drafted to play football for the Cowboys but never signed) knocked home the winner for the Orioles. By the act of embarking on that eighth-inning rally, the Rangers only succeeded in extending the proceedings another hour and a half on getaway day, thereby missing their flight. They were now scheduled to arrive in Minneapolis at three A.M.

Up in the pressbox, Bob Short presented me with an offer that I couldn't refuse. He invited me to fly over to Minnesota with him in his private jet, arriving in time to meet and interview David Clyde and hammer out a quick feature. After confirming that this private jet was equipped with a liquor cabinet, I agreed.

On the plane, it occurred to me that I had perhaps never seen a man as happy as Bob Short appeared to be on that late afternoon westward journey. "This Clyde . . . you're getting to see . . . is a gift from God," Short was saying. "I mean, beyond what the baseball scouts say. Photogenic. Mature. Articulate. A natural for the media. I mean, he's like a fucking Eagle Scout."

Short's little jet landed in Minneapolis and then we drove over to the Leamington Hotel in a limo. Short also owned the hotel, and when we got there he sprinted directly to the front desk. "Walter," he demanded of the desk clerk. "My young friend David Clyde. Has he checked in yet?"

Walter smiled, nodded and answered, "Why, yes, Mr. Short. You'll find him in the bar."

CHAPTER

8

THE FOLLOWING INCIDENT happened on one of those Rangers trips rather early in the season. My tray table, as usual, was in what the flight attendants call the "down position" and cluttered with the customary assortment of miniature liquor bottles. I was scanning the current issue of Reader's Digest and happened upon a feature headlined "Are You An Alcoholic?"

To find out, the reader was requested to answer twenty simple questions "yes" or "no." Well, I knew what an alcoholic was, having seen Ray "One's Too Many and a Thousand's Not Enough" Milland in "Lost Weekend," but decided to take the quiz anyway. I assure you that I am loosely paraphrasing the actual text of the Reader's Digest article.

Question 1. Do you ever consume more than two drinks in the span of one month?

Question 2. Have you ever consumed more than two drinks in one day?

Question 3. Do you sometimes feel the need to drink in order to enhance your enjoyment of certain social occasions?

Question 4. Have you ever had so much to drink that you cannot entirely remember events of the night before on the morning after?

Question 5. Do you ever vary the types of alcoholic beverages you consume at social occasions? By that, I guessed they meant normal drinking patterns where you switch from beer to wine to gin to rye to Clorox bleach or any other damn thing you can get your hands on when you're the only one still left at the party and the supplies are getting short.

Some quiz, I thought. How many of these Reader's Digest magazines do they sell a month? A billion? Why do they think they have to win over the Hare Krishnas, too? Then, whoever concocted the quiz, turned up the volume a little. The questions became more realistic as the thing went along. I don't remember all of the questions word for word, but the last ones went something like this:

15: Do all the girls look prettier at closing time? (Yes, but the boys don't, thank God.)

16: Do you ever hide alcohol? (Ha! My first "no." Hide my booze? Why the hell should I? A man's home is his castle.)

17: Have you ever had grotesque or terrifying hallucinations, like you're being attacked by a giant flying lizard?

18: Have you, after having too much to drink, shaved your head or painted your genitals purple?

19: Have you ever passed out while smoking in bed but didn't set anything on fire because you'd pissed all over the mattress?

20: Have you ever driven your car over Niagara Falls?

What a snap. Five "no's." I hollered to the stewardess—before "flight attendant"—to bring me two or three more of those little bottles while I turned the page and received some very interesting news. The test person said that if you registered even one "yes" then you were a big-time alkie. "Head to the nearest county hospital, if you can manage to get your car key into the ignition, and check into detox right away because, brother, you are fucked up."

Or words to that effect. What a revelation! Not only was I an alcoholic, but according to the standards of Reader's Digest, so was everyone seated on that airplane. So was everyone in the last eight generations of my family and, in fact, every human being I had encountered since grade school, with the two exceptions of the late Walter R. Humphrey, editor of the Fort Worth *Press,* who never touched a drop in his whole life, and Bobby Bragan, also of Fort Worth, the former manager of the Pirates, Indians and Braves who, if he ever *had* touched a drop, hadn't in the last forty years. And do you know what Bobby Bragan's many friends say about Bobby? "Good old Bobby," they all said. "What a great guy. Imagine what an even greater guy he'd be if he got loaded every once in a while."

Most of my more pragmatic social companions and working associates by far had chosen to avoid AA and instead join AAA, an organization that will tow your car out of a ditch in the pre-dawn hours. As the plane drifted into its final approach, I watched while most of the ballplayers began stuffing the little airline booze bottles into barf bags so that relief supplies would be available on the bus ride from the airport to the hotel. How dare Reader's Digest suggest that these professional athletes couldn't control their drinking activities. Having pondered the overall content of the quiz, my initial impulse was to head to the nearest pay phone when the plane landed, call whoever it was who devised that quiz and propose that he do what I had done and sign on with this . . . this roving airborne madhouse for thirty days, after which time, I would wager, he himself would become the first person ever to score a perfect 20-for-20 in the "yes" column.

The reality was that at age thirty-one I realized my drinking easily exceeded the accepted norms of the general population and ranked me in the top half of my class within the ranks of working print journalists. Only after entering into this association with the Texas Rangers baseball team had I found a work-and-social grouping in which my personal consumption fell in at mid-range. After extensive observation, the conclusion was that I drank more than the infielders but not as much as the pitchers.

The off-the-field play habits of the baseball players that I observed, the activities that entailed corruption of the human soul, mostly concerned extended post-game hours in dimly lit refreshment pavilions in which it was difficult to make conversation over the loud clatter of ice cubes. Contrary to what I presume is the popular notion, efforts to consort with female camp followers happened on an extremely limited basis, because most of the players of that long-ago era lived two-to-a-room on the road and privacy was at a premium. "Let's put it this way," a ballplayer complained to me. "If anybody gets lucky, it usually means that somebody else is going to get to watch. And I'll tell you what. I feel a helluva lot more comfortable being the watcher than the watchee."

Since sportswriters are never called upon to function in either capacity, off-hours were largely devoted to extended visits with John Barleycorn. Too many hours, by my reckoning. Actually, a personal agenda that called for a twenty-five percent alcohol reduction program had actually been activated.

When David Clyde had been sworn into the flock I transposed the agenda and began drinking twenty-five percent more. For the first time since spring training, this job was looking like fun. No longer—for a few weeks, at least—would it be necessary to grope for angles and ideas and explanations to enlighten readership on how the Rangers had managed to lose still another game.

David Clyde was all of a sudden the hottest sports story in the state. Sports Illustrated cover material, in fact. Big news.

When I went into the bar at the Leamington Hotel to meet David for the first time on that Sunday night, Bob Short was relieved to find his brand-new asset drinking a Pepsi, although the cigarette he was smoking—a Salem, as I recall—managed to tarnish Short's Eagle Scout assessment. At six-foot-one, with wide shoulders and long appendages, Clyde at least looked like what a pitcher is supposed to look like and, within the shadows of the Leamington Hotel lounge, he looked older than eighteen, too.

When Short introduced Clyde to Harold McKinney, the guy

covering the team for the morning *Star-Telegram,* David said, "It's a pleasure to meet you, sir." Sir!

When McKinney responded, "Cut the bullshit, kid. You sound like Eddie Haskell," Clyde laughed out loud.

The Hope of the Franchise said all of the right things, for print purposes, and was more quotable than most of his allegedly street-savvy big-league companions. My initial impression was that Clyde was totally tuned in to the fact that a person could pass through 1,000 lifetimes and not experience what he was shortly to encounter. Like the rest of the world, Clyde most certainly had his vulnerabilities, but stage fright wasn't among them.

His only special request from the Rangers, he said (after confirming that Bob Short's bonus check of 150 grand had cleared the bank), was to ask for uniform Number 32 . . . same as Sandy Koufax. In that initial interview, my only suspicions that David Clyde might be carrying a couple of loose connections were aroused when he said that (a) he was thinking about getting married and (b) his career ambition was to become a sportswriter.

One night later, when the Rangers were playing the Twins, it seemed almost as if Bob Short's store-bought gate attraction was acting to rejuvenate the attitude of the jaded Texas players. They beat the Twins, 7–2, with Broberg—a product of Dartmouth College, of all places—pitching like Walter Johnson as he picked up his third straight win.

Jim Mason, a backup shortstop from Alabama who came across in person as a rather mean-spirited Gomer Pyle and who adhered to every stereotype usually associated with the rural South, hit his first career major-league homerun and looked like Marty Marion in the field, particularly on a sensational play where he robbed Rod Carew of a base hit.

And the Rangers won *again* the next night, 3–0, behind the shut-out pitching of Sonny Siebert. Whitey Herzog, a wise man, suspected that all of this was a mirage. He had seen too much baseball to believe in miracles. But Herzog and the rest of the team had also watched with keen interest while David Clyde threw batting practice before the game. Whitey was delighted to see the Rangers hitters reluctant to dig in.

"He had 'em bailing out," Whitey said later at his favorite big-league drinking facility, Howard Wong's restaurant in Minneapolis. Whitey was laughing. Clyde, in fact, could not throw as hard as Whitey's other new hired gun, Jim Bibby, and nobody else in the American League could either. And Clyde, with a big leg kick and a sweeping three-quarter overhand motion, clearly showed enough good stuff to convince Herzog that he might not, perhaps, have to ship David back home in a pine box after his major-league debut.

Revved by stout distilled refreshment personally mixed by Howard Wong's gracious and not unattractive daughter, Herzog was second-guessing himself and arguing that Short's scheme for emergency cash flow might not be such a foolhardy one at that. When Whitey was unwinding from a long day at the yard, I never could figure whether he was talking on the record or not. But he said, "Yeah . . . yeah . . . this looks like a gimmick and a pretty goddamn cheap one at that. I know that . . . But lemmee tell you one thing. This kid is the type of pitcher who'll wind up selling a helluva lotta tickets before he's through."

The difficulty that Herzog was facing now was that a week's worth of games remained on the schedule before Clyde would make his much hyped world premiere at home. After leaving Minnesota, the team traveled to Kansas City for a weekend series.

Jim Merritt, an urbane veteran big leaguer well-schooled in the healing potential of fermented grain who had been hand-picked by Whitey to act as Clyde's roommate and mentor in the ways and means of life on the road, picked up another win on Friday. Then the events of Saturday night presented the team with a reminder of who and what they really were. The Rangers blew a three-run lead in the bottom of the ninth and did not record a single out before Kansas City had scored its four runs. Paul Schaal of the Royals singled home the winning run off Don Stanhouse and, afterward, Schaal offered a strange speculation. "That pitch that I hit to win the game looked like it might have been a spitball," Schaal said. "I'm not saying that it was. I'm just saying that the action on the ball made it look like it was. It acted funny."

Schaal, in all likelihood, was simply attempting to enhance his brief moment in the sunshine by yanking Stanhouse's chain. If that had been Schaal's intent, he was entirely successful. Stanhouse hissed and sputtered when informed of Schaal's veiled accusation, then offered an astute assessment of his own professional skill level at that point in his career. "If I knew how to throw a spitter," he said, "my fuckin' won-lost record would be one goddamn helluva lot better than it is right now."

The next day the Rangers lost both ends of a doubleheader and returned to Texas to go through the motions until Clyde's grand entry. That was set for Wednesday's game against the Twins. The ticket office was inundated with fans armed with cash and Bob Short was adrift in a state of ecstasy.

I drove to the park Monday afternoon to gather information for still another feature about the Kid. An exhibition game against the Astros (one that I fully intended to skip) was scheduled that night. I did take the time to visit the Houston clubhouse to glean some quotes from the manager, Leo Durocher. Leo looked preoccupied, seated at his desk across from some old gargoyle of a bullpen coach. Despite my intrusion, Durocher refused to be distracted from other activities at hand. I threw out a generic question about the overall current state of his pitching staff and Leo said, "Injuries, injuries, injuries. Is that the jack of clubs? Gin."

Leo shuffled and made one discard. I threw out another generic question. "What'll it take to get the Astros back into contention? Any way you can compete with the Reds?"

"Things are going dog shit right now but . . ." He shrugged and said, "Look at that. Four queens. Gin." End of interview.

* * *

ON THE TUESDAY before David Clyde's celebrated unveiling, Oscar Molomont scheduled still another great promotion. Hot Pants Night. This was not a giveaway. Instead, Oscar brainstormed a contest open to any female who wanted to win a trophy confirming that she and only she had the best-looking ass in North Texas. The pageant entries outnumbered the paying fans. They don't have promotions like that at ballparks very much any more.

The setting at Arlington Stadium was very different on Wednesday. Fans began arriving an hour before the gates were open. In the press lounge upstairs, Bob Short looked out, surveyed the gathering throng and said, "They told me it would be like this every night before I moved the team down here."

I wandered down to the dugout, where perhaps a thousand people were jammed, waiting to see the young messiah emerge to warm up. The stands were filling up and even Herzog seemed nervous now, pacing in the dugout tunnel. "This is a helluva thing to ask of an eighteen-year-old kid," he said, as if suddenly stricken by second thoughts. "But that's the way they said they wanted it . . . the kid, his parents, Bob Short. One thing I do feel good about. [Umpire] Ron Luciano will be working the plate. A lot of these old heads like to put the squeeze on a kid like Clyde. But Luciano will call a fair game for him."

Herzog then walked out of the dugout and told the crowd, now eager to catch a glimpse of the Rangers' lefthanded prodigy, "He'll be up here in a minute. I told him to drink a couple of beers and smooth out."

Inside, Clyde seemed completely composed. He was reading a telegram. "Go get 'em Number 32." It was from Sandy Koufax. In the stands, a society writer from the Dallas *Morning News* was interviewing Clyde's petite fiancée, Cheryl Crawford. By now, Clyde was warming up to the accompaniment of high-pitched squeals from some adoring teenyboppers clustered around the bullpen. "I think it's great," Cheryl told the reporter, "that other women find David attractive." Within the course of a year, the future Mrs. Clyde would apparently exercise the female's legendary prerogative to change her mind on that particular topic.

The stadium was completely jammed a half hour before game time and special events coordinator Molomont had even arranged a pre-game show. It was a performance—I am not kidding—by some hula dancers. Presumably, the actual date of David Clyde's big night had been confirmed too late for Oscar to line up some strippers.

At last, there could be no turning back. Clyde walked to the mound to a crowd response that would not be seen at Arlington Stadium again for sixteen years—the night that Nolan Ryan got his 5,000th career strikeout.

The first Twins batter, Jerry Terrell, walked on four pitches. The next batter, Carew, walked on five pitches. "The thought then crossed my mind," Clyde would tell me over one year later, "that I was about to fuck this thing up."

Next, Clyde worked to a 2–2 count on Bobby Darwin, a player built like Mike Tyson. Darwin took the next pitch and umpire Luciano signalled strike three while Arlington Stadium was transformed into an orgasmic ocean of delight. On another 2–2 count the next batter, George Mitterwald, swung late and low on a waist-high fastball. Then Luciano called Joe Lis out on another fastball on a full count. Industrial-strength adrenalin was flowing in the grandstand.

Clyde gave up a two-run opposite-field homerun that curled just inside the foul pole in leftfield to Mike Adams in the second inning. But Clyde continued to pitch through five full innings. His pitching line for the night was two runs, one hit, seven walks, eight strikeouts. He left with the Rangers leading 4–2. Reliever Bill Gogolewski, forever unsung for his effort the rest of the way, allowed one run in the final four innings. Not only would Clyde fulfill the wildest expectations of the crowd, he also got the win. The loser: Nine-time all-star Jim Kaat.

The Twins, for their part, were true major leaguers when it

came to their post-game reaction. Said Bobby Darwin: "Big effing [Darwin's word] deal." Said Rod Carew, watching reporters encircle Mike Adams, who got Minnesota's only hit: "I guess they think it's some kind of miracle that Adams hit a homerun off the guy. Jesus Christ."

Meanwhile, tickets were going on sale at once for Clyde's next scheduled home start against the White Sox. In the press lounge, where the beverage lamp was lit, Bob Short could be seen working out a simple math exercise on a bar napkin with a ballpoint pen. "According to my calculations, on the extra gate receipts alone, in two starts I'll make back David Clyde's entire goddamn signing bonus," Short told me. The man could not contain himself.

On the following night, when it was business as usual again at the park with the Rangers losing to the Twins 4–0 before an announced paid crowd of 3,200—two of whom were given the bum's rush by the stadium cops for shouting racial slurs at Rod Carew—the smile had still not left the face of Robert E. Short and wouldn't, I am told, until the day he died in 1987.

CHAPTER

9

DAVID CLYDE'S RESOUNDING, albeit improbable, triumph on the banks of the Dallas–Fort Worth Turnpike elevated the morale of the whole state. When Clyde's stats were flashed on the garish scoreboard in the Astrodome, Houston fans responded with a standing ovation.

In truth, the spirits of most Texans were already stimulated by a long-awaited event in Austin, the signing of the bill that reinstated the death penalty. Unrestrained joy not seen since the repeal of Prohibition greeted this measure. That same year, somebody was campaigning for the governorship of Alabama with the slogan: "I want to fry 'em until their eyeballs pop out and green and yellow smoke comes out of their ears." Texas' own governor, Dolph Briscoe, clearly lacked the zeal of the Alabama politician. But Briscoe did sign the bill with the same pen that a deputy sheriff in San Antonio was using to write a traffic ticket when some goon gunned him down. Briscoe would be reelected the next year, and overwhelmingly.

In Atlanta, the same week of David Clyde's celebrated launch, Hank Aaron was belting career homerun numbers 696 and 697. In California, Nolan Ryan was pitching his second no-hit game of the season. And in Luckenbach, Texas, Willie Nelson and other notables of what was then known as the progressive country music movement performed an outdoor concert before thousands of adoring "dope smokin' goat ropers."

Not all was rosy in that otherwise golden summer of 1973. A former infielder with several big-league teams was arrested by the FBI in Los Angeles on charges that he'd designed a plan to blow up the Love Boat. J. Edgar Hoover's boys alleged that he attempted to extort $250,000 from the Princess cruise line after threatening to set off some bombs placed on a luxury liner off the west coast of Mexico. Denny McLain, winner of thirty-one games just five seasons earlier and a former employee of Bob Short and a Texas Rangers short-timer from the spring of 1972, didn't appear to be experiencing life to the maximum either. McLain was now pitching for Shreveport in the Texas League.

But the competition for the American having the least fun in the summer of 1973 had settled into a two-horse race involving Richard Nixon and Whitey Herzog.

I think that Whitey was probably having less fun than Dick. As manager of the Rangers, Herzog was forced to climb into the skillet each and every day. The American League standings, unlike certain Watergate witnesses, did not lie. Nixon could at least enjoy occasional escapes to his San Clemente White House. That was where Nixon was, wining and dining his Soviet counterpart, Leonid Brezhnev, on the night that Herzog was watching the White Sox beat his Rangers 15–1.

At Nixon's party for Brezhnev, it was reported that the guest list included Jill St. John . . . "a stunning red-headed actress who caught Brezhnev's eye." I'll bet she did. You can't blame Leonid, of course. We've all seen photographs of those Russian women of that day and they all tend to look like Vince Lombardi, with the exception, of course, of the foxy Marina Oswald, who ran off with a Texas boy!

Not so many movie stars seemed to be appearing at the parties that Whitey was throwing at Arlington Stadium, although several ballplayers were offering convincing impersonations of Buster Keaton. With the season grinding toward the halfway point—the point of no return—the high-amusement profile that Herzog had demonstrated so winningly earlier in the year was beginning to vaporize. So was his paternal approach to some of his prized "live young arms"—specifically Pete Broberg and Don Stanhouse.

Mostly, Whitey's big concern was the combative spirit of Broberg, the Dartmouth product who looked like a pumped-up muscle doll with Troy Donahue's head perched on top. Broberg, unlike most players, was the product of rather privileged circumstances. His father Gus had been a World War II hero and was now a prominent lawyer in a prominent town, Palm Beach, Florida, a swank tropical setting where Pete had been endowed with a perpetual tan.

"When the Senators first drafted Pete, they tell me that Ted Williams watched him throw his fastball and told Broberg that he threw the ball as hard as Bob Feller and would never spend a day in the minor leagues," Herzog said. "If that's the case, that might be part of Pete's problem now." Herzog told me on one of the rare occasions he insisted his remarks stay out of the newspaper, "Short is still clinging to that Bob Feller BS that Williams fed to Broberg."

Privately, Herzog had been attempting to arrange a deal to trade Broberg to Boston. The Red Sox seemingly were more impressed with Broberg's Ivy League background than his lack of finesse on the major-league pitching mound. "They've offered me my pick of two young outfielders, Ben Oglivie or Dwight Evans, and either one of them would be a regular with Texas for the next ten years. But Bob Short won't make the deal," Whitey complained.

(As a historical footnote, it might be pointed out that Ben Oglivie would have fit in well in Texas, indeed. On a road trip, Oglivie departed his room at the Lord Baltimore Hotel for the ballpark and left his shower turned on with the drain plugged. The room flooded and eventually the floor caved in, creating a stressful episode for the couple registered in the room immediately below.)

In Broberg's previous start, Rod Carew had stolen home. As it turned out, Carew could have stolen Whitey's Cadillac and not have had Herzog take it quite so personally. "On the pitch before, Carew danced halfway down the line and Pete didn't look over there. So I yelled out at him to watch third base. But he didn't do that, did he? That's typical of Pete, though. He just doesn't think enough out there." Herzog appeared to be suggesting that some of his live young arms might be brain-dead.

Herzog had somewhat more faith in Stanhouse but voiced dire concerns about his concentration. Herzog provided an illustration. "The other day, when Stanley was pitching in Minnesota, I swear, he kept staring over at this big old set of tits that was sitting behind the Twins' dugout. Well, everybody on our bench was staring at her, too. But we weren't trying to pitch to Harmon Killebrew!"

Other petty annoyances were gnawing at Herzog as well. The Rangers' best everyday player up to this point in the season had been the shortstop, Toby Harrah, product of a state best known for its youthful entries in the Mrs. America Pageant—West Virginia. Toby had been hitting a little too well of late, so Kansas City's Paul Splittorff decided to expunge this growing hazard from the Ranger lineup. This was accomplished by the customary expedient of aiming a fastball at Toby's chin. Toby raised his hand to protect himself and the result was a broken left hand.

Harrah found solace by citing what is not only the West Virginia Golden Rule but also the official state motto. "Better a broken hand than a broken face," Toby cheerfully reminded the media, and any youngsters who might have been listening. Still, Harrah would miss at least two weeks and there was no one on Whitey's bench who could adequately replace the major leagues' leading palindrome. Pete Mackanin would be summoned from the minors. "Mackanin has the best glove in our whole organization," Whitey said. "He's overmatched at the plate in Spokane right now, so he might as well be overmatched here, too," Herzog reasoned.

Another recent development was starting to chew at Herzog's

gut as well. The B-e-e-g Boy was finally beginning to h-e-e-t. Rico had socked one about 450 feet against the Royals and looked like Young Frankenstein as he lumbered—that's the only word for it—around the bases. Carty, in fact, had gone 8-for-8 during the home stand, a streak that was threatening some kind of record, which was spoiling Whitey's plans to gracefully hand Carty an unconditional release. About two weeks earlier, Whitey and Rico had almost gotten into a fistfight in the dugout after Carty had cussed Herzog for not backing him in a dispute with an umpire over a called strike. Apparently it occurred to Herzog that while the B-e-e-g Boy might be able to hit the American League version of a curveball, Carty suddenly appeared damned capable of hitting the old skipper, and Whitey wanted him gone.

Bob Short was not in favor of disposing of Carty, since he assumed most of the off-season credit for bringing Rico and his once grand stats over from Atlanta. Herzog's response: "Every other team in the division, including the Angels, is playing about .500 right now. We're at 29–51, so what the hell difference does it make whether Carty ever hits again or not?"

Every brand-new day presented if not a brand-new crisis then at least a new and different category of pain-in-the-ass. Steve Foucault, who most definitely had not attended Dartmouth College, had been the most dependable bullpen resource of the Rangers for the first half of the season. Foucault had the body of the animated hero Fred Flintstone. But his right arm appeared to have been formed from some synthetic and highly flexible substance that enabled him to whip the ball toward the plate and retire hitters with some consistency.

Then, during a pre-game batting practice session, Foucault was apparently running some wind sprints in the outfield when he ran into Jackie Moore, the third base coach who was out there shagging fly balls. Foucault broke his collarbone and would miss six weeks. A joke was circulating in North Texas that summer: "Did you hear about the freak accident? Two freaks in a van ran over a freak on a motorcycle."

In an act of bad timing, Steve Foucault's freak accident happened about an hour prior to the Second Coming of David Clyde.

Again, the stands were almost full. A gathering of 33,000 that was every bit as frantically fired up as the worshipful group in the stadium for Clyde's maiden voyage watched Kid Lefty fire away at the White Sox and duplicate the results he had posted against the Twins. Clyde pitched six innings this time, and left with the Rangers leading 3–2.

With Foucault busted up, Herzog turned to Mike Paul, who was prematurely gray at thirty-three and justifiably so, and then Stanhouse for relief. The results were predictable—the Kid's lead was allowed to slip away. Instead of Clyde coming away with another W, Stanhouse left the park with another L, which put his record at 1–7.

Herzog was philosophical about the outcome. "When you take Clyde out, the crowd hauls ass anyway. But that Clyde. He's somethin'. It looks like he's burning ethyl while the rest of these guys are on regular."

Over in the Chicago clubhouse, the comments were more charitable than those made by the Twins at Clyde's debut. Chuck Tanner, the manager, went to great lengths to explain how Clyde might be the final cog in a big wheel that just might take the Rangers on to a pennant. "As early as next season!" Tanner said.

I chose not to put those comments in public print. Chuck Tanner had not been watching a team that, over the course of eighty games, was not exactly playing the game that Abner Doubleday had in mind when he invented the sport. Actually, the notion that Abner Doubleday invented the game had been incontrovertibly proven to be a myth. But if Doubleday *had* invented baseball, the 1973 Rangers would have given cause for him to reconsider.

Additionally, I sought an appraisal of Clyde from the White Sox pitching coach, Johnny Sain. Yes, I was talking to the very same Johnny Sain of "Spahn and Sain and pray for rain" immortality from the 1948 Boston Braves. "What's not to like?" said Johnny Sain of David Clyde. "What difference does it make if he's only eighteen? It's experience, not age, that counts in this league."

I pointed out to Sain that Clyde had no experience, either. "Well, in baseball and in life, you learn that it's who you rub elbows with that counts. You have to walk down the highway a lot of miles with a man before you really know the size of the shoes he's trying to fill," Sain told me with a solemn nod.

The next day, Sain was quoted in the *Star-Telegram* as having said, "For a young guy, David Clyde sure does have big feet." My readers would have wanted it that way.

Upstairs in the media lounge, Harry (Hol-lee Cow!) Caray, the Voice of the White Sox at the time, known as the Mouth of Middle America, was having his say. At the time, Harry was initiating a career comeback in Chicago. His storied tenure in St. Louis had ended when Caray was run over by a taxi and almost killed. Dark and unsubstantiated hearsay whispered for a time that the accident had been arranged by someone connected with the Cardinals management.

That was in the past and now Harry was telling us his thoughts on young King David. "GOD . . . [twelve-second pause] . . . DAMN! WHERE'D THAT KID COME FROM? JEE—SUS! WHAT A FIND!"

The game the next night would conclude what would always rate as the most eventful home stand in the history of a franchise that has lasted almost twenty-five years. Herzog was offering his State of the Staff message before the game.

"For the first time, I'd say that I'm comfortable with the rotation," he said. In fact, this was the first time since the end of spring training that he could even identify a rotation.

Clyde, of course, was confirmed as a regular. "In two starts the kid has shown that he's not just some two-headed calf we're putting out there as a drawing card. I don't see any reason now why we can't count on him to give us six good innings at least and get a lot of people out while he's doing it," Herzog said. In the course of six days it seemed that David Clyde had established himself as the ace of the staff. And what a staff.

Whitey was also now sold on his other "find," Jim Bibby, who had proved that he was more than just the man with a gargantuan apparatus that might someday qualify for display at the Smithsonian. Buried beneath the hype of David Clyde's first start, Bibby had shut out Kansas City two nights later with a one-hitter.

"The rap on Bibby was that he had a history of control problems, but I really haven't seen that yet," said Whitey. "Of course," Herzog conceded, "if Bibby ever does let one slip, he's liable to send somebody to intensive care. But the hitters know that and it's about time we're able to throw somebody out there that people are a little scared of."

Jim Merritt, the man otherwise known as Bones, had made the roster out of spring training because of his résumé. He had won seventeen games for Sparky Anderson at Cincinnati in 1969 and twenty the year the Reds won the pennant in 1970. Going for his twenty-first win against the Giants, Merritt had said, "I heard something pop in my left shoulder while I was pitching to Willie McCovey." He'd blown out his arm and only a salvage yard like Texas would take a chance on a restoration project such as Merritt. Bones knew that his pitching arm would forevermore maintain all the zing of overcooked pasta, so he was giving consideration to developing a new pitch that might enable him to last the season and maybe one or two more as well without having to rely altogether on chicanery and guile. And so far, Merritt had somehow come away with three wins in four starts.

Sonny Siebert, Herzog's other veteran, had been solid as the fourth starter. Steve Dunning would remain the fifth starter, although Herzog sized him up with carefully measured enthusiasm. Dunning was the player acquired from Cleveland in the Dick Bosman swap, and Herzog cast out a slightly different slant to the time-honored "the trade helped both teams" bromide to justify the transaction. "Dick hasn't done much for Cleveland and Steve hasn't looked too good for us, either," Herzog said.

Out in the clubhouse, suitcases and assorted other stacks of paraphernalia were being loaded into a truck that would haul them to the Ranger 727 charter that would fly to Milwaukee that night. The man supervising the loading was equipment manager Joe Macko, who was also known as Smacko when he was always contending for Texas League homerun championships in the late forties. Actually, more people knew him as the owner of Smacko's beer joint than as an ex-minor-league star.

Two suitcases would not be making the flight. While outlining the membership for his realigned pitching staff, Herzog mentioned in passing that both Stanhouse and Broberg had been optioned to Spokane. Typically, Whitey didn't airbrush the announcement with management jive.

"I don't think anyone doubts the major-league potential of Don or Pete," Herzog said. "But what I do question is the dedication—or lack of dedication—by both of them. If they go to Spokane, join the rotation and learn how to pitch, I think they'll be back. Otherwise, we might not hear from them again."

Earlier in the year, throughout spring training and into the first months of the season, several of the Rangers players had seemed giddy over what they viewed as the emancipating presence of Whitey Herzog. The new manager was not only accessible but actually would listen to their complaints. He appeared tolerant of on-the-field lapses. All of this stood out in what the players unanimously agreed was dramatic contrast to the frosty climate of the Ted Williams regime. According to the never-ending testimonials offered by a variety of Senators-Rangers, Williams mostly came across as Teddy the Terrible, Imperial Czar of the American League basement.

"Ted couldn't understand why everybody couldn't hit .400 like he could . . . Ted thought we were all a bunch of morons and took every available opportunity to let us know that . . . Just because I don't know where the tarpon are running or who

Harry Greb knocked out in 1925 doesn't make me a complete idiot, does it? . . . The only encouragement Ted ever gave me was to suggest I try for a job skill outside of baseball . . . Ted got pissed off because I spent more time working on my golf swing than my baseball swing! . . . Ted didn't have any respect for anybody but himself . . . Ted was a horse's ass . . ."

Such comments represented the litany that came streaming forth from quite a few of the holdover players. They described Williams in various ways, but all agreed that Teddy Ball Game was a relentless perfectionist. It's easy to see how a player with the requisite physical tools to bat .300 but who was hitting .225 because he persisted on swinging at pitches outside the strike zone could, under the intense scrutiny of a man such as Williams, find life sometimes oppressive.

Now some of these same players were learning that the congenial Whitey Herzog, himself no .400 hitter and therefore capable of understanding that most players aren't, also had limits to his well of compassion.

CHAPTER

10

BOB SHORT AND his entire Rangersland operation had become the topic of considerable coast-to-coast public disdain from the high echelons of the Baseball Writers Association of America. His stunt of hauling a high schooler into the center ring was widely pilloried as the kind of dilapidated theatrics and carnival mentality that might be acceptable in a court of law but never within the sanctity of a ballyard.

Here, the baseball press was ignoring or was oblivious to the obvious, something they had refined to a science over the years. Had the traditionalists of the sport not noticed that professional baseball, in terms of general interest and paid attendance, was lingering in a state of advanced constipation? Wasn't the media overlooking the fact that big-league baseball, the American League version of it in particular, had been lapsing into near-obsolescence as an entertainment venture?

To illustrate the sorry state of the American League in 1973, the major-league owners took a vote on introducing inter-league play in future seasons. The vote, for the first time in baseball ownership history, was unanimous. All of the American League owners voted "yes" and all of the National League owners voted "no." Commissioner Kuhn could have cast a vote of his own that would have broken the tie, but he refused to do it and the issue was dead.

The advent of television and its splendid marriage with professional football was largely held out as the root cause of baseball's broadening relationship with the empty seat. Baseball, conversely, was and always will be the paradigm of *radio* sports. An announcer like, say, Red Barber, after developing a following, could make the audio version of a baseball game more captivating to many fans than the version that was being served at the ballpark itself.

Baseball and TV have never really gotten along all that well, at least since the network people quit letting Dizzy Dean guzzle his sponsor's product, Falstaff beer, while on the air. According to the legend, and I presume this to be apocryphal, Old Diz was doing his usual Saturday schtick, swilling down the Falstaff and singing "The Wabash Cannon Ball" when the CBS cameras picked up a youthful couple seated in the outfield at Wrigley Field, ignoring the game and involved in what was known at the time as light to moderate petting. "I know what's going on there," Diz supposedly told his nationwide audience. "He's kissing her on the strikes and she's kissing him on the balls."

I can only presume that Dizzy Dean never actually uttered those lovely words. I do know that in the latter stages of his tenure with CBS, Diz seemed to employ a toned-down approach to his descriptions of the games that to me smelled of network-sponsor-imposed restraint. Whatever. His telecasts were no longer as much fun, and neither, in turn, was baseball.

There's another theory, and this one is entirely mine, as to why baseball drifted from the mainstream of sports-fan attention. I blame Lyndon Johnson and Vietnam. Nobody can deny that with the advent of the Seventies, the American League had ceased to produce the box-office stars. The Mantles and the Berras were retiring and little of replacement value was coming along. Why? The leading teenage athletes were mostly turning to football and basketball. The baseball signing bonus was eschewed in favor of the college athletic scholarship and the draft deferment that came with it.

Plus, the kids were simply beginning to wise up. Why subject themselves to those eternal bus rides in the Alfalfa League when they could go to college for free and devote endless evenings to porking Chi Omegas in the backseat of a new GTO presented courtesy of the booster club. Ten years earlier, I can guarantee you that Joe Namath would have been pitching somewhere in the big leagues and not having to worry whether Coach Bear Bryant might want to smell his breath an hour before a bowl game.

True, the military draft was about over by 1973, but the American League's agenda of new names with any ticket-window magnetism was practically zilch.

Another problem. The baseball owners were not individuals renowned for their cutting-edge approach to the mysteries of modern marketing. At the annual owners' meeting, almost always held at Palm Springs so that the richest of the owners, Gene Autry, wouldn't have to travel too far to get there, the owners were recognizable as the fellows prowling the hotel lobbies with Cream o' Wheat on their chins and approaching strangers to ask them if they knew what day it was.

Bob Short and Charles O. Finley stood alone as American League owners who were equipped with a fundamental sense of direction of where the game was heading, and they knew the exact station where they intended to get off.

Milwaukee, for sure, stood out as a living example of a baseball venue that was not what it once was. Certainly, the American League Brewers, an expansion team that landed in the American Malt Capital only after it had flopped in Seattle, was a watered-down facsimile of the great Braves teams of Henry Aaron, Warren Spahn, Eddie Matthews, Lou Burdette, et al . . . the Braves who left town and moved to Atlanta because ownership sniffed a quicker buck down there.

Crowds of about 10,000 were more commonplace now when the Brewers played in Milwaukee—an old Iroquois word that means "land of many Polish-Americans." That 10,000 was about what was on hand when the Rangers opened a series on Friday night. Jim Merritt, still field-testing his newly lubricated left-handed offerings, picked up still another win and Jeff Burroughs hit a homerun.

Afterward, the thought occurred to me that Burroughs might be the only player in the majors to use a game-winning homer as the topic of a forum for his pet polemic, which was the hostile prevailing winds at his home park back in Arlington. "That homerun? Just a long out back in Texas. Just another long fuckin' out," he was telling Lou Chapman of the *Journal*, who I think was approaching his second century of covering baseball in Milwaukee. (Chapman's special claim to fame was when, so it is said, he hid in an equipment trunk in the clubhouse of the old Braves to eavesdrop on a team meeting.)

"That wind in Arlington has turned me into a singles hitter," Burroughs said. "No reason to swing for the fences down in Texas because if you do, you're going to suffer." Bitch, bitch, bitch. The Texas press had heard it all before. Lou Chapman, though, was taking it all down.

To be fair, by the end of the season Burroughs would hit thirty homeruns, and no Ranger would hit as many for the next thirteen seasons.

The next game, on Saturday afternoon, brought 15,000 to the stands. Few, I suppose, would remember what happened, but this game was memorable because it gave David Clyde an accurate gauge as to exactly where his baseball future would eventually lead. In Clyde's third-ever major-league start, the Milwaukee Brewers, rarely mistaken for a juggernaut at the plate with the lineup featuring Bob Coluccio and Sixto Lezcano, beat David Clyde and the Rangers, 17–2.

This was not a case of the wholesale collapse of a neo-natal legend. The Brewers had already bounced Clyde around to the tune of seven runs in four and two-thirds innings when Whitey came out to fetch him from the mound. By the standards of the 1973 Rangers staff, that effort constituted a routine start. The remainder and uglier portions of the damage were heaped on the relief corps, or what Herzog often termed the "arson squad," the relief tandem of Mike Paul and Lloyd Allen.

County Stadium, by the way, contained (and still does) one of the more startling ballpark features of the American League. Next to the scoreboard in centerfield, high over the stands, a structure resembling an alpine chalet sits occupied by the team mascot, Bernie Brewer. Whenever a Milwaukee player hits a homerun, Bernie Brewer, clad in a traditional Oktoberfest get-up, zips down a slide into a giant beer mug and releases some white balloons that represent, yes, beer bubbles. I am not going to suggest that the Bernie Brewer routine could or should be written off as hokey. That's for greater minds than mine to decide. What I do know is that with Lloyd Allen pitching for the Rangers, Bernie Brewer was working his butt off.

After the game, Herzog tossed out a peculiar reason for David Clyde's rough outing. "David said the ball felt big in his hand," Herzog said. "That's often a sign that a pitcher doesn't have his real good stuff." The kid who had just ascended straight from his manger and into the big leagues offered what seemed a more reasonable explanation: "Maybe I'm not so tough to hit in daylight games," he said.

That night, while pondering the topic of how things could go so wrong so quickly, I would encounter a fact that many Americans probably do not realize. People in Milwaukee do not consume beer in conspicuously vast quantities. But they do drink one hell of a lot of brandy. So, on a Saturday night in the Pfister Hotel, I decided to help them drink it, choosing an inexpensive brand. The label read: "Isaac Newton Brandy . . . What Goes Down Must Come Up." A portion of this particular Saturday evening was spent with young Joe Lovitto, soon to be handed a reservation on Whitey Herzog's transport to Spokane. I recall with some haziness pointing out to Lovitto that "all these women in Milwaukee seem to have fat ankles." Lovitto shot back, "Beats the hell out of Cleveland, then. I'd rather look at a fat ankle than a fat ass." I know, I know . . . what a couple of rank sexist porkers. Real different from the players and sports-writers of today, of course. You bet.

Upon my Sunday afternoon arrival for a double-header at County Stadium, my head was a gelatinous blimp-sized container of tortured nerve endings. That much, I deserved. Richly so. What I did not deserve was Bat Day, an event at which 31,000 representatives of the pride of Wisconsin youth receive a free bat. Why would they stage a thing like that in a steel ballpark, where the pressbox is located immediately beneath the base of the upper deck?

The pounding of wooden bat against metal grandstand started even before the first pitch of the first game, producing the sort of concussive effect that used to happen when we'd drop a cherry bomb down the toilet at junior high school. The acoustics in the pressbox were like the interior of a submarine under attack from depth charges. Wham! Wham! Wham! Louder and louder yet. Why were these children doing this to me? What had I ever done to harm them? Finally, I almost approached a stadium cop guarding the pressbox door and asked if there was any way he could make them stop.

All I could do, finally, was to place my head next to my typewriter and pray for the swift arrival of the Angel of Death. When I finally opened my eyes again, the first game was over. According to the numbers on the scoreboard, the Brewers had beaten Jim Bibby, 7–3, and from the sound of things, Bernie Brewer had been subjected to another active outing.

Now, in the third inning of the second game, the Rangers were already hopelessly beaten and Whitey Herzog was on the field, screaming at plate umpire Bill Haller and flapping his wings like some crazed gander.

Afterward, when the kids with the bats had ceased their assault and were filing out to go home to Oshkosh and Sheboygan and wherever else, I entered the Rangers' clubhouse to inquire as to the source of Whitey Herzog's affliction. His response provided what turned out to be the post-game highlight of my entire tour covering this outlandish baseball franchise:

"It started yesterday, when they were beating up on us with seventeen runs. I knew something was up and figured the third base coach was stealing Suarez's [the catcher's] signs," said Herzog, speaking rapidly and making wild, pointing gestures, like in an old film of Mussolini making a speech. "But today, in the first game, I figured it out. I got some binoculars and looked out there in centerfield where they keep that little asshole in the costume.

"And that's when I saw the other guy and that's when I was positive. He had binoculars, too, picking up our signs. Then . . . the other one . . . in the costume . . . he wears these white gloves and he'd clap his hands. Once for a curve and twice for a fastball. That's how they were doing it. That has to be it. Either they were getting our pitches or this is the greatest hitting team of all time."

Herzog added that after the opening game loss "I wanted to send Bibby up there to Bernie Brewer's little house and kick his goddamn ass. But I didn't."

Herzog concluded with a statement that encompassed the spectrum of what had largely amounted to a season of abject frustration: "Can you imagine," Whitey demanded, "that a team would have to cheat to beat *us*?"

Milwaukee manager and baseball fixture Del Crandall, when presented with Whitey's contention, shook his head. He'd seen Whitey's Rangers on display here, too, and could sympathize with Herzog, perhaps now enduring what health professionals at the time might have termed an emotional breakdown. Some guy in the Brewers' clubhouse took me aside and said that Bernie, in real life, was the son of some team employee. "The kid . . . and please don't print this . . . but his blender doesn't go all the way to puree, if you know what I mean. Steal signs? Hell. It's all he can do to release those goddamn balloons."

The Rangers left town and the Bernie Brewer incident never escalated into anything beyond Herzog's post-game blowup. I didn't know who to feel sorrier for . . . Whitey or Bernie.

* * *

In Detroit, the next stop on the road trip, Herzog's forces continued to swing and sway with the official Rangers Dance. One step forward, two steps back. They won the Monday night opener, even though Steve Stunning gave up three homers. Jim Merritt surrendered two more on Tuesday, both by Dick Sharon, as the Tigers evened the series. On Wednesday, four homers by the Tigers (two by Jim Northrup and one apiece by Dick McAuliffe and Duke Sims) helped capsize the Rangers, 14–2. The starting rotation that Herzog had endorsed back in Texas was falling apart . . . was a shambles, in fact. Sonny Siebert was now out with a bad shoulder. Texas pitching had been lit up for seventeen homers in its previous six games.

The trip to Detroit was not entirely wasted. Several of the players replenished their wardrobes at a downtown clothing establishment called Hot Sam's, which specialized in apparel not frequently found on the floor of the British House of Lords. Hot Sam's featured suits suited for the Seventies. Polyester fibers. Wide lapels. Wider cuts yet . . . sweeping . . . around-the-pants cuffs. Colors that would match a Jamaican sunset. Several of the Rangers wore their Hot Sam's ensembles with pride for the remainder of the season. Some looked like pallbearers at Bugsy Siegel's funeral.

An additional highlight of the Detroit visit occurred at the airport, where I actually shook hands with Linda Lovelace, star of *Deep Throat*. Linda had been spotted by some fans as she was standing near a metal detector and signing autographs. (Other airport sightings that summer included Roy Rogers, Ted Kennedy and Howard Cosell.)

And, according to Detroit *Free Press* baseball writer Jim Hawkins, I'd come within a day of being introduced to Detroit Shirley. This was the lady famous for having shared various intimacies with celebrities in every professional sport from archery to tractor pulls. I wanted to ghostwrite Shirley's book. She had been on the disabled list for almost twelve weeks after an encounter with a hockey player (a Frenchman, naturally) got out of control and now America's Sweetheart was back in commission. "You just missed her," Hawkins said. "Shirley's in Cincinnati now. She just called me in the pressbox and wanted to know which hotel the Cardinals might be staying in. She said she'd never fucked the Cardinals before." Hawkins, a reporter with sources, always seemed to know how to get in contact with Detroit Shirley whenever there was a crisis.

NEXT STOP, BOSTON.

In the novel *Dr. No,* Ian Fleming wrote that James Bond liked Texans better than other Americans. But in my travels I've learned that most Americans do not exactly share the sentiments of James Bond.

Maybe it's because of the notion that Texans make too much noise when they get drunk. Or am I projecting? Or maybe it's because they think that most Texans maintain a primitive outlook when it comes to so-called gay rights. I don't agree with that. Most Texans exhibit admirable levels of tolerance and understanding. If that's their pleasure, then as we say in Texas . . . by God, we're proud for 'em.

Anyway, I'm convinced there is no place where Texans are disliked more than in Boston, and at least in those days it didn't have anything to do with concerns just mentioned. After arriving in Boston from Detroit, I was sharing a delicate Chardonnay with Bill Sudakis, one of the Rangers' utility players. Some guy at the table next to our booth asked where we were from, and when I said, "Dallas," the guy smirked and responded, "Dallas? That's where they shot the President, didn't they?"

Sudakis nodded, stuck an index finger against his right temple and said, "Right there."

In the restaurant of the downtown Sheraton Hotel the next morning, a waitress confirmed some other matters that I suspected about this team I was following. "What's with the Rangers?" she asked me. "Every team in the American League stays here and the Rangers come in for breakfast a whole lot later than the rest. Also, they drink more coffee, smoke more cigarettes and order the heaviest things on the menu." Emerson might call it compensation.

Two tables over, David Clyde, sitting alone, was reading about himself in the Boston *Globe*. A banner headline said: "Kid Sensation To Face Sox Tonight At Fenway." That was not the sports page but the regular front section. The story about John Dean's testimony in the Watergate hearings was positioned farther down on the page. Clyde looked at the headline without expression and took a deep drag off his Salem. The events of the previous two weeks were finally, I figured, about to make a cerebral impact. "Probably wishes now that he'd never left Westchester High. Fenway Park? Hostile crowd? The Green Monster? Carl Yastrzemski? Orlando Cepeda at DH? They're going to light him up like the Coconut Grove fire."

In fact, the near sellout crowd at Fenway Park was not all that hostile. Everyone stood up and applauded when the Kid made the long and lonely march in from the bullpen in rightfield before he started pitching the bottom of the first inning.

They also stood and applauded—and cheered loudly—when Clyde finally left the game after seven innings. He'd given up one run when the Rangers' infield misplayed a grounder and another when Tommy Harper lofted a soft homer into the net atop the Green Monster. Clyde would take the loss, because the Rangers could muster only a solitary run in the way of support. For the night: Seven innings, two runs, seven hits, no walks and eight strikeouts. Not too shabby.

Afterward Yastrzemski told me, "In my second at bat, the kid threw as well as any pitcher I have faced in my career. The ball seemed to come out of nowhere. He struck me out and I wasn't surprised when he did."

Cepeda, now at the end of his career and playing thanks to the advent of the designated-hitter rule, did in fact compare David Clyde favorably with Sandy Koufax. "And that," Cepeda added, "means trouble for the hitters in this league."

Luis Aparicio, in Boston to wind down his Hall of Fame in-field career, allowed that "I've never been so impressed with a young pitcher."

Were the Red Sox simply blowing smoke, setting Clyde up for a rematch later in the season back in Arlington? Probably. But the Sox, to their credit, were making the task of covering a dead-end baseball team considerably less anxiety-provoking. So was Whitey Herzog. Before the start of the series at Fenway Park he jettisoned the immortal "player to be named later" from the Rangers' farm system to make room for Jim Fregosi, a former seven-time all-star shortstop with the Angels and lately of the New York Mets. He brought more to the Rangers than experience and a good bat.

His stay in New York had been a somewhat troubled one. The Mets had traded Nolan Ryan to acquire Fregosi's services. In subsequent seasons, while Ryan was setting the baseball world ablaze, Fregosi was not. Fans in New York are known to have what might be termed a high-gratification-expectation (HGE) quotient, and the media there was ever helpful in reminding Fregosi that the paying customers were displeased.

"Yeah, I was really going horseshit in New York," said Fregosi as he walked with Galloway, McKinney and me from the park to the hotel lounge. "But I've been hard at work on my book," he added. He said he was entitling the autobiography *The Bases Were Loaded And So Was I.*

This Rangers team was ordained to stack up losses in numbers that would be unsurpassed in franchise history. But Herzog was now determined. If his team was going to lose, it was going to lose with style.

CHAPTER

11

According to a two-paragraph item stuck on the back page of my newspaper, the *Star-Telegram,* the city of Fort Worth had just lost a proud citizen. I don't recall the guy's name, exactly, but he did have one of those standard-issue Fort Worth–West Texas names like Bob Ray or Mack Ed. Anyway, according to the paper, this guy had been beaten to death with his own six-pack of cold beer in the parking lot of Donnie's Blue Room Lounge in the honky-tonk district along the Jacksboro Highway, also known as the Old Jizzum Trail. The honky-tonk district in Fort Worth, by the way, begins at the intersection of Twelfth and Throckmorton and extends northward to the city limits of Pawnee, Oklahoma.

Back in the world of baseball, the Detroit Tigers had just experienced manslaughter in Arlington Stadium. The Rangers, for the first time that season, had completed a three-game series sweep, and the ignominious distinction of being the team on the losing end of that proposition belonged to the Tigers. After the third game, I ventured over to the Detroit clubhouse to see if manager Billy Martin might have some kind of explanation.

There was nothing to fear in attempting that, really. My paper, after all, had a comprehensive health-insurance plan. I was met at the door by the trainer of the Tigers. He put his index finger to his lips, said "sshhh," and then we tiptoed back to the manager's office, where Martin bore the eyes of a man who had just been . . . well . . . beaten up with his own six-pack.

Few American citizens could match Billy Martin's legitimate reputation as a back-alley ass-kicker, but the man's voice was misleadingly soft. He sounded like Mr. Rogers, the kiddie show guy in the cardigan sweaters. "Give all the credit to those guys," said Billy, gesturing toward the Rangers' dugout. "They played damn solid ball for three days. No mistakes." That much was true. Martin simply had to be wondering what cosmic disturbances were at work that called for his Tigers to be in town on this rare occasion when the Rangers performed like a major-league baseball team instead of a warm-up act for the Flying Walendas.

More than anything on the planet, Billy Martin desired to manage in a World Series. The year before, he had been deprived of that opportunity because of a dreadful call by a first-base umpire that cost the Tigers the deciding game in the league championship series against Dick Williams' Oakland A's. Martin now suspected, and with good reason, that this season's Tigers might lose the Eastern Division race to the superior pitching and defense of the Orioles. Dropping three games in Arlington spelled doomsday.

Lyndon Johnson once noted that the only event a political candidate could not overcome was "being caught in bed with a dead woman or a live man." If one wished to draw comparisons between politics and baseball, it could safely be alleged that pennant contenders in a close race might as well gargle with Drano as drop three straight to a recovery-room outfit like the Rangers. Billy Martin could not have realized it at the time, but something else involving the Texas baseball franchise was looming in his future about sixty days down the road, and it was a destiny far more daunting than the mere loss of a three-game series.

Whitey Herzog probably thought that he had accidentally tiptoed into the Twilight Zone. First his team had swept the Tigers. Then, two nights later, Herzog gazed at the lineup card hanging next to the bat rack in his dugout with an air of quiet reverence, as if it had been painted on the wall by Claude Monet. Herzog probably didn't know the difference between Claude Monet and Clint Courtney, But to me it seemed that Whitey was tilting his head, as if attempting to capture the lineup card in various shadings of light.

He searched the card up and down and nowhere on it was there a Carty or a Maddox or a Mason or a Steve Stunning. The names on his team this night would include Bert Campaneris, Rod Carew, John Mayberry, Reggie Jackson, Carlton Fisk, Bobby Murcer and Brooks Robinson. His starting pitcher would be Catfish Hunter. This was the starting lineup that the American League would put on the field at the major-league all-star game in Kansas City, and American League manager Dick Williams had invited Whitey to serve as his third-base coach.

I suspect Williams had, at least in part, extended that honor as an act of compassion. Everybody in the league seemed moved by the dignity that Whitey had shown while playing with the cards he had been dealt in his first managerial post. Of course, not everybody had been exposed to Whitey backstage and after hours, when he was saying what he actually thought about his extended baseball family of yo-yo's and castaways. So, in Kansas City, Herzog was like a soldier with a three-day furlough, soaking in the R and R of all-star talent before returning to another ninety days of digging latrines.

Some personalities of interest stood out among the National League contingent, too. Pete Rose, Joe Morgan, Johnny Bench, Ron Santo. But this was the summer of 1973, which meant that the barbaric media horde would be ignoring most of this collection of smokeless tobacco luminaries and cluster at the feet of Hank Aaron. The mob had gathered around Aaron's locker and the NL clubhouse looked like the banks of the Ganges on a holy day. I don't know to what extent the average fan had been consumed by Aaron's inexorable advance on Babe Ruth's career homerun record, although nobody could doubt the depth of the media's obsession with what amounted to the changing of an historic statistical guard.

Aaron seemed to withstand the mass interrogation with all the patience that he could reasonably muster, but he also, upon reading his quotes from afar, seemed to me to be becoming a trifle peevish. For one thing, he had been receiving considerable written correspondence from some Mississippi barnburners and others of that ilk who were unhappy that a black man was encroaching into the hallowed homerun territory of the Great White Hedonist himself, the Babe. But what, I think, Aaron found to be far more burdensome was simply enduring the task of answering, again and again, the same questions from these reporters. Only in this case, he was repeatedly faced with the same question (singular), and that question always began with the word "when."

He told the mob in Kansas City that the anxiously awaited "when" of homeruns Numbers 714 and 715 would not happen in the season of 1973 but more likely early the next year. That satisfied the troops and most soon abandoned the area. I stood among perhaps a remaining dozen when Aaron said something interesting. He had just smacked Number 700 off George Brett's big brother Ken of the Phillies. And now Aaron was seriously miffed at none other than Bowie Kuhn, the commissioner of baseball.

"I got dozens and dozens of congratulatory telegrams when I got the 700th," he said. "I got one from Jesse Jackson. I got one from Chub Feeney [National League president]. But I didn't get one from Bowie." Aaron then paused and for the first time all day, he smiled. "I didn't get one from Nixon, either," he said, "but I wasn't expecting one from him."

Having finished listening to Hank Aaron, I also needed to extract some comments from two all-stars wearing Rangers uniforms. One was Dave Nelson, whom Dick Williams had selected for the team because, according to the guidelines of the event, at least one player from every team had to be included. Then, just the day before, Carl Yastrzemski was out of the contest because of an injury. Maybe Yaz had popped a gut string trying to hit David Clyde. Whatever, Dick Williams stunned the baseball world by naming Rangers first baseman Jim Spencer as Yaz's emergency replacement.

Spencer, who had joined the Rangers from California in May in the swap for Mike Epstein, seemed as flabbergasted as anyone else. I asked Spencer to explain to my readers What Being In The All-Star Games Means To Me, in twenty-five words or less. "Messed up some plans," he answered. "We were having some people over to watch it on TV." He also volunteered deeper reflections on this 1973 season that had brought him such a large serving of the unexpected.

I recalled the expression on Spencer's face that afternoon in Anaheim when I ventured into the clubhouse to get his reaction to being traded to Texas . . . and it wasn't the reaction that I had anticipated. "Trade? What trade?" Spencer had said. Nobody from the Angels had gotten around to breaking the news to him. "Guess somethin's up, huh? I better go talk to [Manager Bobby] Winkles."

Spencer had seemed cheerful enough when he came back out of Winkles' office. "I've played over there before," said Spencer, groping to locate a bright side. "El Paso, in the Texas League. The ball carried damn good and the fence was only about 280 feet down the rightfield line. I poked a bunch of 'em out of that place and whenever I did, these Mexicans would stick dollar bills through the backstop and I'd trot over there and gather the cash. Do they do that in Arlington?"

In his first and last career at-bat in the all-star game, Jim Spencer almost hit a homerun. His deep fly ball hooked past the wrong side of the flagpole by about three feet. In the end, while Herzog and Spencer might have been sharing the dugout with a dream lineup, the results were all too familiar. The American League got stomped, 7–1.

*   *   *

BACK IN ARLINGTON, after the traditional three-day all-star break, the Rangers' clubhouse was alive with what is now known as an attitude. Buoyed by the three-game streak against the Tigers, the players seemed actually to be strutting. Plus their sense of honor had been violated by something that had appeared in a newspaper.

Their recent ex-teammate Mike Epstein was the printed source of some surprising declarations appearing in a Washington paper—not the *Post* but the *Star,* that would eventually be replaced by the Moonie-owned *Times.* Both Washington papers had mostly been covering the Orioles since Bob Short had moved the Senators to Arlington. Epstein's history was kind of odd. He had actually worked for Bob Short twice and been a Senator in the Ted Williams regime before Short had traded him to Oakland; then he had rejoined his ex-boss for his brief tenure in Texas.

Epstein, now playing with the Angels and on a road trip to Baltimore, made these comments to a Washington writer: "Getting out of that Texas mess was all I could ask for this year," Epstein was quoted as saying. As for the trade that had brought him to Texas, Epstein said, "I never did go for that deal. Short said that things had changed since Ted was gone and I said, 'No, Bob, they haven't.' Oh, the faces have changed and Ted is gone, but the attitude is still the rotten same. Those guys don't pride themselves on anything but getting to the ballpark. Some guys can adjust to that and live with it, but I can't."

Several of the Rangers got steamed up when that clipping was passed around, suggesting that Epstein had hardly busted his ass during his truncated stay in Texas. These guys were accustomed to being kicked around in the papers by sportswriters, but who cared about that? Most players regarded journalists as a besotted assortment of old poofters who didn't know shit from wild honey. Like Dave Nelson cheerfully told me one time: "The only reason you're a sportswriter is because you're too damn stupid to operate a forklift.''

But catching grief like that from a fraternity brother ranked as the ultimate insult. Catcher Rich Billings said, "You might think that he was misquoted, but that sure sounds like the way Mike articulates himself." Lloyd Allen, the pitcher who was involved in the four-player trade that sent Epstein to Orange County, recalled that, "He [Epstein] walked up to me in the Angels clubhouse after the deal was done and said, 'You don't know me and I don't know you, but I want to assure you that you're going over to one of the best organizations and best owners in the game.' Looks like he changed his mind.''

A SCHEDULING IRONY placed Epstein and the California Angels in Arlington for a double-header on the Thursday night that opened league play after the all-star break. The pitching match-ups came with real marquee value for a change. Big Tex himself, Nolan Ryan, already with two no-hitters for the season and enjoying a record-pace strikeout binge, would pitch the opener for the Angels. Bill Singer, the ex-Dodger now scorching the American League with a 15–5 record, was due in the second game.

Herzog was impressed. *"Phew.* Ryan and Singer. Next to Jack Daniels and I. W. Harper, that's about as potent a combination as I can think of." The Rangers would counter with two hot arms of their own, Jim Bibby and David Clyde. Up until now, and I had written this in the *Star-Telegram,* they could have taken the love scene from *Deliverance* and used it as the Rangers' highlights film. (That observation managed to find its way into print because the person working the copydesk that night was not a moviegoer). Now, inspired by Mike Epstein's put-down, the Rangers took on the aura of a team on a mission.

The F-Troop, by God, wasn't going to take it anymore. In the opener, Nolan Ryan would retire twelve straight batters at one point, but in the seventh the Rangers finally stopped shooting blanks. Vic Harris whistled a triple to left center. Alex Johnson followed with a double into the same territory. Then Larry Biittner, a lefthanded hitter with a stance so open he looked like he was straddling a creek, ripped a liner that banged off the centerfield fence on the fly. Winkles, the Angels manager, was not used to seeing his ace get kicked around, and certainly not by this gang of vagabonds and buffoons, the Lost Tribe that Epstein had described. Ryan was pulled from the game before his psyche was further damaged.

Jim Bibby, and not Ryan, looked like the pitcher with the Hall of Fame fastball. He paralyzed the Angels with eleven strikeouts, gave up three hits and the Rangers breezed, 7–1. Happily for ownership, a crowd approaching 30,000 was there to witness the feat. This was Farm and Ranch Night at Arlington Stadium, and the first 10,000 paying customers got a certificate they could redeem for a free bag of Rangers fertilizer.

Between games, in an exhibition of udder (sorry) nonsense, Angels pitching coach Tom Morgan beat Rangers pitcher Jackie Brown in a cow-milking contest. Whitey Herzog missed that. He was back in his office enjoying the final results of the Ryan-Bibby match-up. "That wasn't the real Nolan Ryan out there tonight," he said, "but by God, it *was* the real Jim Bibby. He threw 150 pitches, but hell, I've seen him pitch 200 in the minors and keep on coming. He's big, he's strong and he can throw with any of 'em when it comes to strength."

Whatever interplanetary force-field that had pulled the earth so drastically away from its customary flight plan in the first game was also at work in Act II. Jeff Burroughs, whose soul had been so tormented by the malignant Texas south winds that had snuffed the life from so many of his best whacks, connected with a grand-slam homerun—first ever by a Ranger—in the first inning off Bill Singer.

Meanwhile, the Angels seemed just as helpless against David Clyde as they had when Jim Bibby was pitching. True, the Angels lineup consisted of the once-great Frank Robinson—who, like most of the designated hitters that year, was getting on—

and eight nobodies. But they wore major-league uniforms with haloes on their caps and they scarcely touched David Clyde, who pitched seven scoreless innings and gave up three hits and three walks, striking out five. This would be just about the last flare in the cartridge of David's 1973 Roman candle, but he picked an ideal night to fire the thing off. Jackie Brown had sufficiently recovered from his disastrous loss in the cow-milking competition to come in and pitch two scoreless innings in relief and the Rangers won, 8–0.

Texas' "When You're Hot, You're Hot" cavalcade beat the Angels again the next night, 5–3, and Diamond Jim Fregosi was batting .400 since coming over from the Mets. So the Rangers not only had their revenge on Mike Epstein, they'd also won six straight.

In Dallas, people were rioting in the streets. Not because of the Rangers' winning streak but because a Dallas police officer (he would eventually be convicted of murder) shot and killed a twelve-year-old Mexican-American boy who was sitting handcuffed in the back seat of a squad car.

At the airport, though, as the Rangers left for a four-city, two-coast road excursion, there were indications that Rangers Mania was taking hold in this area known as the Metroplex. A cheering crowd of well-wishers met the team at Love Field in Dallas (D-FW wouldn't open for another six months) carrying signs with "Go Rangers!" type messages.

Well, maybe not actually a crowd. It was about a half-dozen sweet-looking old ladies who probably should have been at home watching Lawrence Welk. These were not exactly the Dallas Cowboys cheerleaders. And probably it would also be less than accurate to say that they were cheering, although they *were* smiling.

These ladies were showing their support because they were certain that this Rangers team would refuse to quit and they were right, by God. This team wouldn't quit until it had lost 105 games, the most in franchise history.

CHAPTER

12

ON A PLANE ride to Oakland, one Ranger was talking to another about a recent occasion when he had not only "nailed a couple of fuckin' dingers" off some pitcher but had "smoked his tits" as well. A big leaguer doesn't simply hit an occasional pitcher hard. He "smokes his tits," one of the milder expressions that color conversational patterns of players. In terms of social refinement, some of these sportsmen are not what might be recognized as finished products. Some are.

The behavioral ethos put forth by the men of the ballyard was a significant departure from my earliest professional beat. For the previous five years a lot of my work as a reporter had been interviews with people such as Elizabeth Montgomery or Lucille Ball or Barbara Eden or Sally Field or Mary Tyler Moore, and these exchanges were happening at the Polo Lounge in the Beverly Hills Hotel or maybe the veranda of the Royal Hawaiian.

These job assignments occurred when I was employed by the Fort Worth *Press,* a storied little Scripps-Howard tabloid. I was writing some sports but mostly occupied myself in my other persona as television editor-critic. This was during the golden age of lavish junkets financed by networks and production companies. In the modern age of hypocritical newspaper "ethics," the writers can no longer accept those kinds of freebies lest the partiality of the oracle become tainted. So a network or movie outfit or whoever would fly you around first-class and set you up in a five-star hotel with instructions to sign anything to your tab but prostitutes and alligator shoes.

I can remember sitting with two other writers and a publicist in the Garden Room of the Century Plaza. We interviewed Dick Clark for about four hours and I signed a drink tab that exceeded $500, which was a hell of an accomplishment according to 1970 prices. I then left to have dinner with Lana Turner, who was starring in some prime-time soap that regrettably flopped on ABC after thirteen weeks.

Why, you might well ask, would I want to trade what I will always regard as the greatest scam in the history of journalism for this baseball assignment, in which I spent my Saturday nights in pressboxes in towns like Bloomington, Minnesota (no offense intended) drinking Grain Belt beer and watching grown men hit foul balls? Two reasons. First, in 1971, the editor of the *Press* dropped dead and was replaced by a guy who wanted me to spend less time with Ann-Margret in Montreal and more time watching football practice at TCU. This editor, his name was Delbert, thought I might be having too much fun on the job (he was right, too) and told me that I lacked the dedication to make it in the "newspaper business" over the long haul. I told Delbert that I never thought of myself as being even slightly involved with the newspaper business. "And you ain't either," I said. "Some heir to the Scripps-Howard fortune, as we speak, is down on some private island with Miss Teenage Sweden and eighty cases of Dom Perignon. *He's* in the newspaper business, Delbert. You and me are not."

Reason Number Two for slinking onto the *Star-Telegram* baseball beat like a starving rodent was the notion that the *Press* was about to fold at any minute. It actually hung on for three years after I left, but when Scripps-Howard finally did close the place at high noon on a June Friday, a few dozen of the most talented and loyal people ever involved in the newspaper "business" were given a whole week's pay and told to get their asses out of

the office pronto. Most of them didn't even have time to finish
the can of Vienna sausage they were having for lunch before the
building was padlocked.

Those were some of the quirks of fate that led me to the
coffeeshop of a hotel near the Oakland Coliseum where the
Rangers were about to play the A's in a doubleheader. I was
eating a bowl of Rice Krispies and listening to some woman who
had sat down, I'll swear, at my table after somehow guessing,
perhaps by the cut of my jib, that I was connected somehow with
the Rangers entourage. She was hoping that I might point out
or somehow locate a particular Rangers pitcher whom she
averred she wanted to screw. Just like that. This woman, I took
it, was the Bay Area's equivalent of Detroit Shirley.

Without my asking, she proceeded to rattle off the names of
her personal 1973 baseball all-star team, along with an MVP, a
rookie of the year and a comeback player of the year. I was
surprised that she didn't also give a Sigh Young award. The criteria for making this all-star lineup didn't, of course, include
homeruns or batting averages but rather an array of skills that
she described so graphically that my Rice Krispies became prematurely soggy. Then she mentioned the name of a fairly well-
known player with the White Sox. "He wanted me to do a two-
on-one with some other guy but, hey, my head's screwed on way
too good to get involved with something as kinky as that. I told
him to fuck off." Those were her exact words.

I felt a strong urge to get away from the table. Not so much
because I was afraid of compromising my potential placement in
the hereafter but for the simple concern that this woman was
probably an undercover cop. In light of the litigious realities of
more up-to-date times, I am told that professional athletes
largely tend to shun the "kindness of strangers" like the woman
in Oakland in fear of being set up with rape charges and civil
suits. And who has been most damaged by the lawsuit craze?
The poor groupies themselves, mostly. Business has dried up in
the lobbies and lounges of the nice hotels and the girls have
been relegated back to the truck stops.

Later, at the ballpark, having recounted that coffeeshop vignette to Harold McKinney, he said, "Hell, you should have turned her on to Bibby. Then she could claim that she not only scored another righthander but made it with Mr. Ed, too."

DOWN ON THE field, Whitey's Rangers remained on a tear. With Sonny Siebert still on the shelf, Herzog was having to resort to random selection to fill out his rotation again. When Jackie Gene Brown of Wewoka, Oklahoma, had been called up from Spokane, his role was to replace Don Stanhouse on the roster in the bullpen.

Now Brown was starting against the past, present and future world-champion Oakland A's. Brown went the distance and pitched a shutout. In the second inning of the game, Sal Bando hit a ball that landed in the leftfield stands at least fifteen feet to the foul side of the flagpole. Frank Umont, also known to the players as Old Helmet Head, appeared to have been aroused from a short nap by the sound of the ball landing in the seats. Umont looked toward leftfield, raised his right hand and twirled a finger around, signalling homerun. It was, in fact, a two-run homer, and Bando could scarcely keep a straight face as he trotted around the bases.

JIM FREGOSI, PLAYING third base, was not particularly amused. In fact, the usually blasé Fregosi had taken enough spins around the block in the major leagues to realize that disputes with umpires were not only futile but involved dialogue that was less than elegant.

Now Fregosi was thrashing about in a self-choreographed performance punctuated with grief-stricken wails not put forth since Flaubert's deathbed scene in *Madame Bovary*. For a moment, I thought Fregosi was about to put his hands around Old Helmet Head's throat. The umpire quickly disqualified Fregosi from the remainder of the afternoon's proceedings. Oakland went ahead and won by three.

"I can't remember the last time I got chased but I think it was when I was nineteen years old and playing for the Dallas-Fort Worth team in the American Association," Fregosi would say later. "But I also don't remember seeing an umpire make such a horseshit call." Herzog seemed less agitated. "Ah, the old f—, wait a minute. You gotta be careful what you say about the umps," Herzog said. Umont told me that the ball went straight over the top of the foul pole. And I asked him how in the hell such a thing was possible. If the ball had gone above the foul pole it would have landed in the parking lot. Bando's ball came down in the lower deck.

"But," added Herzog philosophically, "that is exactly the kind of crap you can expect from the umps when you are a last-place team playing a first-place team. And"—Whitey concluded with an air of resignation—"the situation doesn't look too good tomorrow, either. We're catching Vida Blue. His record isn't that good, but if I had my pick of any pitcher in the league, Vida would be the guy."

What I remember most about what happened the next night was that in the open-air pressbox on a midsummer's night at the Oakland Coliseum, it is very possible for the visiting journalist to freeze his cojones off if he isn't wearing attire suitable for an NFL playoff game in Green Bay, Wisconsin.

In the top of the first, Dave Nelson, Vic Harris and Alex Johnson each reached base against Vida Blue. Five nights earlier, Jeff Burroughs had hit the franchise's first ever grand slam. That had come off Bill Singer. Now, after the first pitch, Vida Blue had yielded grand slam Number Two. That was a promising enough beginning. So I turned to Burt Hawkins, the traveling secretary seated to my left, and wisely noted, "The last time I was this cold was in New York." The Rangers got ahead 7–0 that night and blew it.

In the bottom half of that inning Jim Bibby got Burt Campaneris to pop up, struck out Bill North on three pitches, all chest-high fastballs, and then got Sal Bando to swing late and pop up. After the inning Bando trotted past Hiller, who was going over to coach first, and said, "Don't tell me he can throw that damn hard for nine innings." Hiller looked at Bando and replied, "Just wait. He gets faster." In the Rangers' dugout, pitching coach Cha-Cha Estrada turned to Herzog and said, "Bibby's got it tonight. They won't touch him. I bet he pitches a no-hitter."

In the third inning, Ray Fosse finally hit a ball hard, but Pete Mackanin, still filling in while Toby Harrah's broken hand was on the mend, made a slick play on the ball, moving to his right, and threw Fosse out. In the fourth Vic Harris, the centerfielder, got a decent jump on Deron Johnson's looper and ran down the ball.

Then, as the innings rolled by, Bibby was relying essentially on one pitch, the fastball, and it was becoming increasingly apparent that none of the A's were up to the task of hitting the thing with any kind of authority. In the vernacular of the trade, Bibby was bringing serious gas.

When he walked to the mound to start the bottom of the ninth, Bibby had walked six A's, but according to the scoreboard, had yet to yield a run or a hit. The Oakland crowd of 23,000, with the A's trailing 6–0 and now beaten, was on Bibby's side now. They wanted to witness a no-hitter. So did Catfish Hunter, watching from the A's bullpen. "The game was out of reach so why not?" Hunter would say. "I know how the kid felt. I'd been there myself."

The "kid" that Hunter was watching was actually twenty-eight, had served a tour in Vietnam and two years earlier had been bedridden for weeks after undergoing a spinal fusion. With one out, Bill North walked. Now Reggie Jackson was up and Bibby's little flirtation with history had reached its point of crisis. On a 3–2 count, Jackson swung, literally, from the heels, and then sat down. "That," Jackson said afterward, "was the fastest pitch I ever saw . . . or rather . . . never did see."

One out to go now, and Gene Tenace lifted a pop fly into

short right center. This was a ball that I had seen the Rangers
misplay with numbing frequency. Sure enough, second baseman
Dave Nelson was backpedaling, and just as the ball reached his
glove he was rammed by the onrushing Harris. "Dave was calling 'I've got it! I've got it!' but the crowd noise was so loud I
never heard him," Harris would say later. Somehow, though,
the ball stuck in Nelson's glove, and Bob Short's last-place team
was back in the national sports headlines.

Billings, the catcher, was availing himself of Charlie Finley's
lavish post-game spread of Velveeta and white bread, drawn
from the menu of maximum security, and raving about Bibby's
effort. At what Billings conceded was "the twilight of a mediocre career," the last thing he expected was to catch a no-hit
from a Rangers pitcher. "The big guy was absolutely unbelievable," Billings said. "I don't think there is a man in baseball
who could have touched some of those pitches. I've never seen
smoke like that." Bibby had thrown 148 pitches and struck out
thirteen A's.

Now Bibby himself was virtually alone in the dugout, wearing
earphones and transmitting his thoughts to the folks back home
in Texas on the Rangers' post-game radio show. Actually, Rangers' broadcasts were carried on a clear channel AM that, this
time of night, could be picked up throughout North America.
At this peak moment in his career, Bibby had one thought on
his mind. "Man, it was cold out there when the game started
and I thought I was gonna freeze my ass off," he informed his
audience. "But I bet I lost ten pounds by the time it was over.
But I'm gonna get it all back in the clubhouse with some of that
good cold beer and I'm ready for it right now."

Bob Short was on the trip, probably, I presumed, to consult
with Finley about any possible good ideas on how best to unload
the franchise. Short, at least, had the good luck to be around to
see what would certainly now stand out as the premiere on-the-
field moment of his ownership tenure. He might have been taking a colossal bath with this thing, but Short walked up to Bibby
in the clubhouse, hugged him and handed over a bonus check

for five grand. The spectacle of a no-hit game was hardly a commonplace event in the Texas-Washington franchise. Bibby's was the first since a Senator pitcher named Bobby Burke accomplished the feat in 1931. The only one prior to that happened in 1920 and was thrown by Walter Johnson.

On the flight to Anaheim (actually Los Angeles, followed by about a ninety-minute bus ride to the outskirts of Disneyland, after which I had to find my room and write three stories about the no-hitter . . . it was two hours earlier in Texas and my deadline for the first P.M. editions was fast approaching . . . talk about a suck-ass job), I was wondering how many more total improbabilities this team might have left in it. For a team that was essentially DOA, it still persisted in making a ridiculous amount of noise.

According to the blueprint, the Rangers should quickly return to the basic, feeble performance standards in Anaheim. "Don't," Herzog had been quick to remind me before the series opener against the A's, "go expecting too many more fucking miracles out of this bunch."

That much was evident in the latest candidate in Whitey's Amateur Hour auditions for starting pitcher, a lefthander from the Cardinals minor-league system. His name was Don "Bull" Durham. Bull had a lousy outing, but the organist at Anaheim extracted some convincing "m-o-o-o" sounds from his instrument.

Then here came David Clyde. When the Kid was on top of his game, it had already been demonstrated that Carl Yastrzemski couldn't hit him. Neither, then, could the Angels' Richie Scheinblum, Art Kusnyer and Rudi Meoli. Clyde gave up one run in a seven-inning outing, and now the Rangers had won nine out of their last eleven games! One night later, on an all-night flight to Chicago for a weekend series, one of the veteran players handpicked by Herzog to act as a father figure to the teenaged pitcher, came to Clyde and offered him a traditional big-league performance booster. He slipped a black capsule into Clyde's hand and said, "Here, kid. Take this and you won't have to go to bed for a week."

Harold McKinney had a cheerful reminder for David as well. "Just remember," he told the pitcher, "that on the twenty-seventh of this month the legal drinking age in Texas will be lowered to eighteen."

CHICAGO STOOD OUT as a favorite stopover for many of the Rangers players. The City with Broad Shoulders offered many attractions, and the one most appealing to many of the Rangers caravan was that Chicago was the home of Channel 61, the Action Channel, they called it, that showed nothing but Superman and Spiderman on a twenty-four-hour basis.

The Rangers finally began to flounder at Comiskey Park, that grand old South Side arena surrounded by tough dives owned and operated by women all named, it seemed, Wanda Skutnik.

Burroughs, on Saturday, hit his third grandslam in ten days. By now, Burroughs had decided not to surrender to the bedeviling winds back in Arlington and try to become a singles hitter like Wee Willie Keeler. "Well, the club expects me to hit homers," Burroughs conceded, "so I might as well try."

But the team, like some of the suits the players had purchased at Hot Sam's in Detroit, was rapidly coming apart at the seams. On Sunday, they got beat in the ninth inning on a hit provided by the unknown shortstop of the White Sox, Bucky Dent. "Bucky Dent?" wondered Dave Nelson after the game. "What kind of wimp name is Bucky Dent? Sounds like some kind of kid in a cartoon. It's embarrassing to lose to a Bucky Dent."

On Monday, another scheduling diversion awaited the Rangers. They flew to upstate New York to play the Pirates in the exhibition game that always accompanies the Hall of Fame inductions at Cooperstown. That year's group included Warren Spahn. During his acceptance speech, a man in the front row pitched over with a heart attack. Spahn stopped in mid-sentence, looked into the audience and said, "Oh my God! It's

George." George was Spahn's brother-in-law. The only way a Hall of Fame induction ceremony could be screwed up, it seemed, would be with the Rangers in town.

THE LONG LONG road trip finally was ending. In New York, on the bus ride to the stadium from the Essex House Hotel up through the Bronx, we passed by a standard Seventies American Gothic street scene. Two representatives of the nation's future, waving what appeared to be machetes, were attempting to assault a leader of tomorrow who was actively fending off the other two with a broom handle. Alex Johnson, the stoic outfielder, spoke rarely but when he did his message was usually profound. The kid swinging the mop had caught AJ's eye. "I guess he's the designated hitter," Johnson said.

Yankee Stadium, like everyone in the Rangers traveling party, had seen better days. At the end of the season, it would be shut down for two years for much needed renovations while the Yankees played their home games at Shea Stadium.

The pressbox at Yankee Stadium is arranged in an open area behind the plate on the mezzanine level. Halfway through the final game of the series—Bibby salvaged the only win with a two-hit, fourteen strikeout effort—I got hit in the back of the head with a rock. I turned around, staring into the crowd behind the press area and attempting to locate the son of a bitch throwing the rocks when . . . *kabam* . . . a chunk of concrete that must have weighed fifty pounds fell from the bottom of the deck overhead and shattered between me and Harold McKinney. If the mass had landed one foot to either side, Harold's head or mine would have been squashed. I heard a moan from the fans in the mezzanine. They were, I guess, disappointed that nobody was killed. Some of them would probably demand their money back.

Bob Fischel, who had been the Yankees' vice-president in charge of PR and media relations for probably forty years and wore those circular wire-rimmed glasses like Woodrow Wilson's, heard the crash like everybody else and came trotting over. Fischel was grinning like Robert Young on a Sanka commercial and said, "Don't worry. No problem. That stuff's been happening all the time lately."

An hour or so later, when I walked out of Yankee Stadium and was still alive, it occurred to me that I had just replaced Lou Gehrig as the luckiest man on the face of the earth.

CHAPTER

13

MY FAVORITE PASSAGE in *The Grapes of Wrath* depicts a conversation involving a couple of filling-station-pump jockeys on Route 66 in New Mexico. They had just finished providing full service to the Joad family, which was headed west to golden California.

"Jesus, what a hard looking outfit."

"Them Okies? They're all hard looking."

"Jesus, I'd hate to start out in a jalopy like that."

"Well, you and me got sense. Them goddamn Okies got no sense and no feeling. They ain't human. A human being wouldn't live like they do. A human being couldn't stand to be so dirty and miserable. They ain't a helluva lot better than gorillas."

If the author, John Steinbeck, wished to produce an account of American life in the summer of 1973—at least the version that my colleagues and I were experiencing—that might be accomplished by substituting "baseball writer" for "Okie." With the regular season four-and-a-half months old and no end in sight, travel with the Rangers was starting to take on the aspect of riding on a wagon train to Destination Unknown. "Well, this beats shootin' rivets at the bomber plant," Randy Galloway, the Dallas *Morning News* baseball guy, used to say. One night, during a two-hour rain delay in Chicago, he said it about seventy-five times.

Galloway probably could not fully appreciate what life was like inside the bomber plant. I could. A part-time position in the sports department at the Fort Worth *Press* was my first employment experience that didn't entail a mop, a hoe or a shovel . . . and where everyone on the crew wasn't humming "Old Man River." Immediately prior to becoming a media whiz I was steam-cleaning floors at a General Motors assembly plant, a job that even a John Steinbeck Okie wouldn't take.

So why the carping about the baseball chore? OK. For one thing, not too many baseball writers were seen driving around in what was known in Texas as a fancy Eye-talian sports car. And their wives didn't wear fine furs and Cartier jewelry, because if they did, they'd look out of place working their customary double-shifts as "salad girls" at the Mexiteria.

But the money wasn't the big rub either. The baseball reporter, unlike the guys covering city hall, could at least draw a small bundle of cash in expense money before heading out on a ten-day road swing and then dash over to the credit union to plunk down a car payment.

There was one task that made the job a real ordeal. For twenty-three games I was supposed to take my turn in the barrel and carry out the duty of what was known as "the official scorer." That diabolical aspect of the baseball writer's call of duty amounted to one living color 3-D hemorrhoid.

As such, I was to be the arbiter of what was a base hit and what was an error, along with other intricately detailed matters that are associated with the vital statistics of the game. And there is no other activity known to man for which statistics are as vital as they are for major-league baseball.

After each game the official scorer must also complete a ledger sheet that would stagger a senior accountant of Price Waterhouse. The numbers on that document account for every put out, assist, broken bat, belch, yawn and whatever else happened from first pitch to last of every game. The ledger sheets were to be promptly mailed to the American League office, where they were entered on the sacred parchment of the major-league annals and laid to rest throughout eternity in the mausoleum of statistical lore/bore.

According to bylaws set down by God knows who—the Continental Congress, probably—the official scorer must be a member of the Baseball Writers Association of America who sees a minimum of 100 big-league games a season. Which means the baseball writer must do some traveling to be certified as the official scorer, and in Texas there weren't very many of those who could qualify. My portion amounted to twenty-three games that I was assigned to score at Arlington Stadium. I told Harold McKinney that I didn't want to do it.

"You have to," he said. "Besides, the league pays you fifty dollars a game to score." I calculated that twenty-three games at fifty a game might translate into a weekend of fulfillment in New Orleans in the off-season. But I had already witnessed the angst and grief that characterized the day-to-day drudge of the official scorer.

The sportswriter could, in the public print, suggest that a player's job skills were insufficient for the major leagues and receive no reaction from the player himself. The players all said that they never read the papers and most of them probably didn't. The writer could accuse a player of engaging in perversions too weird to be listed in a criminal forensics textbook and that player might, if sufficiently oiled, even cheerfully acknowledge the comments. But if the same player thinks you, as official scorer, might have stiffed him out of a base hit, you can anticipate most sincere threats to life and limb.

The act of ruling on a hit or error can never affect the outcome of a game, like the "safe" or "out" rulings of an umpire. But it should be remembered that the majority of the ballplayers were most keenly absorbed in the progress of their individual stats. Whether his team was winning or losing games was often of secondary concern. If a player was robbed, in his personal judgment, of a base hit, then his batting average might read .258933 instead of .258934 at the end of the season. Ever wonder what ballplayers might actually be thinking about while they sit hour after hour in the dugout sucking on sunflower seeds? Many at least are pondering how that final digit in his batting average might round off at the end of the year. Enough change in the digits added, of course, to dollars plus or minus.

Another unfortunate feature was that unlike the umpires, the official scorer had twenty-four hours to change his mind on a call. In other words, if the scorer could be convinced or coerced into believing a call was indeed horseshit, the scorer could reverse himself. Which meant that the scorer was continually exposed to endless heartfelt, emotional appeals from the men on the field. "You're stuck way up there in the pressbox. You've got a crappy angle and can't see those plays the same way we see them," was the conventional argument. "So what do you want me to do? Cover the game from second base? I didn't invent the goddamn system, ya know," was the conventional reply.

Now, late in the season, the complaints against scoring rulings would be louder and more persistent. That was because many of the players had entered what they termed their annual "salary drive." With most of the pennant races already determined, many teams would be bringing in untested talent from the minors in the dying weeks. So this was a good time for the regulars to inflate their stats in hopes of gaining a little leverage at contract time in the off-season.

Actually, in the three seasons that I endured the trauma of acting as official scorer, only one encounter became really acrimonious. It involved Pat Dobson, who was pitching for the Yankees. Because I did not charge New York first baseman Chris Chambliss with an error on a bad-hop grounder, the world spun a couple of degrees off its axis and the resulting tidal wave killed a billion people in Bangladesh. But more importantly, the scoring decision stuck Dobson with a couple of earned runs that looked unsightly on his stat sheet. The names that Pat Dobson called me are not usually associated with honorable conduct or normal human sexuality. Because of the play in question, Dobson came away with a loss instead of a win. But that earned-run average was Dobson's primary source of concern.

This interchange led me to ponder a couple of philosophical issues. First—since I could not locate any salary checks in my name that carried the signature of Pat Dobson, I wondered why he thought I might be even minutely concerned about the state of his fucking earned-run average. And second—I wondered what kind of grown man would desire to hang onto a job where he had to put up with crap like that.

As a final insult, it had also been ordained that for the sake of appearance the official scorer should not consume alcohol during his term on the hot seat. Instances had been reported over the years in which an official scorer was seen facedown by the sixth inning, the kind of scenario that might be regarded as bad form in the modern era. Thus, my beverage caravan from the pressroom lounge to my seat in the pressbox would be discontinued for the final twenty-three home games. What next? Mandatory chapel? Scoring presented yet another annoyance. Since the scorer's obligation naturally involved concentrating on the game, I was distracted from working on my self-help account of my baseball travels fancifully entitled *Men Are From Fort Worth, Women Are From Bakersfield.*

On a typical night, the routine at Arlington Stadium worked like this: The official scorer sits at the far left end of the pressbox next to Burt Hawkins, who handles the pressbox PA. A batter hits a grounder past the pitcher up the middle. The shortstop gets a glove on the ball but can't make the play. The scorer turns to Burt Hawkins and says either "base hit" or "E-6," meaning an error on the shortstop. Since the unwritten criteria in rendering such judgments is that these guys are major leaguers who are amply compensated for making tough plays, you tell Hawkins "E-6" and Hawkins gets on the pressbox PA and says "E-6." About five seconds later, way out atop the leftfield stands on the huge scoreboard shaped in the outline of the state of Texas, the notation E-6 appears in lights up in the Panhandle portion of the state, right around the community of Dumas.

Twelve seconds later a phone rings in the pressbox. Someone wishes to speak to the official scorer. This would be the batter, calling from the dugout. The message is always the same: "MOTHER FUCKER! HOW THE FUCK CAN YOU CALL THAT AN ERROR? YOU'RE STEALING FOOD OUT OF MY BABY'S MOUTH. AARRRGGGHHH!"

Almost always the source of the phone call in the dugout will be the batter. The fielder involved in decisions like that rarely carps. Nobody pays that much attention to fielding averages. Golden Glove awards are nice but they don't get you the bucks a 300-plus batting average does or a 30-plus homerun season does. It was ironic, by the way, that the top-echelon players with all-star credentials rarely if ever phoned the pressbox. The man on the telephone would usually be hitting .235. The only other party known to protest over a scorer's ruling was none other than the Chicago broadcaster Harry Caray, who would burst into the writers' section of the pressbox to complain.

So naturally I looked forward to my personal initiation as official scorer with the same enthusiasm I'd felt a week earlier when I'd sat in Dr. Horne's office waiting to have two wisdom teeth yanked out. The first night proceeded without difficulty, with no plays that might challenge the keen intuitions of the scorer—until the eighth inning. The Orioles, now asserting themselves in a late-season push that would separate Baltimore from the rest of the pack in the AL East, were in town and the Birds were leading the Rangers by about six runs, surprise, surprise.

In the eighth, a Rangers batter hammered a hard shot right down the third base line. By the time Brooks Robinson made his patented lunge, the ball was already past him and into leftfield. Since I'd been told that the big leaguers were supposed to make the tough plays, I figured Brooks Robinson should make *all* the plays, shouldn't he? Hell, I'd seen a picture of Robinson actually making that same play on the cover of Sports Illustrated when he turned the 1970 World Series into a one-man show.

I looked at Burt Hawkins and said, "E-5." Whee! What a

power trip! Brooks Robinson will think twice before he lets another one like that slip past him in Texas, by God.

After the game, I was confronted in the Rangers clubhouse by one of the catchers, Ken Suarez. "Were you the scorer tonight?" he said. I nodded.

"Jeez . . . what happened to you in the eighth inning?" Suarez demanded. "Have you got a tank of laughing gas up there, or what?" My response to Suarez was, word for word, what Spiro Agnew had said that very same afternoon when news reports had surfaced that the vice-president of our country was being investigated for accepting kickbacks while governor of Maryland. "Those charges are false and scurrilous and malicious . . . damned lies!" That's what Spiro told the media and that's what I was telling Ken Suarez.

"Well, that call you made giving Brooks Robinson an error was brutal," Suarez said. It occurred to me now that he was absolutely right, since the batter was not even Suarez but his competition for the catcher's job, Rich Billings. "I mean," said Suarez, "Billings has been going bad and if anybody ever needed a break it was him. You really screwed him on that call."

Like most of the players in the summer of 1973, Billings was sporting mutton-chop sideburns and looked like someone in a Matthew Brady photograph of Abraham Lincoln's cabinet. And, like some of the members of Lincoln's cabinet, a lot of these Rangers looked like they should perhaps go somewhere and get a chest X-ray.

Billings was sitting on a stool in front of his locker, smoking a cigarette and appearing perplexed. He presented the general appearance of a man who could not make up his mind whether he wanted to go get some Mexican food or climb a light tower in the outfield and jump off. I walked up to Billings and said something like "it has been, uh, suggested, er, that I might have, um, made a bad call on that ball in the eighth inning and—"

Billings cut me off. "Didn't you see that batting average they

flash on the scoreboard when I come up to hit?'' he said. "It's
.169 and that says it all. When you're batting .169 this late in the
year you don't go whining to the official scorer . . . you consult a hypnotist. Know any good ones?

"Last year, I hit about .292 and had the best average on the
team. This year I can't buy a hit and that means that with the
contract I get next year I not only won't be able to buy a hit, I
won't be able to buy a pack of cigarettes. I don't know what in
the hell is wrong. I've tried everything. I've taken extra batting
practice. Sometimes I've taken no batting practice. I'll bet I've
tried two dozen different bats this year. Nothin' works,'' Billings
said.

With that soliloquy, Billings put forth a candid appraisal of his
season of discontent and, while doing so, encapsulated a summer's worth of frustrations for the whole team. Billings had un-
complainingly served as sort of the poster boy for the wayward
Rangers, baseball's unorthodox franchise, from the beginning.
None other than Denny McLain, who had worn a Rangers uniform for about fifteen minutes before being traded in the
spring of 1972, had cautioned writers to "watch out for Billings.
He's as crazy as I am."

I decided to compose a story on the demise of Rich Billings.
Any topic would do, actually, at this point of the season. For a
team that could traverse the long season, wire-to-wire, in last
place, the 1973 Rangers had put forth some rare theatrics for
the benefit of the struggling journalist. On an irregular basis
the Rangers' act had been one to rival Abbott and Costello.

But now it was getting late and the fatigue factor seemed to
lurk everywhere. Players walked about like zombies. Nobody was
threatening to throw any more no-hitters. The novelty of David
Clyde was beginning to wear off. Most of the baseball fans
around North Texas mostly now remember Clyde as a one-start
wonder.

David Clyde, in fact, had been sent forth from the trenches
and directly into the face of enemy fire on a twice-a-week basis

over the span of a month and a half and had pitched as consistently well as just about anybody in the American League. His record coming into this late home stand was 4–4, with more innings pitched than base hits given up and a solid two strike-outs for every one base-on-balls ratio. In his last three starts at Arlington, though, a seven-inning winning effort against the Yankees had been sandwiched between a couple of disastrous appearances.

Suddenly the Kid was on estranged terms with his curveball. Once he finally started to overthrow his breaking pitch, it just sort of packed up and moved away, never to be seen again. The Orioles and the Red Sox had chased Clyde after a couple of innings, and his most recent start at Arlington attracted only 9,000 paying customers.

The writers no longer had the B-e-e-g Boy to put on display for comic relief, either. Rico Carty was a Cub now. The Rangers had put Carty on waivers, and Chicago had claimed him for $20,000. Reports that the Cubs had also thrown in a new hot-water heater for Bob Short's guest house in Minneapolis were unsubstantiated.

So a story about Rich Billings seemed as good as any. I found Whitey in his office, buck-naked and blow-drying his hair. Years later, when he won a World Series managing the Cardinals, Herzog wore his hair in a classic flat-top, but with the Rangers in 1973 he sported a much fuller, Conway Twitty look. In 1973, Whitey could have found work as a tent evangelist.

"I got no complaints with Billings," Whitey said, responding to my inquiry. "You don't give up on somebody who's busting his butt every night. Sometimes I might get on Toby Harrah's case. There have been nights when I wonder if Toby might not have been in some kind of accident as a kid and paralyzed from the neck up. But that kid's got great instincts for the game and will be a helluva player someday. In most aspects, he already is.

"Look. It's not like I'm playing den mother to a bunch of winos. Just about everybody on this team has played his guts out," added Herzog, "and that's what has to concern a manager. You gotta wonder when your team is giving it the old 110 percent effort and their record's still 45–86."

On the surface, the project of elevating this franchise to respectability seemed overwhelming. Jim Russo, one of the leading scouts in the game, had surveyed the Rangers' major-league roster, looked at the reports as to what was available in the farm system and told me, "I don't see how they can be .500 even four or five years from now. Pitching is the name of the game and, well . . ."

I asked Herzog about the scout's evaluation and he simply grinned. "I've got a catcher in AA, Jim Sundberg, playing at Pittsfield in the Eastern League, who's better than anything we've got on this roster. He'll start here next season and will stay in the big leagues for fifteen years. Bill Madlock down at Spokane will play third base for us next year and bat .325."

That sounded nice. So who was going to pitch? Nobody needed to tell Whitey Herzog that his staff had topped the majors in one category: in late August, the Rangers had used fifteen different starting pitchers. At times it seemed as though Whitey were auditioning extras for Charlton Heston's latest Bible movie. Of those fifteen, the Rangers could count on exactly one, Jim Bibby, for any kind of stability in the coming season.

"Well, you can't put this in the paper because it'll queer the deal, but when we dumped the B-e-e-g Boy on the Cubs," Herzog said, "we made another little transaction that'll be announced in the off-season. Ferguson Jenkins is burned out at Wrigley Field and the Cubs are kind of burned out on him . . . so Fergie's gonna be a Ranger next year. Got him cheap, too. They're giving up AJ [Alex Johnson] and Vic [centerfielder Vic Harris]. Vic's a nice player but he'll never hit much."

Herzog wore an everything-is-under-control look. "The wind has been blowing out at Wrigley Field a lot this year and I hear Fergie is getting a little weird." Whitey laughed. "He'll like it in Arlington next year. And he'll win twenty-five games, too."

Whitey was a prophet in one aspect. Ferguson Jenkins *would* win twenty-five games for the Rangers. But due to circumstances that Herzog had not yet foreseen, while Fergie was holding up his end of the proposition, Whitey would be coaching third base for the California Angels.

CHAPTER

14

THE EAST COAST media in particular was snapping at Spiro Agnew's trousers leg. According to all the papers and TV newscasts, the vice-president was accused of all manner of malfeasance: tax fraud, bribery, conspiracy, driving on the wrong side of the road.

Julie Nixon Eisenhower was in Williamsport, Pennsylvania, throwing out the first ball at the Little League World Series. Her father couldn't make it, being preoccupied with some distracting affairs back in the capital. President Richard Nixon appeared on television in late August and delivered a speech in which he said he had now determined, for sure, that he had been "misled" by some of his "subordinates" and, having concluded that, declared that it was now high time for Congress and the media to "end the obsession with Watergate so that I can return to the urgent business of the nation."

The President had perhaps been moved by the inspiring words of Eddie Fisher . . . "count your blessings." The real success stories in American life repeat that passage to themselves every day. It triggers an attitude that keeps men like Jim Merritt on a major-league payroll. So what if this was a major-league team that was poised to rank with a handful as one of the most feeble of all time? Jim Merritt had a plan and he was about to light a single candle rather than curse the darkness.

"I'm scheduled to pitch the first game of the double-header on Sunday. If I win, make sure to come down to the clubhouse between games because I'll give you a fucking good story." Merritt told me this on a flight to Cleveland where the Rangers would play a weekend series.

Merritt, in fact, was one player on the team that the sportswriters generally regarded as somebody who *belonged* in the big leagues. Certainly his battle-weary left arm was not the weapon that it was when Merritt won twenty games with the 1970 Reds. That didn't matter (not with the Rangers, at least) because he looked and acted the part of the big leaguer. Unlike certain Rangers, Merritt gave the impression that he knew his way around in The Show.

Unlike certain Rangers, Merritt did not shop at Hot Sam's Men's Wear in Detroit. Unlike certain Rangers, Merritt did not order a cup of Everclear with his breakfast. Unlike certain Rangers, Merritt did not travel with a "fart machine" that consisted of a metal washer and rubber band that, when activated against the plastic surface of the chair at the gate of some airport, would make a foul and disgusting noise that old women found unsettling. So when Jim Merritt said that he might have a meaningful post-game announcement, I believed it would be something worthwhile.

Besides, now I had something to look forward to, since this, after all, was the dreaded Cleveland weekend. Dick Bosman, already an ex-Indian, had been traded back from the Rangers to Cleveland in May and had taken the news gallantly. "There's a bright spot to this," Bosman pointed out at the time. "When you're playing for Cleveland, at least you don't have to come in there on the road."

As stated earlier, anybody facing a life sentence of summertime in Texas should never complain about the opportunity to escape to a place where the temperature at midnight might creep beneath 110. From a societal viewpoint, some might argue that the state of Ohio was substantially more advanced than Texas; it was, after all, in the same summer of 1973, I believe, that the environmentally sensitive Ohio legislature voted to add the pink plastic flamingo to its list of endangered species.

Also, it had been reported that civic-minded citizens wanted to reignite the Cuyahoga River as part of Cleveland's Fourth of July celebration. Unfortunately, it was raining and they couldn't get it lit. A Rangers pitcher did voice one complaint: "I made the mistake of trying out a Mexican food restaurant in Cleveland. The food wasn't so bad but a rat crawled up on my plate and started fucking my enchilada."

It becomes so easy to get sucked into all of the negativism. For some reason I wrote in the paper that "a few thousand fans stopped by Municipal Stadium en route to the shores of Lake Erie, where they go to watch the fish die." Even if that had been the case, the view from the lakefront had to be more picturesque than the Rangers' onstage performance. Clobbered by the Indians on Friday night. Stomped again on Saturday afternoon. Ken Aspromonte, the Indians manager, said that if his team had played like that in the first half of the season it would now be neck-and-neck with the Orioles in the AL East. If they played every game against the Rangers, hell yes they would.

Yearning for a drastic change of scenery, I avoided the Rangers' postgame Saturday gathering at the Hairy Buffalo Club in suburban Rocky River and, instead, rode a commuter train out to Shaker Heights to take in a movie, *Last Tango in Paris*, that was getting some interesting reviews. Pitching coach Chuck Estrada rode out there with me and when it was over we both agreed that Marlon Brando had gotten laid more times in that movie than the entire Rangers traveling party had in the last two years.

On the train back to the hotel I started to ask Estrada about what sort of mystery announcement Jim Merritt was planning for his postgame comments the next afternoon if he won. But I decided not to. Estrada might not have been briefed on whatever it was that Merritt was planning and I didn't want to spoil his surprise.

Back in the Hollenden House Hotel, the Rangers media forces were assembled in the lounge where, once again, a political debate was in full flower. Burt Hawkins, the traveling secretary, was defending President Nixon's recent address to the nation and Harold McKinney expressed other opinions.

"Get on with the urgent business of the nation! Urgent business!" McKinney was screaming. He waved the front section of that day's edition of the Cleveland *Plain Dealer*. "Just look at this story, buried in the back of the section of this Republican rag!" Harold probably had no way of knowing whether the *Plain Dealer* was Republican or not and his description of the paper as a "rag" was ironic, I thought, for someone employed by the Fort Worth *Star-Telegram*. But that was not the point here. "Look here!" McKinney demanded. "Thanks to the fact that Nixon gave the Turks a bunch of money to burn away all the poppyfields, there's now a worldwide shortage of codeine! And then he stands up there and talks about urgent business."

The mystic effects of bottled imports from the Scottish Highlands had carried Harold's mind away to a special place and being a damned fool, I decided to join him there rather than go to the room and prepare for the following afternoon's doubleheader.

When I arrived at the park on Sunday, about ten minutes before the start of the first game, a rare assembly in excess of 20,000 was gathering in that enormous grandstand and the fellows with the rightfield drums were already feverishly expressing what I supposed they deemed as their First Amendment right to free speech. Too late, I discovered that this double-header had the discomfort potential of that frightful afternoon in Milwaukee—Bernie Brewer Day—seven weeks previous. After reflecting on the words of a popular bumper sticker of the time, I thought, "If this is really the first day of the rest of my life, then pass the hemlock, please." In the meantime, it would be necessary to maintain a pulse rate until the completion of the first game, at least, since the readers back home needed to learn about Merritt's major announcement.

The first batter Merritt faced in the first inning, Buddy Bell, rapped a simple two-hopper that Jim Fregosi picked up cleanly at third. But his throw to first sailed over Jim Spencer's head by a good five feet. "There goes his perfect game," Harold McKinney said. "There is no such thing as a perfect game in Cleveland," Randy Galloway responded.

Although that opening play was characteristic of the Rangers, it was not what was customarily expected of Fregosi since he had been transferred into Whitey's menagerie. For some peculiar reason, though, Fregosi was laughing out loud and, on the mound, Merritt also appeared clearly amused.

The next three batters for the Indians went quietly, though, and so it was for the rest of the game. Merritt pitched a three-hit shutout, effectively silencing those menacing outfield drums while the agony within my cranial regions diminished to a point just below the danger zone. Now marginally coherent, I marched down to the Rangers' clubhouse in hopes that Merritt, as promised, would deliver something beyond the usual post-game winning-pitcher jive.

Merritt was waiting in front of his locker. "I am announcing today," he began, "that I am officially coming out of the closet." Then Merritt reached inside his locker and produced a tube of K-Y jelly, a well-known lubricant sometimes used to enhance acts that some practitioners preferred to keep back in the closet. Initially, I didn't catch on to what Merritt was perpetrating here and momentarily panicked. "Not that!" I was thinking. Remember, this was 1973.

No. It wasn't that. Jim Merritt was coming clean and confessing that his three-hit shutout against the Indians was accomplished mostly with a new pitch that he called his "Gaylord Perry slider." He had smeared the lubricant on the back of his neck and "elsewhere on my uniform" for the purpose of throwing a pitch that had been outlawed in organized ball since the early Thirties. A pitcher who makes the spitball or greaseball correctly operational will moisten the fingertips of his pitching hand. The customary spin on the pitched ball is then altered and aerodynamics cause the ball to dip at a sharp angle just as it reaches the plate.

Throwing an effective spitball, like buying off a judge, is not always as easy as it might appear. "It's like any other new pitch. You can't just start using it and have instant success," Merritt said. If confession is good for the soul, it's even better for newspaper baseball stories, and Merritt's was improving by the second. "So the last time the Indians were in Texas, I went to Gaylord Perry, asked him about certain mechanics, and he gave me a few valuable tips . . . how to hold the ball differently and so forth.

"Then I experimented with it in that last home stand against the Orioles. We were losing 14–1 when I got into the game and I thought that was a good place to see if the thing worked. The Orioles hit it pretty good . . . but not Cleveland today." Merritt was beaming. He couldn't have been more pleased if someone had told him he'd just been traded to the Dodgers.

But why was Merritt now going public with his declaration? "I'm not doing it to make the umpires or anybody else look bad," Merritt said. "It's just that three or four pitchers are using a spitball or a greaseball and having success with it. So I am just admitting that I did something today. So make it legal for everybody or illegal for everybody. Maybe next year it will be legal."

The Bernie Brewer incident back in Milwaukee was a good story for Texas Rangers purposes, but it did not gain any national attention. What Jim Merritt was doing here stood out as something altogether different. One year ago this time, Merritt was pitching for the Reds AAA farm team at Indianapolis in the American Association. Life beyond the major leagues had not agreed with him, and Merritt did concede that the addition of a K-Y greaser to his repertoire of pitches might forever prevent future work assignments in the corn belt. "I never thought about [a greaseball] before this season. But I was getting desperate and this could mean my career."

Like the man in Fort Worth who had recently accidentally killed himself with his own shotgun "burglar trap," Merritt at least now had the satisfaction of knowing it worked. "The only misfire came on Fregosi's throw in the first inning," Merritt explained. I realized now why Fregosi thought his throw to first base, which nearly floated into orbit, was so hilarious. "Half the ball was loaded up," Fregosi said. "I thought about calling up the official scorer and asking him to charge Merritt with the error instead of me."

Sonny Siebert, scheduled to start the second game for the Rangers, stopped at Merritt's locker and asked to borrow the magic tube. With Merritt's marvelously self-styled exposé, it was altogether necessary to venture into the clubhouse of the home team and extract some reaction from the man known and revered throughout the game as Mister Grease . . . Gaylord Perry himself. Upon hearing of Merritt's post-game comments, yes, Perry was surprised and, no, he was not happy.

"I remember Jim Merritt coming to me in Texas and asking me about, uh, certain pitches," said Perry. "I don't remember exactly which ones. Down in Texas, I don't ever throw a greaseball. It's so hot there and you sweat so much, you never have to." Perry went on to say that he thought Merritt was "very foolish" for making the disclosures that he had . . . "considering the way he pitched." Perry didn't actually say so, but he felt that a more prudent man, given Merritt's mastery of the over-the-counter pitching enhancements, would have kept matters to himself. And nobody would doubt that Perry was an honest man. A tobacco farmer in North Carolina, Perry would tell me on a future date that some agronomist told him his land offered ideal growing conditions for marijuana, but "I just won't plant the stuff," he said.

Throughout baseball, official reaction to Merritt's gambit varied sharply. Speaking of marijuana, Boston's Bill "Spaceman" Lee came out strongly in favor of Jim Merritt and what he was attempting to accomplish. (Lee later would be the first big leaguer to publicly admit marijuana use.) "I don't smoke it, but

I do sprinkle it on my pancakes." Lee said that "if they're going to make a grand jury case out of this, I hope every pitcher who has experimented with it [a greaseball, not marijuana] will come forward and admit it," Lee said. "Almost every pitcher I know has tried something like that when he's going bad."

The next day, in Baltimore, Merritt would learn that league president Joe Cronin did not share some of the enthusiasms expressed by others over his actions in Cleveland. Cronin announced that Merritt would draw a fine . . . "although the league has no positive evidence that an illegal pitch was used except [Merritt's] own admission." Cronin added that Bill Lee was being fined $250 for popping off like he had.

Merritt appeared relieved by the results. "I hadn't checked the rule thoroughly," he said, "and while I do not particularly care to part with my money, it turns out that I could have been suspended and that the game could have been forfeited." True, it would appear here that AL president Joe Cronin was a man of immeasurable capacities of empathy, leniency and mercy. Had Cronin chosen to exercise his option of forfeiture, the Rangers would have completed the 1973 season with 106 losses instead of 105.

So thanks to the ingenuity of Jim Merritt and the advanced technological techniques at the K-Y laboratories, the Rangers were once again giving us amusements that extended well beyond the commonplace. Now in Baltimore for another three-game series, the Orioles were riding a fourteen-game winning streak that had left the Tigers, Red Sox and Yankees gasping, collapsed and hopelessly beaten for any type of further competition for the AL East title. But most space in the local papers was devoted not to Earl Weaver and the almighty O's but rather Whitey Herzog and his greaseballing Rangers.

Then, in front of a crowd in Memorial Stadium that included the entire plebe class from Annapolis, the Rangers ended the Orioles' fourteen-game winning streak, 5–3, and ended Dave McNally's personal seventeen-game streak against the Rangers-Senators franchise in the process.

"I wonder," said Whitey Herzog after the game, "if anybody could have possibly calculated the odds of us winning tonight . . . bucking one seventeen-game streak and another fourteen-game streak, and pitching a guy who managed to find a way to shoot himself in his pitching hand . . . Can you imagine the odds?" Yes, Charlie Hudson was back.

LABOR DAY WEEKEND was fast approaching, a vantage point from which the end of the season could be seen lingering mirage-like somewhere in the distance. The cumulative fallout from the long campaign was understandably taking its toll on Whitey, on the players, even on the humble media. Dissention erupted in a taxicab after we had finished filing our stories.

The idea of going for a late meal had been agreed upon, but now, in a city that offered some of the best, if not *the* best seafood restaurants in the United States, Randy Galloway was making loud braying noises and insisting that we try to locate some joint he'd heard advertised that served all-you-can-eat catfish for a quarter. I demurred. "How come you only like to eat at restaurants where the waiters all wear those little sailor-boy costumes, huh?" demanded Galloway. Harold McKinney was on my side in this dispute and, as the cab drove past Johns Hopkins Hospital, McKinney yelled at the driver to put Galloway out at the emergency entrance. "His brain is so fucked up, I'll bet they treat him for free," McKinney told the driver. "Of course, they'll never let him out, either."

The cabbie said he thought it might be a better idea if we all got out. I was the only who did, promptly finding myself wandering the streets of Baltimore, carrying a Smith-Corona portable in one hand, a Xerox telecopier in the other and wondering if the Peace Corps might have any openings for a baseball writer.

CHAPTER

15

A DOZEN OR SO curious onlookers gathered at the gate at Love Field in Dallas, where the Rangers' charter was due to arrive momentarily as the team returned from its trip to Cleveland and Baltimore. The onlookers weren't there to gawk at the players and get autographs; they were ogling the players' wives and live-ins who had assembled to meet the flight. Almost without exception, these women looked sensational, like soap-opera starlets with the posture and bearing of Philadelphia debutantes.

Baseball players are universally successful in attracting high-quality lifetime companions. And why not? Like their wives, most ballplayers seem to have been manufactured in a special cloning laboratory. Ballplayers can generally be identified by their extraordinarily long arms and low foreheads, giving them that primitive appearance that a lot of American women seem to go for.

Plus, baseball players apparently bring most of the assets these same women require in a husband. First, of course, they make lots of dough and, second, they're on the road for—if you count spring training—over 110 days a year. Even when they are in town, ballplayers spend virtually every waking hour at the golf course or in a bass boat, so they are rarely around or underfoot to impede the wives' leisure pursuits or modeling careers. No worries about fooling around with the hometown cheerleaders, because in baseball there aren't any cheerleaders. Another key asset: unlike pro football, basketball and hockey players, baseball players strongly tend toward passive behavior when they become house-drunk. Rather than smashing furniture and spouses, they pass out in the flower bed. So, ladies, if you're looking for Mr. Right, head for the ballpark.

When the Rangers' charter landed at Love Field, the players piled out like conquering heroes, back now from their most successful road trip of the season: three wins and only four losses. Also, the team had been the focal point of some national news, thanks to Jim Merritt's greaseball declaration. ESPN had not yet been invented in 1973, and neither had *USA Today,* but Merritt and the Rangers had at least earned some mention on NBC's "Today" show. Two of the players were so exuberant they rode from the gate in wheelchairs for the simple reason that they were too impaired to negotiate the long walk out to the parking lot.

Merritt's daring stunt continued to sustain its ripple effect around the league. The top wire-service baseball story of the day concerned Billy Martin. In Detroit, the proud skipper, now seemingly locked into a state of terminal frustration by the Tigers' late season disappearance from the race against the Orioles, had ordered two of his pitchers, Fred Scherman and Joe Coleman, to coat their fingertips with a mixture of Vaseline and water when they took the mound against Cleveland. The entire league was arming itself with petroleum jelly and seemed poised to engage in a retaliatory war against the poor Indians.

As a result, Martin received a telegram from American League president Joe Cronin, whose Western Union tab had been hugely enlarged since the Merritt episode of the previous Sunday. Cronin's telegram to Billy read: "This is to inform you that you are suspended for three days for directing your pitchers to throw illegal pitches. Your endorsement of such tactics cannot be tolerated." An interior decorator could paper the walls of a Billy Martin museum with telegrams such as this one that the self-ordained "Little Dago" had received from various types of defied authority over the years.

Still, the seismograph readings on Earthquake Billy had been more active than usual in recent days. After a loss at Baltimore, Martin didn't talk to reporters about the game itself but rather how somebody had broken into his hotel room while he claimed he was asleep and tiptoed off with $330 cash. Martin told the gentlemen of the press that the next night he had attached a coat hanger to the chain lock in his room to make future incursions more challenging for the intruder. "In other words, Billy was trying to catch Art [Tiger pitching coach Art Fowler] in the act," Whitey Herzog said with his characteristic cackle.

The manager was having to rely on events from afar more frequently as a source of mirth since the events in and around his own field headquarters didn't seem that funny to him. Jim Merritt's first appearance since arousing the league-wide clamor turned out to be a wasted evening. Merritt was blasted by the Twins. Plate umpire Jim Odum inspected the ball three times but detected nothing suspicious. "I think Merritt threw a few," Herzog said. "Those were the only pitches he actually threw for strikes the whole game."

On Saturday, the Twins beat Jim Bibby in a game that lured 4,000 paying guests into the park, a sickly number even for the Rangers on a Saturday night. All of the sports fans in the area were at home watching a Dallas Cowboys exhibition game on TV. Then, on Sunday, David Clyde pitched against Minnesota. The last time Clyde faced the Twins had been back in June when his big-league debut had packed the stadium. In his second effort against Minnesota, Clyde attracted 7,700 paid admissions. Results on the mound against the Twins in the rematch would take an awkward turn as well. Clyde lasted an inning and a third—this was a trend by now—and Texas got soaked, 10–7.

Afterward, the team skipped town with an absence of fanfare. A quick three-game trip to Chicago was on the schedule that included, happily, two day games at Comiskey Park after a night-time opener. On the flight to O'Hare I sat beside Toby Harrah, the shortstop, who outlined his off-season plans. In those days most of the big-league players occupied their autumn and winter months by taking prolonged hunting trips and earning cash by greeting customers at new-car dealerships. Not Toby, who so loved the game that he would be playing baseball, from Halloween until Ground Hog Day, in Venezuela. Zulia, to be exact. Plenty of up-and-coming U.S. talent migrate to various Latin leagues in the winter to polish their baseball technique and pick up a nice paycheck. But Toby Harrah was one of the very few well-established major leaguers who continued his annual pilgrimages to the Piña Colada provinces.

"Aw man, it's great down there," said Toby. "The fans are unbelievable. Not as stodgy as the ones who come to most of the Rangers games. Down there, every time somebody gets an extra-base hit they shoot pistols into the air. And the visiting teams catch hell. Those fans, they'll pour cans of piss into the visitors' dugout and throw fireworks and big poisonous snakes in there. Nice people, basically. Nice area, too. I rent a little house there in Zulia. One day I came home and found a dead horse in the front yard . . . but mostly, Zulia's really OK."

AFTER THE OPENING game of the short series at Comiskey Park, still another loss, the writers were quick to finish their account of the latest fiasco. Nobody wanted to miss the team bus that always left forty-five minutes after the game and run the risk of being stranded at night in South Chicago. Ed Fowler, one of the Chicago writers, amplified the paranoia by warning us: "If you do get stuck on the streets around the ballpark, do not, under any circumstances, make any outward show of fear. Because if you do, the people around there will sense it, and there will be nothing left of you but a pile of bones and a pair of tennis shoes."

Back at the Executive House Hotel, most of the players hopped from the bus and transferred directly into cabs that would carry them to nocturnal explorations of Rush Street. My stamina was shot and I went to my hotel room, turned on the TV and learned that Billy Martin was back in the news. The Tigers had fired him.

Now Billy was establishing an employment pattern. In 1969, he had managed the Twins to a division championship. The next season Billy was canned and placed on the shelf next to the peas and okra for ongoing skirmishes with front office management. Billy's Detroit Tigers had taken the Eastern Division pennant in 1972 and now, a year later, Martin was out. Why? Was it this spitball suspension? According to Jim Campbell, the Detroit general manager: "It was a breakdown on company-policy matters. There were misunderstandings. From foul line to foul line, he did a good job. I cautioned Billy about making comments about the commissioner, the league president and club executives." Jim Campbell concluded his statement with the immortal Billy Martin epitaph: "WE CAN'T HAVE THAT SORT OF THING." Martin and Jim Campbell did not part as friends. For the next two years at least, Billy, in polite company, liked to excuse himself, head for the john and announce, "I've gotta go take a Jim Campbell."

Billy's players in Detroit appeared mystified by the sudden departure. Al Kaline, who would be finishing his Hall of Fame career in another three weeks, said, "The last two weeks have been very hectic. It wasn't just the spitball thing. I can't see him getting fired over that."

Persons who actually knew Billy Martin were also certain that wasn't the case. They suspected his dismissal in Detroit was likely due to what the engineers at Three Mile Island would one day refer to as an "incident." It was later, maybe a year or two, that a Detroit sportswriter, seated near the jukebox at the Lindell AC, described the "incident" to me this way: "John Fetzer, the Tigers' owner who also owned Upjohn Pharmaceuticals and lived in Kalamazoo, made a rare visit to a game at Tiger Stadium and sat in the owner's box next to the Tigers' dugout. He was there with some family and friends, including one who might be described as an attractive young woman.

"Some time after the game started," the writer contended, "somebody, allegedly Billy Martin, reached out of the dugout and handed the woman a note. It read something like: 'Why don't you meet me in the players' parking lot after the game and we can go have a drink. Love, Billy.' So the girl hands the note to Fetzer, who's a nice old fellow with straightlaced values, and says, 'What's this all about, Uncle John?' That's pretty much what happened." Another episode in the The Saga of Billy Martin.

"WE CAN'T HAVE THAT SORT OF THING."

Repercussions of the upheaval in Detroit extended down to Texas. After the short series in Chicago, the Rangers were back in Arlington for a weekend engagement against Oakland. Friday afternoon, Burt Hawkins called me at home. "Get out to the park early," he said. "Bob Short is having a press conference." Well, a Bob Short press conference ordinarily did not give cause for network alerts that began, "We interrupt our regularly scheduled programing . . ." Jim Merritt gave good press conferences. Mike Kekich and Fritz Peterson of the Yankees gave an outstanding press conference when they announced they were trading wives. Bob Short, up to this point, had failed miserably in his occasional attempts to rouse the rabble.

This one would be different. Short sat behind a desk in his stadium office. Whitey Herzog sat immediately to Short's left. Short began the press conference by announcing that he had fired Whitey. His reason, he said, was "the artistic state of the Rangers."

The relationship between the Rangers' management and the Rangers' press corps had, from the first, been more informal than what is more commonly seen in professional sports. This press conference was typical. Harold McKinney began calling Bob Short the same names that McKinney called his ten-year-old Buick Skylark on the frequent mornings that it wouldn't start.

"Jesus Christ, Bob! Artistic state of the Rangers! Whitey's not the one who went and rounded up Rico Carty and Mike Epstein to be the heart of the batting order! You were! Some fuckin' art you collected there!'' People out in the parking lot could probably hear Harold yelling at the owner. Now the cameras were clicking and Bob Short found himself pressed into a defensive posture. Short said that Del Wilbur, the AAA manager from Spokane, had been pressed into service on an interim basis. The full-time guy for 1974 had not been identified yet, Short kept insisting.

Here was where Bob Short could have made matters easier on himself at the press conference . . . by simply confirming that the instant Billy Martin was ousted in Detroit, he had found a warm nest awaiting in Texas. It made sense. All around Dallas-Fort Worth suburbs like Blue Mound, Joshua and Grapevine, guys were roaring up and down the blacktop roads in pickup trucks adorned with bumper stickers that read: "The West Wasn't Won With A Registered Gun." They had money to spend, but they were spending it all in bowling alleys and head-shops and not at the ballpark that Short had presumed would have established itself by now as the Poor Man's Country Club.

Short's long-range plan to sell the team to Texas ownership needed a boost, and a Texas baseball team with Billy Martin as the manager stood out as exactly the sort of attraction that might justify the ten-million-dollar price tag that the vendor had hung around the neck of this turkey of a franchise. Exactly the right touch. To these potential buyers . . . when it came to making a luxury purchase, it was the size of the hood ornament that mattered more than what might be under the hood.

At his press conference, though, Short was trying hard to fox-trot around the topic of Billy Martin. His strategy there was simple enough. Herzog had received Short's full assurance that he was in the boat for the long cruise when he signed on the previous fall. Now Herzog was being dumped for no reason other than the obvious one: Short had stumbled over what he figured was a rare gem in Billy Martin.

"I thought that the emphasis here was supposed to be more

on development than winning right away," Herzog said. "I guess I was wrong about that, and when you're wrong with a 47–91 record, you are not going to get very far." Whitey, once again, was demonstrating his usual candor and rare ability to sit on a media platform and place matters into correct focus while those around him could not.

If Bob Short didn't want to talk about Billy Martin, then Whitey Herzog would do it for him. "If he can get Billy Martin, then it would be a great move for the organization," Whitey continued. "I think that Bob has made him an offer and hopes to get his shot in before Houston or New York or somebody. You can't blame him for going after Martin. I have a lot of respect for Billy Martin."

Certain members of the Texas media "corral" were not as convinced that Short was doing the right thing, certainly not at the expense of Whitey Herzog, whom the writers realized was a once-in-a-career departure from the array of dull tools and craftsmen of the con who populate the realm of sports in staggering numbers.

McKinney called Bob Short more names, and the owner, now backpedaling, said, "B-u-u-t, all of you have been saying that the team is better than its record." Herzog interrupted and for the first time indicated that he might be marginally irritated.

"No—I don't think that's what's been said," Herzog asserted. "What they said was that this team was more interesting and colorful than last year." And Whitey Herzog was understating his point.

Down in the clubhouse, the men most responsible for drawing the blueprints for the unsightly 47–91 record that Herzog had mentioned, the players themselves, seemed appropriately chagrined by the events of the early evening. "They said a team meeting had been called for six o'clock and I figured it was something routine . . . like to announce that I had been traded to some team in Japan in exchange for a broken bat," said Rich Billings. "When they said Whitey was fired, it was a shock. In fact, it was one hell of a shock."

Several of the others went on the record, agreeing that "if you can't play for a man like Whitey, you can't play for anybody." Professional athletes have been reading from the same weary script that conventionally appears when the coach or the manager comes to work and discovers that somebody has changed the locks on his office door.

They never say so, but the players are usually elated when the boss goes stumbling out like a gutted snowbird. That was *not* the case with the 1973 Rangers and Whitey Herzog. But Herzog's formal dismissal had been posted for less than an hour, and already the unofficial presence of Billy Martin was hanging heavily in the clubhouse. You couldn't actually see Billy yet, but he was up there in the rafters and the players were watering down their comments accordingly.

The next day—Saturday—I showed up at the stadium in mid-afternoon. I wanted to bang out a story for the Sunday edition about the lingering aftertaste of Whitey's abrupt dismissal. Then I planned to skip out early and spend the remainder of my Saturday at an agreeable ballpark alternative—the Cave. That was a location in Arlington that encouraged the development of area vocalists and string musicians who performed Texas ballads like "When The Moon Goes Down On Medina, I'll Be Going Down On You."

Good old Merle Heryford, the *Morning News* guy, had agreed to substitute for me as official scorer. I didn't have to ask him twice. Merle was probably the only person in the history of the game who actually liked to score.

After arriving at the mostly deserted ballpark about three-thirty, I walked into the pressbox elevator. One other person was also stepping into the same elevator—none other than Billy Martin. So when, I asked Martin, do you start? Billy was casual. "Tonight," he said. "They're sewing the old Number 1 on the back of my Rangers uniform as we speak." We talked for about two minutes, and he assured the readers of the *Star-Telegram* that General George Patton was there and that the ranks of the old Rangers F-Troop, the Dark Command—beginning next season and not at the tail end of this now-forgotten campaign—would either shape up or consider a career in vacuum-cleaner sales.

One more question was left to ask. "This team has some fairly controversial characters on it. How do you plan to deal with those people?" His eyes seemed to spark momentarily as he answered a question with a question.

"Who do they have who's more controversial than I am?" said Billy Martin.

CHAPTER

———

16

CERTAIN ARCHITECTS MAINTAIN a distinctive talent for designing structures that actually seem to frown. Mostly, this look is reserved for criminal-court buildings, Internal Revenue Service offices and other such facilities that the average citizen attempts to avoid like the cholera. Pompano Stadium was probably the only baseball park that had that kind of ominous facade.

Spring training, 1974, was about to begin, and the Rangers' Florida headquarters exuded the same aura of defeat that had radiated such a striking impression when I arrived there exactly one year before. Even when this ballpark was full of people, which it always was when the Yankees rode the bus up from Fort Lauderdale for an exhibition game, the place still seemed somehow abandoned.

On the field, the players went through the routine of the workouts with the same attitude of world-weariness, earmarked by a distinct absence of vigor and élan, and the same contagious ennui that had been so much in evidence the last season. The white home uniforms were the same, with red-and-blue trim and the word "Rangers" stitched across the shirts in that hokey-type style that sign painters in the Old West seemed to have favored.

Old Captain Jack still maintained his vigil in the little lunchroom down the leftfield line, making sure that the hot dogs were the ones for which, in Bob Short's estimation, there could be no ersatz replacement, no matter how well disguised. The palm trees beyond the fence still seemed to be battling tuberculosis and the kids from Pompano Beach's talented and gifted magnet high school were still smoking reefers on top of the pressbox.

Beyond the surface elements, however, the concept of change was manifesting itself in many critical areas of Rangers spring training. First of all, the "quality of life" of the 1973 season was mitigated this year. Essentials such as nightlife venues were limited because of the gasoline shortage brought on that year by the latest ceremonial war in the Mideast. Lines at the pumps in South Florida were absurdly long. Finally, the equipment guy of the Rangers, Smacko Macko, had arranged exclusive access at a Gulf station for the baseball "group" . . . as long as you showed up at three A.M., an hour at which I was hardly up to operating the pump. Another downside feature of that spring was a swamp fire just to the west of Pompano Beach that blanketed the whole area for the entire month of March with a god-awful stench.

The most significant alteration of Pompano lifestyle was that my on-the-road partnership with Harold McKinney had been dissolved. During the previous year, the ownership of the Fort Worth *Star-Telegram* and its TV station, Channel 5, had been transferred from the hometown Amon Carter group to Cap Cities in what at the time had been the biggest media sale in the history of the country. Cap Cities apparently employed something novel in its operational setup—people who were known as accountants—and when they began researching the bar tabs of the two *Star-Telegram* baseball writers, I am told that gasps could be heard throughout the corridors of Manhattan.

So "the big boys in the home office" had ordained that McKinney and I would split spring training and all of the regular season road trips, an act that I regarded as benign, humane and entirely unnewspaper-like. It also meant double the workload on the road. Translation: I might have to cut my hours in the Florida bistros sometimes as much as one hour a day.

The arrival of Billy Martin late in the 1973 season naturally meant that the working mood around the baseball team would be different, although one could not determine just *how* different from the pace of the new manager's spring-training approach. During much of the off-season Martin had assured the good people of the Dallas-Fort Worth region that the burlesque show at Arlington Stadium was closing for good, to be replaced with a more sophisticated version of major-league baseball. Billy also told the people not to be surprised when his Rangers negotiated a Worst-To-First gambit—which the fan base and certainly the media cheerfully wrote off as the hollow and opportunistic rhetoric of a politician six points down in the polls. But Martin swore that the Rangers, fresh from a 57–105 showing in 1973, would, through the magic of a Billy Martin Makeover, contend for the division championship in 1974.

Billy's demeanor in his first spring training in Pompano was tactically keyed down. He well realized that the material on the field was fifteen percent silk purse and eighty-five percent sow's ear. From all the way across the diamond, Martin could hear Lloyd Allen—one of the remaining refugees from Whitey Herzog's Lost Battalion of Live Young Arms—warming up in the makeshift bullpen out by the leftfield flagpole. The sound was not the "thud" of Lloyd Allen's sonic boom fastball into a catcher's mitt but rather the "bang" of Lloyd's high hard one hitting the fence after it had sailed several feet in various directions beyond the reach of the catcher.

One of Billy's ample corps of "trusted lieutenants"—Art Fowler—was openly appalled at what he was seeing. It was Art Fowler's self-embraced destiny to follow the same checkered job path as Billy Martin—the Human Cannonball—to be hired and fired on the same day. Fired in Minnesota and on to Detroit. Fired in Detroit and on to Texas. Art, the pitching coach, traveled with Martin every step. Fowler, whose nose should have rated mention in Ripley's *Believe It or Not* as a replica of W.C.

Fields', wore a blank expression as he sat behind the plate and watched the Rangers mound prospects warm up.

"Just throw strikes, kid," Art would mutter, mostly to himself in a soft South Carolina lament. "Babe Ruth's dead." Art would shake his head, gesture toward a Lloyd Allen, a Don Stanhouse or a Steve Dunning and proclaim, "If these kids can't get people out simply throwin' the ball over the plate, then I'll eat this batting cage. But . . ." Then another "bang" would resound from the fence behind the leftfield bullpen and Art would shake his head again. Billy Martin and Art Fowler could now readily understand why Whitey Herzog, at times, had been on the verge of storming the altar at a Billy Graham crusade, begging for salvation.

Given the characteristics of the personnel at hand, Billy shrewdly abandoned—for spring training at least—his favored leadership techniques. Better Living Through Confrontation wouldn't work down here. Billy usually liked to stress that "the way to a man's heart is through his chest" but he would put that policy on hold, too. He told me that his only ironclad rule for spring training was this: anybody who missed a workout would be fined unless the player could offer proof that he had been fishing.

Martin, this year, was Mister Congeniality, and that profile was on display nightly at the dear old Banyan Lounge at the Surf Rider Resort, right there at beachside on Highway 1. Billy was a regular there with his coaches *and* his ballplayers. Most big-league managers decree, as Baseball's First Commandment, that the players' cocktail-hour congregations be conducted anywhere but the bar in the same hotel where the team is located. The reasoning is simple. Often fans, autograph-seekers and assorted other curious members of the private sector are known to hang out at baseball hotels. Therefore, the Lords of Baseball are characteristically reluctant to allow the general public to witness the field hands at play. To express it bluntly, a gathering of five or more big-league baseball players in those days had the potential to make the U.S. Navy Tailhook convention look like a Mormon prayer convocation.

Because of what Billy considered his natural paternal instincts, he professed that he felt more comfortable with his players lingering closer to the house. "It's a hell of a lot easier to ride an elevator up to the room than it is to get back from a strange part of town," Billy reasoned. "I don't want to get any three A.M. phone calls from the cops or some shithead in an emergency room telling me that my cleanup hitter has driven up a telephone pole and that I need to come pick up what's left of him."

So the Banyan Room then became the baseball hangout of 1974, but the ballplayers were the supporting cast. Billy Martin was the star. In the history of American celebritydom, there has probably never been a recognizable personality who went out of his or her way to be seen to the extent that Billy Martin did.

The "Little Dago"—he persisted in calling himself that even though persons familiar with Billy's lineage believe him to be more Portuguese than Italian—adored his fans. At least, he did until exactly seventy-five minutes past midnight. Then Billy would undergo a swift transformation of personality in which he suddenly became the reigning poultryweight champion of the world and apt to practice uppercuts and jabs into the faces of some of these same adoring fans. He didn't require New York's Copacabana nightclub to stage the main event of the evening. The County Line Tavern in Grand Prairie, Texas, could serve as a more than adequate facility. Indeed, any old dive would do. But that aspect of Billy's enigmatic disposition would not come to the fore until much later in the season. The Billy that everybody encountered in the Banyan Room in 1974 looked and acted like a man playing the lead in a toothpaste commercial.

And why not? In Texas, Billy was in everyday sipping proximity to his adored companion, Mickey Mantle, now immersed in his golfing retirement in Dallas. Billy was avidly proclaiming to the world that Texas was his kind of place. He wore Levis, cowboy boots and occasionally even a cowboy hat. All that was missing was a set of pearl-handled six shooters. "The Little Dago" appeared at home in his new identity as "Bronco Billy," the Baseball Bushwhacker. Martin's black Lincoln, seemingly as long as Bob Short's yacht, was conspicuous by its presence in the Banyan Room parking lot, with personalized Texas license plates emblazoned with the numeral "1."

Martin further realized that he had stumbled into the closest facsimile to a "win-win" managerial situation that baseball had to offer. The Rangers had only one direction available to them and the one man who might enable Martin to punch the "up" button was now at work in a Rangers' uniform. The trade that Whitey Herzog had initially orchestrated with the Cubs had, indeed, taken place over the winter. It was not quite the deal that Whitey had outlined. Herzog had a tacit agreement from Chicago to send Alex Johnson and Vic Harris over in exchange for the treasure in the deal, Ferguson Jenkins. Instead, the Rangers retained Johnson but parted with Harris and Bill Madlock, the prime prospect in the Rangers' farm system. Madlock wound up winning three National League batting championships.

That seemed inconsequential in 1974. Standing among the kamikaze corps that was competing for jobs on Martin's staff, Fergie Jenkins appeared to have drifted down from another planet. He could throw strikes and he had long ago mastered the nuances of the craft of pitching that seemed so baffling to the majority of the cast assembled in Pompano Beach.

This man alone meant that the Rangers figured to be at least fifteen wins better than the 1973 season. He sure as hell looked the part of a man who would eventually surpass the hallowed 300-win milestone in the major league. Almost six-foot-seven, his towering presence on the mound could petrify the hitter.

Jenkins now sat serenely atop the picnic table down the leftfield line that served as the pressroom at Pompano Stadium. He watched a rookie centerfielder field a line drive during an intra-squad game and then run about eight strides forward before relaying the ball back to the infield. "That young man ap-

Billy Martin turns on the charm at the Rangers Women's Club picnic.

Ted Williams shows
off his Texas-style
baseball shoe,
opening night, 1972.
Arlington mayor
Tom Vandergriff is
in background.

Jim Bibby demonstrates his
"no-hitter grip" to Martin.

Billy Martin.

Whitey Herzog presides over a
comedy of errors in 1973.

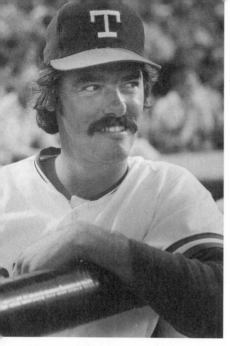

Jim Merritt owned up to throwing a greaseball.

Rich Billings, behind the plate for Jim Bibby's no-hitter.

Owner Bob Short (right) talks over the plight of the team with Herzog and general manager Joe Burke (left).

Future manager Jim Fregosi provided personality to the early Rangers.

Jeff Burroughs overcame the ill winds of Arlington to win American League MVP honors in 1974.

The REAL Texas Rangers of law-enforcement fame seem dubious of their baseball namesakes.

The new Texas franchise joins the rodeo.

Baseball history and empty seats—a Rangers tradition.

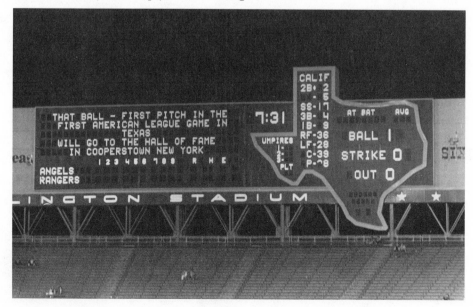

Bugs outnumbered the fans in
the early days of the Rangers.

David Clyde,
teenage rookie sensation.

Fans and media went nuts over David Clyde's big-league debut.

Rangers cheerleaders were a
temporary novelty.

Arlington Stadium in midsummer—
one hell of a place.

The TV Lone
Ranger, Clayton
Moore, offers Jim
Sundberg more
ammunition.

Owner Brad Corbett and Rangers are host to the President, Gerald Ford, who threw out the first pitch opening night, 1976.

From left: David Clyde, future Rangers general manager Tom Grieve, coach and future A's manager Jackie Moore, Billy Martin, coach Merrill Combs and another future Rangers manager, Frank Lucchesi.

parently thinks he's involved in a javelin competition," Jenkins observed.

I sat there scribbling notes, trying to collect items for a Sunday article on Jenkins' life story. He told me that he had played for the Harlem Globetrotters for a season before deciding that pitching baseballs would become his life's work. Born in Chatham and having grown up on a farm in Ontario, Jenkins also said that scouts assured him he had all the necessary requirements to become the first black star in the National Hockey League. Jenkins laughed and said, "Now why in the world would I want to do *that?*"

Billy Martin, naturally, was delighted that a force like Jenkins was working for the Rangers. What Billy saw in Fergie was a Manager of the Year plaque. It was obvious that Jenkins and Jim Bibby would constitute a two-man starting rotation for this team, and the candidates for the fill-in spots gave Martin some interesting choices.

One was David Clyde. "Having saved the franchise, David Clyde now tries to make the team." I wrote that in the *Star-Telegram* one afternoon, after my sensitivities had been heightened by a husky cabernet and some expensive incense provided by a New Age woman—in those days, I think they were still known as hippies—who was sharing my room during this spring training of 1974.

Clyde would indeed make the team and not, Martin assured me, "because of who he is but because he's got guts, throws hard and is one of the few who appears to know what he's doing."

Jim Merritt—sans greaseball—was back by popular demand, although his starting assignments would be widely spaced to mostly coincide with the appearance of comets and an occasional lunar eclipse. The remaining starting job was being won by a righthander who had come to the Rangers via the team's favorite talent pool—the American League's "physically unable to perform" list. Steve Hargan, another rehab project, told me that he had been delivered to Pompano Beach "in a truck from Goodwill Industries."

Like Jim Merritt, Hargan had compiled a winning major-league track record until his arm had blown up. Now he was attempting a comeback in Texas. The mainspring in Steve Hargan's pitching arm might not have been as tight as it once was, "but," he said, "at least I can throw again without my shoulder making noises like somebody stripping the gears on a Model T."

Hargan showed right away that he enjoyed natural instincts that enabled him to excel not only on the pitcher's mound but also in what is known as the Game of Life. Such people also tend to be endowed with inquisitive minds. Hargan, for instance, was devoting an afternoon to patronage of the poolside bar at the Surf Rider when he encountered a Canuck whose bathing suit emphasized a physical configuration that was strikingly similar to that of a showgirl who had been Jack Ruby's top stage attraction in Dallas: Chris Colt and her twin 45's. The pitcher gazed at the lady's God-given assets in admiration and wonderment and finally asked, "Don't you ever let the air out of those things?"

Billy Martin had little doubt that Steve Hargan would conform nicely to this unit that might be described as "The Little Dago's Foreign Legion." Like the 1973 Rangers, this group was largely composed of outcasts and renegades, but Billy had hand-picked a few operatives who were proven survivors in the big-league jungles. One of these was Cesar Tovar, who had been one of Martin's key guys when he won the division with the Twins. In Minnesota, Tovar had once played all nine positions for an inning apiece in a single game. The quintessential blithe spirit, Tovar insisted that everyone call him "Pepi," although other names probably came into use as well since it was rumored that he was married to three women in three different countries when he joined the Rangers.

If such was the case, Tovar apparently was recruiting a possible Number Four after the Rangers had won their exhibition season opener against the Yankees. At the Banyan Room bar, he sat beaming next to what Hargan described as a "pageant-quality" Scandinavian woman. "Tovar have good day," he explained. "Get two hits and score blonde."

One of the holdovers from the Rangers' shipwreck of 1973, Jim Fregosi, was also assured membership on Billy's somewhat modified and redecorated Texas roster. Fregosi had agreed to a reduction in his previous salary of $90,000—a fat salary in the paleolithic, pre-free-agency era of major-league baseball. "You have to figure out how to prolong your shelf life. That's the key to longevity in this racket for players like me," Fregosi insisted. "Don't get pushy at contract time and wear out your welcome. Baseball players are just like motor oil and toilet paper . . . a commodity with a set market price. If more players thought like I do, they'd last longer."

Fregosi, of course, was another of those troops who adhered to the label of "the kind of guy Billy likes to have around." There was still some life in Fregosi's bat, he knew how to play the game and could hold his liquor. Not only that, Fregosi ranked near the absolute top of the major-league heap when it came to overall handicapping skills at the horse and harness track.

Above all else, Fregosi, with his perspective built from years of service, was simply happy to be a Ranger. "That team last year . . . I've been in the majors a dozen years and I've never been around anything like that," he reflected. "That was not only the worst team I've ever been associated with, but also it had the best morale, far and away. Very loose. Imagine how much fun it would be around here if these guys actually started to win a few?"

CHAPTER

17

SOMEBODY ONCE DEFINED the meaning of life as "the interruption of an otherwise peaceful nonexistence." My extended off-season vacation, mandated by company-calculated "comp" time, had amounted to exactly that, a peaceful nonexistence devoted mostly to playing tennis and working on the original draft of my first novel, *Teenage Milkman,* a title that I must confess was supplied by Rangers outfielder Jeff Burroughs. He recommended another one as well—*Nurses On Horseback.*

This prolonged separation from the Rangers' ordeal had proved therapeutic for the spirit and cleansing of the liver. In late January 1974, however, I made one trip to Arlington Stadium. The occasion was a small party in the press lounge. It was scheduled for an all-important announcement: for the coming season, Schlitz had signed on as the main sponsor of games broadcast on the Rangers' radio network. The Beer That Made Milwaukee Famous was now also the official beer of the Texas Rangers.

As far as media parties go, this one was not particularly lavish. Refreshments were the same as what you'd find in the bedroom of the average Texan—a washtub full of ice and beer cans and a bowl of potato chips. Several high-powered ad guys showed for the announcement party for some reason, account executives from Dallas, Milwaukee and New York.

Ad guys and sportswriters are not always a safe philosophical mix in certain social circumstances. My partner on the Rangers newspaper beat, Harold McKinney, had in fact recently been decked by an ad guy at Harold's second home, the Press Club in Fort Worth. Harold had no choice, he assured me, other than to retaliate by pushing the ad guy down a flight of stairs.

Now I have no quarrels with individuals associated with the advertising industry, although the true value of their contribution to what they themselves might refer to as the highways and byways of American life is something that I do often find to be ill-defined and fuzzy.

So there was absolutely no motivation to foment agitation and certainly not the smallest trace of what the courts call malicious intent when I embarked on a conversation with one of the Schlitz ad guys that I guessed was from New York. "These Schlitz commercials that I see on TV all the time," I began, "they're all filmed on big sailboats and you see a bunch of guys rigging the sails and diving off the deck and drinking Schlitz and having a great time and all, but you never see any women on the boat . . . and you don't see any women after the boat is parked on the beach and the guys are having a clambake and they're singing and throwing Frisbees and still drinking all that Schlitz. So I was watching some of those commercials on a football game and got to wondering if maybe Schlitz is going after the gay market with these TV commercials." My intent in making these remarks was solely to inject some levity into what was shaping up as a colorless gathering, perhaps bring some life to the usually dismal small talk that happens among strangers, even when free beer is being served. It never occurred to me to notice that, like the Schlitz sailboat, there weren't any women at this press party.

The ad man seemed offended. Well, he didn't seem offended, he *was* offended. "Listen . . . we just finished filming a new series of commercials in Tokyo," he told me in a tone that car-

ried a sharp edge, "and these spots feature a young actor . . .
Michael . . . and let me tell you this . . . Michael is all man.
Strong shoulders, beautifully sculpted back, trim hips, magnifi-
cent thighs. I'd like to see you call Michael a fag to his face and
you'll really get what's coming to you—" Whoa. A tense moment. Fortunately, further discussion of the matter of Michael
was cut off with the entry of Jimmy Piersall into the press
lounge. Piersall had recently been hired by Bob Short in a public relations capacity for the Rangers. He was supposed to make
speeches to civic organizations, hawking season tickets, telling
funny stories and serving as the Rangers' Ambassador of Good
Will. This was the same colorful Jimmy Piersall who played
centerfield so spectacularly during the latter-day Ted Williams
tenure in Boston and the same Jim Piersall who was portrayed
by Anthony Perkins of *Psycho* fame in the film *Fear Strikes Out*—
the story of how Piersall had some kind of major psychiatric
episode, then came back to play more baseball.

Piersall was exactly the kind of person that Bob Short liked to
hire—a name that carried celebrity connotation. The ad guy
who was so disenchanted with me sure as hell knew who Piersall
was. So he turned from me and said, "Jimmy! Have a Schlitz!"

"I don't drink that goddamn goat piss," Piersall said, and
kept on walking. Jimmy might have added that it wasn't Schlitz,
specifically, that he regarded as goat piss. Piersall didn't drink
alcohol—period. But the poor ad guy didn't know that and his
mouth fell open. I felt like rushing over to Jimmy Piersall and
giving him a warm embrace, then decided against that, lest I
wind up on a Schlitz commercial.

A brief conversation with Piersall did take place. He admitted
that he would rather, by far, be associated with baseball on a
more direct basis. But Jimmy said he had managed a team in
the low minors and was disillusioned by the experience. He said
that he suspected most of his players "were on dope."

Perhaps six weeks later, when I was billeted at Pompano
Beach for spring training, some strange stories were filtering out
of Texas concerning my new idol, Jimmy Piersall. According to

information arriving at Pompano Stadium, the Rangers' Ambassador of Good Will was successful in attracting attention to the ball club but was churning up some now heavy seas of discontent in the process.

In a speech to the Fort Worth Chamber of Commerce, Piersall supposedly castigated the group because of slow Rangers ticket sales in what is known (depending on one's origins or view) as either the City Where The West Begins or Where The East Peters Out. "Fort Worth," Piersall assured his audience, "is a horseshit little town. It even smells like horseshit."

Fort Worth people might echo such feelings to each other, but they do not take warmly to such an evaluation from an outsider. So the Rangers' office in Arlington received perhaps a half-dozen complaints about Piersall, including a couple from individuals volunteering to come "whip the sumbitch's ass."

Now Jimmy was on the prowl. In a speech to various Dallas big shots, Bob Short's ambassador announced that cities like Dallas made him uneasy. The reason? Too many doctors and lawyers. "The only people more crooked than lawyers," Piersall assured the group, "are doctors." Not too many doctors were in the audience, but apparently, officers of the court were in plentiful supply and they were angry. More calls to Arlington Stadium, this time from insulted lawyers. They didn't sue, but maybe they were thinking . . . How dare that man insinuate that doctors are more crooked than lawyers. I'm only partly joking.

Apparently Jimmy had also found himself at times on the periphery and often at the core of some flare-ups around the Rangers' officials. So Bob Short left spring training aboard his private Sabre Liner jet, traveled to Arlington and formally excommunicated Piersall from the Rangers' temple. The ambassador's credentials were jerked and he was to be deported.

Piersall apologized to Short and swore to repent. So Short hired him back. "The poor guy is having all sorts of problems. I think he is going through a divorce and he told me he needed a heart transplant. He was in tears. How could I let him go?"

Short was telling me all of these things during a party on his yacht back in Florida.

IN EARLY APRIL the regular season opened in Arlington with a good draw. Texas would open the grind with a weekend against Oakland, the same players that owner Charles Finley was paying bonuses for growing handlebar mustaches, which now stood above the rest as the prime attraction in all of baseball since the A's had won another World Series with names like Reggie Jackson and Catfish Hunter. They blitzed Jim Bibby in the Friday opener, and in the press that night I was approached by Roy Parks, sales director for the Rangers' radio network, and informed that "Piersall is really steamed at you."

Parks said that the ambassador had expressed dire displeasure over something that I had written in spring training. The gist of the story was that the players were sulking about catching a seven A.M. bus for an exhibition game against the Royals at Fort Myers . . . "at an hour when some of these players are used to getting in." That's what the story had said and that's why Piersall was now angry. I wondered why. Closing time was four A.M. in Florida, after all, and by the time it took to find your car, it was not unreasonable to make it to bed at seven.

On Saturday night Piersall, as promised, appeared in the pressbox, loudly offering, sure enough, a negative critique of that article. He began with an unusual preamble . . . "most of that shit you wrote down there was actually pretty fuckin' good. I was using your stuff in my speeches. But that . . . that . . . crap about the players dragging in at seven in the morning . . . that really sucked."

"Well, Jimmy," I said, "given the makeup of these teams that have been on display the last two years, we take a lighter view of things around here."

Piersall wasn't through. "Listen. If I was still playing and you wrote something like that about me, I'd punch your fuckin' lights out."

How does one respond to that? "I know you would," I said. "I saw that movie." Piersall's mouth formed what I interpreted as a smile. Everybody else in the pressbox was smiling for sure and I thought nothing else of it.

Ferguson Jenkins was making his first regular-season appearance in a Rangers uniform and performing as advertised. Jenkins, a precision marksman, was pop, pop, popping away and hitting his spots with the nonchalance of a darts hustler in a Manchester pub. Jenkins toyed with Oakland's powerhouse lineup like a mean kid pulling the wings off flies. When Jenkins finally completed this preliminary demonstration of his throwing technique to the American League, he had fashioned a two-hit shutout.

The finale to the series was a day game on Sunday. They played a few of those in Arlington in April, before the heat became too insufferable. After the seventh inning I ventured back into the lounge area for a quick shot of liquid anesthetic and was followed in there by who else but Jimmy Piersall. Once inside, Piersall exploded and I suspected for a moment that he might be about to redecorate the walls and ceiling with the contents of my skull. From the corner of my eye, I noticed that Al Panzera of the *Star-Telegram,* a man who claimed with some justification to be the best sports photographer in the United States, had picked up a butcher knife from the barbecue buffet table. I yelled at Piersall: "For God's sake, Jimmy. Keep your voice down. Can't you see? People are trying to drink in here!" Piersall, thankfully, stomped off.

Al Panzera promptly assured me that "if Piersall made a move, I had the knife and was ready to jump him from behind." I suspected that Al's actual motive here had been self-preservation. Panzera figured that after Piersall had finished me off, he might well turn his attentions to Al. After the game, en route to the Rangers' clubhouse, I literally bumped into Bob Short under the stands and told him that his ambassador might be suffering some sort of meltdown. Well, not that term, exactly. The miracle of American nuclear engineering technology had not quite advanced to the point where "meltdown" was in common-place usage in the modern vernacular.

Ten minutes later in the clubhouse I was asking Toby Harrah to tell my North Texas reading audience all about how he had gotten the game-winning RBI off the A's. All of a sudden, an expression of distress crossed Harrah's face as he took note of Piersall's arrival. "Short just fired me and it's your fault, you son of a bitch!" Piersall said. I presumed that he was once again addressing me. He looked about to charge. Harrah jumped in front of me, holding a bat, and then Billy Martin heard the commotion, came out, grabbed Piersall around the shoulders and pulled him into his office. Conflict and friction are territo-rial hazards in the working life of the sportswriter, but I hadn't encounted it in a dosage like this since I'd found a death threat under my windshield wiper six years earlier. A reader was plan-ning my demise because I had suggested TCU might win more games if the school offered scholarships to black athletes.

The next day, Monday, was one of those all-too-rare off-days that happen during the regular season and still, the shadow of Jimmy Piersall was refusing to vanish from my life. All day, the phone rang at my house. People from news outlets around the country were calling to find out why I had wanted to thrust more difficulty into Jimmy Piersall's already troubled life. My response to all was the same: "What in the hell are you talking about?" I was not aware, at this point, that David Fink had pre-pared an essentially erroneous account of the whole sorry epi-sode that ran in the Dallas *Times-Herald* and was picked up by the wire services. The last thing, the very last thing that a sports-writer desires is to see his own name appearing in the *news* col-umns. According to Fink's account, I had gone running to Bob Short, demanding that Piersall be axed. At least, that's the way I interpreted it. There was nothing in Fink's story about how Pier-sall, within the month, had already been fired and defired. Now I knew what it was like to be screwed by a newspaperman.

The next time I encountered Fink I did my best to evoke an icy tone. "I 'demanded' that Short fire Piersall? If I'd known I had so much influence over Short's personnel decisions, then I'd be managing the Rangers instead of Billy Martin. Get your facts straight!'' This was my message to David Fink. And the real facts in this case were that I actually *liked* Jimmy Piersall and hated that he was fired. Besides, what other team in baseball had a guy who viewed his full-time job as going around telling lawyers and ad executives to fuck off?

ONE WEEK INTO the 1974 regular season, the happiest event in Bob Short's life took place.

When Short had confirmed in late September 1971 that he was moving the Senators franchise to Texas, a fan crept into his box at RFK Stadium and dumped a jumbo-sized cup of beer on Bob Short's head. For Bob Short, the months that followed brought a procession of events filled with ridicule and humiliation. Now Short was finally attaining his long-term goal. He was unloading the franchise on some Texas people who had tapped on his door and offered cash.

The true story was that Bob Short's lawyer, friend and trusted ally, Frank Ryan, was between flights in the Atlanta airport and waiting in the bar when he overheard a man with the kind of voice that fills a room tell another traveler of his growing desire to purchase an existing franchise in the National Basketball Association and transfer it to the Dallas-Fort Worth area. Ryan approached the man in the airport bar, introduced himself and said that while he could be of no assistance in the world of hoops, he could provide quick access to somebody with a major sports product.

After a negotiation that lasted less than two weeks, Bradford G. Corbett, an individual bearing a remarkable resemblance in face and torso to modern-day actor John Goodman, would head an investor group that had obtained necessary financing to take the Rangers off Bob Short's hands.

Corbett, who lived in Fort Worth but was a native of Staten Island, had started a chemical company called Robintec with a

Small Business Administration loan. Somehow, Robintec had perfected a patented process that could mass-produce polyvinyl-chloride pipe that met recently imposed and rigid environmental standards. With the oilfield service-supply industry now at its zenith, Corbett had turned Robintec into a publicly held company, had become rich and now wanted to have some fun.

That was to be anticipated from a man who had grown up in modest circumstances and gone on to achieve the big financial hit while still on the cool side of forty. Corbett told me that when he was going to school in New York State at Wagner College he was hopelessly, terminally in love with a striking Norwegian beauty named Gunnie who was the school homecoming queen. "I helped push Gunnie's float down the street in the Wagner homecoming parade," Corbett told me one time.

Homecoming queens traditionally marry into the family that some large campus building is named after, and failing that, they might marry the president of the Young Repubicans or perhaps even the quarterback. Homecoming queens do not marry float pushers. But Corbett persisted and eventually claimed his prize. Now Brad was lusting to own a big-league sports franchise.

At the press conference called to announce officially that Bob Short could now safely evacuate the badlands of Texas and return to the Land of 10,000 Lakes with his head high and his bank account sufficiently nourished, Corbett was accompanied by a few other well-heeled wheelhorses from Fort Worth and Dallas who had bought into the Rangers deal. One was Amon Carter, Jr., the publishing heir who had recently sold to Cap Cities the paper that employed me. Another was Ray Nasher, a dapper little man who had developed North Park, the first massive shopping mall in Dallas.

The new Rangers deed-holders at the hastily arranged meeting with the media were woefully ill-prepared to answer any specific questions concerning who actually owned what and how much they had paid for whatever it was that they weren't sure that they owned. Corbett was asked when he expected to receive

formal approval of the franchise sale from the American
League. He shrugged and rolled his eyes, as if to say, "You
mean the league has to okay this deal? Nobody told us that."

But Corbett could definitely confirm one item that was a side-
issue to the sale. A former Rangers employee had been hired by
Corbett's company Robintec. Jimmy Piersall was going to work
as a plastic-pipe salesman.

Piersall spent a lot of time at the ballpark for the remainder
of that 1974 season and treated me like a long-lost brother.
"Jesus . . . Corbett's paying me twice what I was making with
Short and the Rangers," he told me. "What a deal."

Indeed.

CHAPTER

18

"In this day and time, people are excitable and it doesn't take much to set them off."

—DICK BUTLER,
*Supervisor of American League
umpires, June 1974*

BILLY MARTIN WAS perplexed.

For much of the entire month of April, the Texas Rangers remained listed in first place in the baseball standings for the American League West, just like Billy Martin had said they would be. In Texas, the fans were responding. Attendance might not have been skyrocketing, but a persistent pulse rate was at least in evidence in the turnstile-count at Arlington Stadium.

Only now, in late May, Martin was being beleaguered by a problem fan—a season ticket holder who sat behind the Rangers' dugout shrieking obscenities at the home-team manager and bewailing his every strategic ploy.

"I found out who the guy is," Martin said, referring to his irascible critic after the Rangers had beaten Kansas City to stay one-half game ahead of Oakland. "He's a doctor. Can you believe that? Before long I'm going to bust in on him while he's operating on somebody and start yelling, 'Don't cut on his gall bladder, you stupid goddamn quack! It's his liver that's fucked

up!' and see how he likes that. This guy is a real son of a bitch
and one of these nights . . .''

What Billy was trying to say, of course, was: "Look here at the
feisty New Fan this team is bringing to the park." He was right.
Granted, the ticket-buyers who were finally discovering major-
league baseball in North Texas were not exactly conducive to
the wholesome family atmosphere that the tourist bureau of Arlington claimed would be showing up for the games in this middle–to–upper–class suburb. Rather, the fans who were turned on
by what certain sportswriters had termed Ranger Madness took
on the aspect of a motorcycle gang crashing a Pentecostal
church service. But, to paraphrase Jimmy Swaggart, if they're
leaving money in the collection plate, then who gives a big rat's
ass?

Slowly, Martin watched as the personality of his team gradu-
ally appeared to fit the contours of the New Fan attitude, and at
one Wednesday night game against Cleveland everything fell
into place. One of a few new Rangers who had not seen any
service with Whitey Herzog's memorable F-Troop of 1973 was
Lenny Randle, who could be plugged in to play second or third,
center or left. Randle stood only about five-foot-eight, but was
built like Mighty Mouse, biceps and calves like bowling balls,
and was Billy Martin's kind of guy. That was not surprising because Lenny Randle had also been Frank Kush's kind of guy on
the football team at Arizona State. Kush had been the coach
who eventually punched out his own punter after he shanked a
kick in a big game and in deportment made Woody Hayes look
like Captain Kangaroo. So, when Lenny Randle slammed his
shoulder into the midsection of Jack Brohamer, the Indians'
shortstop, to break up a double play in the fourth inning, this
was a tactic that came naturally to Lenny Randle.

When Randle came to bat in the bottom of the eighth inning,
Cleveland pitcher Milt Wilcox decided to retaliate against Randle for attempting to rearrange the Indian shortstop's innards.
Wilcox whistled a pitch that actually passed about six inches
behind Randle's head, the ultimate signal that a batter has done

something to arouse considerable disfavor from the opposing team.

Randle ducked the pitch, looked at the Cleveland catcher, Dave Duncan, and said, "What's going on?"

"The pitch just slipped, I guess," Duncan told him. Baseball, at the professional level, revolves almost entirely around the arts of intimidation and, in this game, the pitcher commands the entire munitions supply. The man on the mound can direct his telemetry toward the temple, larynx or kneecap whenever the whim strikes him, and the batter has virtually no means of counter-argument except to lower his head and look the part of the fool as he rushes the mound like a jealous husband barging into a wayward wife's motel nest *d'amour*.

There is one artful ploy that is sometimes discussed and that involves the batter dropping a bunt along the first base line and then extracting his vengeance when the pitcher comes prancing over to field the ball. But because of timing and location, that tactic is hardly as easy as it might sound, and Lenny Randle is the only player I ever saw actually make it happen.

On the next pitch after the one that sailed behind his head, Randle bunted the ball toward first. The bunt was not perfectly placed but close enough for mayhem, and Randle had only to veer about four feet from the base path in order to level a fore-arm in the direction of Milt Wilcox's jawbone. Then, to continue his demonstration, Randle kept running and tried to butt first baseman John Ellis square in the nuts.

Ellis, who picked up extra money in the off-season working as a bounty hunter for bailbondsmen, was not the sort to take kindly to Randle's show of pugnacity. Fists began to flail, players from both teams joined the brawl, people were punched, kicked, stomped. Unlike the fights that happen in pro football and ice hockey, players can actually get hurt in some of these baseball uprisings because they are not encumbered by helmets, face guards and skates.

In this particular fracas, nobody became disabled. But some of the Rangers' fans decided that this should be an audience-participation program and were slinging cups of beer onto the visiting players. One, a bearded guy in cutoff Levis, a tank top emblazoned with the printed slogan "Eat More Possum" and wearing sandals, had climbed atop the Indians' dugout and issued a direct challenge to Dave Duncan to join him there for a rumble just before being hauled off by the stadium cops. Afterward, Duncan said the man on the dugout "looked like Ben Hur and for a minute I thought I was going to have to fight him."

"Our fans," said an obviously pleased Toby Harrah, "are getting more and more like the ones in Venezuela." The Rangers' shortstop was talking about the patrons of the winter leagues who embellish the ballpark setting with live serpents and firearms.

ONE WEEK LATER, the Rangers were scheduled to visit Cleveland and Municipal Stadium, the big hollow canyon by the lake. Some of the Rangers' players had hinted that the resumption of unpleasantries might not come as a surprise. If that were to be the case, a ballpark promotion scheduled for the opening night of the series was well-timed to accelerate any hostilities. Wednesday was to be 10-Cent Beer Night at Municipal Stadium.

The same celebration had been conducted in Arlington a couple of times and, according to rumors, action in the cheap seats had resembled an old Clint Eastwood spaghetti western by the seventh inning. There could be little doubt that with the summer approaching, fans in Cleveland could certainly match those in Texas in the category of uninhibited behavior. Alcohol, adrenalin and testosterone can be a high-combustion combination in the bloodstream when mixed in the correct proportions.

On certain recent occasions I had found it more convenient to make travel arrangements separate from the baseball team. That had been the case when I arrived in Cleveland at six P.M. on Wednesday, an hour and a half before the start of the game. On the commuter train from Hopkins Airport into downtown it became clear that something really special—or at least different—was looming at the ballpark on 10-Cent Beer Night. At each stop the train was filling with young people obviously headed for the game to take advantage of the promotion. Everybody was wearing Indians baseball caps and Indians batting helmets. As a court-certified expert on brain abuse, it was my educated guess that most of these fans were already loaded on Wild Turkey and whatever medicine it is that truck drivers take to stay awake on long hauls. Their condition suggested that they might be on their way home from, and not on their way to, a 10-Cent Beer Night game. It appeared that many had been preparing for this event for perhaps a couple of days.

A paid crowd of 23,000 was in the stands when the game began at dusk—quite a gang for a weeknight game in Cleveland. Throughout the first inning little detonations that sounded like cherry bombs could be heard in the stands. The cadence of the drummers in rightfield was faster than usual. It was nice to see fans like these in such a jolly mood. Every Ranger was robustly booed as he stepped up to bat. That was, I felt, because of the afterglow from the big fight with the Indians in Arlington one week before. Of course, while those suckers in the stands were paying a dime for their cups of Strohs beer, we were drinking it free in the pressbox.

In the top of the second inning a fan climbed from the stands and appeared to stagger into the on-deck circle near the Indians' dugout. This was a large female fan and she exposed her breasts to the crowd, spurring an ovation so thunderous that it must have eclipsed anything that Luciano Pavarotti would hear on his best day. Now the mood of the evening was clearly in place. A cop escorted the lady from the playing field. From the pressbox set up along the facing of the upper deck between home plate and first base, I was afforded a superior vantage point for that spectacle and most of those that would follow. If it is true the decade of the Seventies was earmarked by behavioral residue of the spirit of the late Sixties, then Beer Night in Cleveland was the archetypal illustration of what all of that was to represent.

The Rangers jumped out to an early lead on Beer Night and when Tom Grieve crossed the plate after hammering his second homerun of the game in the top of the fourth, a naked man slid into second base. No—it was not a Rangers ballplayer but a fan who had escaped the stands. In the fifth, two males who were later identified by police as a father-and-son act, trotted out to an infield position and mooned the stands. Again, the Cleveland police were there to take this family unit into custody. In anticipation of fraternity-house ritual behavior at the stadium on Beer Night, the police had doubled its customary squad for ballpark duty. Forty-eight uniformed officers had been stationed in the stands, and the crowd, now eager to get on with the hunt, sensed that forty-eight cops would be a poor match against 23,000 drunks. After the seventh-inning stretch, the playing field was the place to be. The primary point of entry was an area near the rightfield foul pole. Many stopped by to say hello to Jeff Burroughs, the Rangers' rightfielder, who looked like a campaigning politician glad-handing a procession of workers at the factory gate.

When the game reached the bottom of the ninth inning, the temperament of the crowd became strikingly like that of Billy Martin when he reached his hour of belligerence in the cocktail lounge. What had been a largely congenial gathering turned combative. Woodstock had become Kent State. Rangers outfielders were under missile attack now, bombarded with bottles, rocks, golf balls and other debris. Someone ran onto the field and attempted to snatch Burroughs' glove. Burroughs responded, first shoving the intruder and then chasing him back over the rightfield wall. And now, people poured onto the field like ants.

From the Rangers' dugout along the third-base line players surged out with the "yahoo" élan of the old Third Cavalry, racing out to rescue Jeff Burroughs, armed with baseball bats instead of sabres. Cleveland players were on the field, too, fighting off their own fans.

Nestor Chylak, the chief umpire, trotted into the Indians' dugout and placed an urgent phone call to the public-address announcer, who then informed the crowd that the ballgame was over—forfeited to the Rangers. At this point they presumably ceased the sales of the dime beer as well. From my safe haven in the pressbox I was delighted by the entire spectacle since my dispatch to the newspaper back in Texas would offer something out of the ordinary and I figured that the players' post-game quotes might not be as clichéd as usual.

This beat the hell out of Jim Merritt's greaseball press conference here the previous August. By God, if a sportswriter is looking for a story, then come to Cleveland.

My first stop was not the visiting clubhouse but the little dressing room occupied by the four umpires. In the big leagues I believe a game is forfeited approximately every third decade. Chylak, the head ump who made the call to terminate the proceedings, was in a state of total rage. Nestor did not necessarily conform to the typical physical image of the major-league umpire in that his silhouette was never mistaken for that of a sumo wrestler, Ringling Brothers elephant or Boeing 747. But in attitude, style and overall delivery, Nestor Chylak was an umpire's umpire.

"ANIMALS! FUCKING ANIMALS! THAT'S WHAT ALL THESE FUCKING PEOPLE ARE!" Nestor was shouting. I saw no reason, at this point, to ask Chylak to elaborate on his reasons for forfeiting the game.

"I even saw a couple of knives out there in that mob. Then they [the Rangers] charged out, they had to because those fucking animals wanted to kill somebody. I personally got hit with a chair and a rock."

Case closed.

When I talked to the Rangers, most of them appeared rather shaken by what they had clearly regarded as an ordeal. Billy Martin was predictably verbose. "We got hit with everything you can think of," Martin recounted with an air of seeming wonderment. "Chairs were flying down out of the upper deck. Cleveland players were fighting their own fans. First they were protecting the Rangers and then they were fighting to protect themselves. Somebody hit Tom Hilgendorf [Indians pitcher] with a chair and cut his head open."

Martin offered special exoneration for two Cleveland players. One was Dave Duncan, the catcher who had been so involved in the saloon brawl that had happened in Arlington the week before, and the other was Rusty Torres, an outfielder. "They tried to reason with the fans and then laid a couple out when they wouldn't listen." Of course, Billy would pay box-seat prices to witness a production like that.

Jeff Burroughs, who had been the focal point of the concourse of fans, said, "It started in the third inning. One guy came out of the stands, then two or three and then they came by the dozens, mostly between innings. They were friendly at first, yelling and having a good time. Then it got mean."

With Toby Harrah's comments about the fans in Venezuela in mind, I asked Cesar Tovar—himself a card-carrying Venezuelan—if he might draw some comparisons between the Beer Night throng in Cleveland and the baseball enthusiasts of his homeland. "These people are different, very different. Got no respect for the police," Tovar declared. "Of course, they'd shoot the people who tried that at home."

Over on the Cleveland side, the Indians players were clearly less than thrilled by their night of adventure. Interestingly, the then most recent major-league forfeit had happened at the Senators' final game at RFK Stadium, before the franchise moved to Texas. Spectators had taken to the field and refused to leave. Indians pitcher Dick Bosman, an ex-Ranger and ex-Senator at the time, said, "That experience was entirely different. Those fans in Washington were out on the field digging up souvenirs . . . it was the last game there, ever. This business tonight was mean, ugly and frightening."

Ken Aspromonte, the Cleveland manager turned sociologist,

was disgusted. "What happened in Arlington last week was part of baseball. This was a riot. This is what happens in our country when our people are angry and ready to fight at the drop of a coin [sic]. We complained in Arlington when people threw beer on us and taunted us. But look at our people. They were worse."

Quite a few hundred of Aspromonte's "our people" still lingered in the stands as I made my way back to the pressbox to write and transmit the story back to the *Star-Telegram*. The stadium smelled of beer and reefer smoke. After finishing the stories I was faced with a dilemma. The team bus had already left for the hotel behind a four-car police escort. Now the cops had sealed off the stadium area and no cabs were venturing down. So, carrying my portable typewriter and telecopier, I walked some four miles back to the Hollenden House Hotel, where the lounge, I was thinking, had goddamn sure better still be open. En route, in a downtown park, I heard a gunshot and, like Ichabod Crane in the dark forest, panicked, broke into what might be described as an elongated stride, and gratefully realized that I was experiencing the rich and glamorous life of the sportswriter at its fullest.

About a dozen players were in the bar when I got there. One—Burroughs—pulled me aside. "Hey," he wondered, "do the stats count in a forfeit? I hope not. I went 0-for-4, but the marijuana smoke was so thick out there in rightfield, I think I was higher than the fans."

Various debriefing sessions were held the day after. What had been largely overlooked in what was now nationally labeled the Cleveland Beer Night Riot was that the Indians had rallied to tie the game in the ninth and had placed what probably was the winning run on third base when Nestor Chylak decided to pull the plug. Now Ted Bonda, the Indians' vice-president, said his team would formally protest the forfeit.

Bonda was blaming Billy Martin. Clearly born to enter corporate executivehood, he conceded that he had left the game in the eighth inning and had missed the main event, but, he said, he had received a "full report" on what happened in the ninth. "It wasn't the Beer Night promotion . . . our fans were excited and really keyed up after the business in Arlington the week before," Bonda insisted. "At some point Billy Martin started throwing gravel and shooting our fans the finger and when he led his men out of the dugout, that was when matters got out of hand."

Someone might have pointed out to Ted Bonda that Billy Martin was probably throwing gravel and shooting people the finger at his first communion and so his activities on Beer Night in Cleveland were in no way generated by any motivations to incite a riot. The Indians' protest of the forfeit was hastily denied. The whole episode could and should have been written down and then written off as a footnote on what can take place when there is a full moon over Cleveland. (I don't know if there really was a full moon in Cleveland that night, and if not, one can only marvel at what could have taken place had there been one.)

Unfortunately, the Beer Night calamity would produce one everlasting ramification. The people in charge of both big leagues met and ordained that dime-beer nights or any similar promotions were taboo, and henceforth guideposts to happiness would be labeled Clean and Sober. So it should be historically noted that the graceless puritans who write all of the house rules of the Nineties gained their initial foothold on that June night in 1974 when the fans went nuts in Cleveland.

CHAPTER

19

THE LATE AND oft-lamented publication called the Fort Worth *Press,* in truth, probably would have been rated by industry analysts as "uneven" in its overall presentation of the news. Nobody from the *Press* ever got close to being nominated for a Pulitzer Prize. Faithful subscribers could always rely on the same front-page photograph whenever the temperature reached 106 or higher. Some downtown secretary with big jugs would be recruited to pose beneath the digital thermometer outside the First National Bank and the caption always read "P-H-E-W-W!" And when the old Blue Northers blew through town and the temperature dropped under 25, another secretary would strike a similar pose, this time captioned: "B-R-R-R!"

But on one shining moment in 1962, the readers of the *Press* were given a once-in-a-lifetime treat. On the occasion of Richard Nixon's defeat in his campaign for the governor of California, the *Press* ran a short UPI feature describing Mrs. Nixon's disappointment at the setback. At this historic juncture, a headline writer at the *Press* composed the following masterpiece: "Pat Loses Composure As Dick Sinks."

Apparently Mrs. Nixon had become more accustomed to the sensation by 1974. She appeared rather serene on the portable set that everyone was watching in the pressbox at Arlington Stadium while the President told the nation that "I've never been a quitter, but . . ." Nixon's speech took place during a Rangers-A's game. In the bottom of the fourth inning the Rangers' public-address announcer, Bob Berry, told the crowd that President Nixon had resigned, and I later read in some wire-service story that the folks in the stands in Arlington responded to the news with "hoots and catcalls." I'm not sure what catcalls are, actually, but if the nation was "grief-stricken" by the event, as the media had suggested, then that part of the nation did not include Arlington Stadium.

Baseball annals will note that on the night Nixon took a hike, the A's beat the Rangers, 8–1. Afterward I approached Reggie Jackson, who next to Hank Aaron was the closest thing to a celebrity that baseball had to offer at the time, and asked him what, if anything, had crossed his mind out there in rightfield when it was announced that the President was no longer the President. Reggie Jackson looked at me like I was nuts. "Announcement? I didn't hear any announcement, did you, Sal?" Jackson said, turning to the man at the adjacent locker, Sal Bando. Bando merely shrugged.

"I get paid a lot of money to hit homeruns. I concentrate on that and nothing else. Why should I be interested in politics?" Jackson said. "Why worry about that crap? What I'm worried about is the Texas Rangers. We're trying to win a third straight World Series and they're not making it easy for us. They're in the race and they'll be in it until the last because if they were going to fold, that would have happened long before now."

I did not doubt for a nanosecond that Reggie Jackson was completely sincere when he said that this transcendent event—Watergate—was of absolutely no consequence to him. In the one-and-a-half years that I had been covering the Texas Rangers, the media had become habitually devoted to this story, but I had yet to encounter a baseball player who maintained even an obscure knowledge or interest in the topic of Watergate or could name even one of the people involved. If anybody in baseball was "grief-stricken" over the news events of that week, it was because Dizzy Dean had just dropped dead in Reno (pall-bearers included Pee Wee Reese, Roy Acuff and Bear Bryant). And if ballplayers were absorbed by anything beyond their own stats, it was Evel Knievel's upcoming jump across the Snake River canyon on a jet motorcycle.

While Jackson meant what he said about politics, considerable doubt remained about the sincerity of his expressed concerns about the Rangers' role in the pennant race. Still . . . the Rangers had been consistently chugging along in the A's shadow, and as Billy Martin was pointing out—nightly and with great elation—the Rangers were not about to choke. Martin's reasoning: There is no way to choke when you're under no pressure.

On the charter airplanes and in the bistros throughout the land, this new Rangers team was quick and willing to replicate the behavior of the 1973 outfit that was so well-suited for a sideshow on the midway. On a trip into Boston in late July the team was sharing the Sheraton with a convention of the Massachusetts state-teachers union and perhaps 300 delegates. Like the Rangers, it turned out that some of these Massachusetts school teachers were no rookies in the party-league themselves. Around midnight I encountered a pitcher, Jackie Gene Brown, the pride of Weewoka, Oklahoma, in charge of a large hospitality suite and wearing a badge that identified him as Ernest Blumenthal of Brookline, candidate for treasurer of the teachers union. "The guy said he'd let me pretend to be him if I could get free tickets tomorrow," Brown explained to me. "Come in and have a drink . . . and I appreciate your vote."

That same night another player told me of something harrowing that had just happened to him. "I was in the bar across the street and putting my best cheap moves on this gal with great tits and asked her to come up to my room," the player said. "Then she . . . or it or whatever it was . . . said that she couldn't because she hadn't had her final operation yet. God awmighty. When I was dancing with her I felt a hard-on. But I thought it was mine."

Off the field it was the same act as 1973. On the field, the team stayed four to six games above .500. Fergie Jenkins would stand out as the root cause. Jenkins, certainly, ranked as a paradigm alternative to the "live young arms" of the previous season, the ones who had given Whitey Herzog cause to consider seeking electroconvulsive therapy to help him through the campaign. But Jenkins could only pitch every fourth or fifth game. What this new 1974 contingent, deemed "The Turnaround Gang" by the Rangers' pre-season media publication, amounted to was an ensemble of players—Lenny Randle, Cesar Tovar, Alex Johnson and Toby Harrah—who were getting on base consistently, and Jeff Burroughs, who was driving them in. Burroughs, in June, came within a game of tying an American League record, shared by Jimmy Foxx and Lou Gehrig, for RBIs in consecutive games.

Beyond Jenkins, Jim Bibby, Steve Hargan and Jackie Brown were pitching just consistently enough to avoid calamity. Steve Foucault, the only Ranger who would someday become an Arlington cop, was a one-man bullpen.

The added factors that enable teams to win pennants—pitching depth, quality defense and a reliable bench—remained in absentia. Billy Martin's centerfielder, Tovar, had been colliding with other fielders so frequently that the manager employed an emergency measure. He tied a whistle around Tovar's neck with instructions "to blow the shit out of the thing whenever he was chasing a fly ball."

The new catcher, Jim Sundberg, up from AA, was measuring up to standards and would actually be selected to the All-Star game. "That makes me the second most famous native of Galesburg, Illinois," Sundberg was fond of telling people. Numero Uno was George Reeves, TV's original Superman, who blew his brains out during a party at his house in Beverly Hills. Another welcome asset was the first Texan in the history of the franchise, one Dudley Michael Hargrove. (David Clyde had gone to high school in Houston but was basically from Kansas). Hargrove was the product of Perryton, Texas, a Panhandle community iso-

lated away in the most primeval regions of the vast Texas Out-
back, a town where all of the little old grannies have the slogan
"The Only Good Indian Is A Baptist Deacon" embroidered in
needlepoint and hanging over the mantel.

Hargrove had been invited to spring training on the basis of
having hit .365 for the Rangers the previous season—the Gas-
tonia Rangers in the Western Carolina League. "In spring training the guy [Hargrove] tells me that he was destined to be a
Ranger," said Billy Martin, "because his team in high school
was the Rangers and then he'd gone to some hick college in
Oklahoma and they were the Rangers, too." Martin rolled his
eyes. "I figured I'd have to locate some team called the Rangers
back in the Lickskillet League just to accommodate him. And
then I saw him hit."

Sharing first base with Jim Spencer, Hargrove hit over .400 for
the first half of the season, and the average was not tailing off
too considerably with the stretch drive now in plain sight. Hargrove maintained a country boy aw-shucks attitude about the
whole thing. Joe Garagiola interviewed Hargrove before the
Rangers' first-ever appearance on the NBC Game of the Week
(the world was starting to notice this team) and Hargrove said,
"Well, I've been flat lucky this year . . . a bunch of chinkers
have fallen in for me."

Chinkers. Joe Garagiola could talk about little else for the
next three months. The chinkers just kept dropping for Hargrove, who, despite the naïve front that he was employing for
his first season in the majors, was actually (as they like to say
back in the Panhandle) tougher than a bus station steak.

The one player in this Rangers' alignment not experiencing
an exceptional season was the salvation of the franchise himself,
David Clyde. As Martin's fifth starter, Clyde had gotten out of
the gate nicely with a 3–1 record that included a complete-game
shutout against New York at Shea Stadium, where the Yankees
were temporarily playing their home games while Yankee Stadium underwent structural renovation. As the season pro-
gressed, Clyde was less and less effective and, on certain morn-

ings on the road in hotel coffee shops, took on something of the air of Jack Lemmon in *The Days of Wine and Roses.*

Clyde avoided missing a morning charter flight from Boston to Detroit only because the plane was late taking off and escaped a substantial fine. Martin said he later learned Clyde himself had called the airport gate and successfully convinced someone to delay the charter for a few minutes. "I've got to hand it to him . . . Clyde saved himself a couple of grand," Martin said. "But that's about all he's done right lately." The fact that Clyde might actually have sacrificed a sterling career so that Bob Short could secure emergency funds at the box office was of no consequence to Billy Martin. He wasn't around when that happened. What Martin cared about was that his fifth starter was a wreck.

And this team didn't require any novelty attractions to bring the fans in. When Bob Short brought the franchise to Arlington, he said the break-even point rested at 800,000 paid attendance for the season. In the first and second seasons the Rangers' sad numbers had not surpassed the 570,000 mark. Now, with Billy driving the bus and the team actually winning, the 1974 team would bring almost 1.2 million paying fans into Arlington.

Brad Corbett, the point man on the new ownership regime that bought the Rangers from Short in April, was in ecstasy. Corbett, as owner, had not yet advanced past the fan stage. The players were his idols and on off-nights Corbett had been hosting huge parties for the team at Shady Oaks Country Club in Fort Worth, an exclusive layout on Roaring Springs Road in West Fort Worth that happened to be the only locale where Ben Hogan would still agree to play golf. Brad bought Billy a membership in the club, and Martin later denied to me—more or less—that he and Mickey Mantle had almost run over Hogan one day in their golf cart. (Now that Billy and Mickey have been reunited in the hereafter, one wonders if they have golf carts in heaven. If so, watch out.)

Martin did confirm that some event had taken place that had demoted him to persona-non-grata status at Shady Oaks. "Look at this," he said in his office one day as he showed me a delinquent food-and-drink tab of over three grand from Shady Oaks. Billy grinned. "How in the hell do they expect me to go out there and pay that bill if I am no longer welcome on the premises?"

In his exuberance Corbett was offering players off-season jobs with his company, Robintec. "Brad asked me if I knew anything about irrigation," Steve Hargan said the day after another soiree at Shady Oaks. "I told him that I'd had my bladder irrigated one time and he said, 'You're hired!' He's a hell of an owner."

Corbett's principal investment partner in the Rangers deal was considerably less conspicuous. That was Amon Carter, Jr., who was still the figurehead publisher of the Fort Worth *Star-Telegram,* although he had recently sold the paper. Carter's father had been the original media magnate of the Southwest, owning not only the paper but also the first radio and TV stations in Texas. In Fort Worth the name Carter was on a par with Rockefeller in New York and everything from the TCU football stadium to an airport to a YMCA camp to a blood center was named after Amon, Sr.

When Amon, Jr., was captured by the Germans in World War II, his father actually arranged to fly to Switzerland to "bail my boy out of that German jail." But when he arrived overseas Carter, Sr., was told that "little Amon" had already escaped. He was recaptured and later related to a friend that the Germans "told me that if I ever tried it again they'd shoot my ass off."

This was a great and colorful family. Actually the only conversation that I can recall having with Amon Carter happened in the pressbox at Arlington and was nickle-dime stuff. "I worry about all these foul balls. Those baseballs are more expensive than you'd think," he told me. "But I've noticed that three or four cups of beer are knocked over by people scrambling for the foul ball and then they all buy another beer, so I guess we just about break even."

What stood out in the early phases of the new operational package that had taken over from Short was that this group had

absolutely no background in the arcane world of baseball ownership. An experienced and talented marketing executive from
Fort Worth, Jerre Todd, approached Brad Corbett with what
Todd called "a comprehensive promotional and advertising
plan" to provide the team with a better image and take full
advantage of the revenue potential not just from Dallas and Fort
Worth but also from Oklahoma, Arkansas and Louisiana.

"I made my pitch to Corbett thoroughly and elaborately . . .
it was a damn good plan," Todd told me, "and then Brad got
this faraway look in his eye and he yelled, 'Parking lot! We'll
have a big barbecue in the parking lot!' And he sent me away
and that was that." Corbett, as well as every Rangers owner before and after him, was chronically retarded when it came to
baseball-marketing insight. But Corbett did bring forward one
strategically wise decision during the ownership transition. He
convinced Dr. Bobby Brown, a cardiologist in Fort Worth, to
suspend his medical practice, temporarily at least, to join the
Rangers full-time with the title of president.

This was the same Bobby Brown who had played third base
for the Yankees during the late Forties and early Fifties, the tail
end of the Joe DiMaggio era of postwar baseball when the Yankees were at the absolute pinnacle of public esteem. Brown was
leaving the Yankees just as Martin was arriving. Bobby Brown,
with his air of dignity and smarts, commanded the total respect
of everybody associated with the team—including Billy Martin.
So Doctor Brown was the ideal person to be at the controls
whenever Billy began to exhibit his "authority problem" as ulti-
mately he always would. In early August Martin decided to ship
David Clyde to the minor leagues. "What I'll do is send him for
less than a week and then bring him right back up . . . but I'm
not going to tell him about the recall," Martin told the Texas
sportswriters. "Sort of like what they do to little hoodlums. Send
them to prison just long enough to give them a taste of what it's
like and then turn 'em loose so maybe they'll learn their lesson.
If I do that with David, maybe he'll wake up."

When Bobby Brown got word of Billy's scheme he called Martin and told him that he was vetoing that plan. "David Clyde has done too much for this franchise to be manipulated like that," Brown ruled, and now the first traces of friction in Martin's Texas Era had become evident.

As Billy's 1974 Rangers established themselves as a team that would refuse to turn back into the pumpkin of 1973, and probably even something more than a complete imposter in the American League West, Martin began to assert himself more frequently in his more familiar role of instigator-agitator.

At a Sunday doubleheader in Milwaukee, when Martin took out his lineup card for the pre-game meeting with Brewers' manager Del Crandell and the umpires, he casually announced to Crandell that "your pitcher threw at our shortstop four times yesterday. So I'm telling you now that your shortstop [rookie Robin Yount] will be going down today."

According to the unwritten rules of baseball there are two things to which a manager must never confess: marital infidelity and intentionally throwing at an opposing batter. In the sixth inning of the opening game at County Stadium, as advertised, Rangers' pitcher Pete Broberg zinged a fastball directly at Robin Yount's chin. After the game, in which Crandell's Brewers had responded in kind, home-plate umpire Ron Luciano became livid over Martin's pre-game declaration when he said that he intended to launch a beanball conflict. "Martin and Crandell both manage their teams with an iron hand and it really pisses me off that they'd go out there and intentionally create a situation like that."

WE CAN'T HAVE THAT SORT OF THING!

Martin got a three-game suspension from the American League office for his part in the subplot in Milwaukee, but now that he had whetted his built-in thirst for controversy and conflict, Billy wanted some more.

CHAPTER

━━━━━━

20

IN HIS BOOK, *The American Scene,* published in 1919, the late H. L. Mencken, the Sage of Baltimore, expressed his disdain for American journalists. Stupid Philistines, was his judgment. And many would agree that people are attracted to journalism because they are too lazy to work at the post office but not lazy enough to become lawyers.

Hell, if I didn't know better, I'd swear that H. L. Mencken was talking about *me.* Even more, he might have been targeting the Baseball Writers Association of America and a clique within that group known as the Seamheads. Since Mencken lived his life in Baltimore, the womb of organized ball, it's a real possibility that in his harangue against the American newspaper, the Seamheads were who he had in mind.

To the Seamheads, baseball is their passion, their opiate, their universe. There is no statistic too remote to remain unexplored by the Seamhead as long as the figures relate to baseball. Seamheads call other Seamheads at three A.M. to talk about how, say, the Braves are hitting .213 with runners on first and third with less than two out, except, of course, against lefthanders and then, hoo boy, that's a whole 'nuther story.

I envied the Seamheads. I really did; the same way I envied the rock hounds who majored in geology in college as they blissfully wandered through creek beds in search of Precambrian shale. If somebody earned a living writing about baseball, imagine the delightful circumstance—being so absolutely absorbed by the topic—of living all day, every day at the ballpark. But there was no chance in hell that the Seamheads would ever allow me to become part of their society, not even as an apprentice or on some other provisional basis. A Pima Indian would be elected to the board of the Los Angeles Country Club before they'd let me call myself a Seamhead.

An event that happened at the end of the 1974 season not only guaranteed that I could never become a Seamhead but also got me more or less blackballed by the Baseball Writers fraternal order in general.

In late September, Billy Martin's Quixote-like quest of the Oakland A's would die of natural causes. On the Sunday that Gerald Ford officially announced that he was granting Richard Nixon his pardon and Evel Knievel botched but still survived his jet-motorcycle jump over the Snake River canyon, the Rangers were in Oakland beating the A's for the third time in a four-game series. Back in Texas the following weekend, the Rangers beat Oakland on Friday and again on Saturday, and if they won again on Sunday night the A's lead would be sliced to one game. But the Rangers would not win that final game. The tank was finally empty.

Thanks to Billy Martin's time-honored formula for witchcraft, sorcery and voodoo magic, blended with the sensational pitching contribution of Fergie Jenkins and an MVP year at the bat by Jeff Burroughs, the Rangers had ventured into a territory where they really did not belong—the perimeters of Oakland's championship estate. In the long run (and the baseball season is indeed the longest of runs), no amount of luck or peculiar gamesmanship could make up for the talent chasm that separated the Rangers from the A's.

After the A's left Texas, they kept on winning while the Rangers, playing at home against Chicago, did not. Two losses in a Friday doubleheader to the White Sox officially extinguished the Rangers' quest of the impossible. All that remained was a quick three-game visit to Kansas City and then Minnesota to complete a season that would see the Rangers finish in second place, a feat that gained Manager of the Year honors for Billy Martin.

But Martin presented symptoms of acute digestive distress at the prospect of receiving a consolation prize. After the loss of the second game to the White Sox that mathematically eliminated the Rangers—an occurrence that more traditionally happened around the Fourth of July in Arlington—I walked onto the Rangers' charter jet for the midnightish flight to Kansas City. Martin, seated on the aisle on the third row, grabbed my sleeve as I headed toward the back of the plane and said, "You know who cost us the pennant? That fucking little David Clyde, that's who. Put that in your goddamn newspaper."

I shook my head and kept on walking. Two things struck me as odd about that little encounter. First, of course, was the notion that Billy Martin would actually single out Clyde as the source of the Rangers' inability to pull off what would have ranked as the most outrageous pennant-chase upset in the history of the sport. Martin probably was saying that had Clyde somehow developed as a reliable third starter in a big-league pitching rotation instead of the game but struggling teenager that, in reality, he was, then the Rangers would have somehow pulled off the feat. But following that reasoning, Martin could just as easily have attached the blame to, say, Jim Sundberg because he didn't bat .415 and hit forty-five homeruns.

What seemed even more odd was that Billy had apparently already lapsed into his post-midnight, Red Alert, clear-the-flight-decks-because-I'm-fixin'-to-kick-somebody's-ass mode. Usually, at least three-and-one-half-hours worth of persistent consumption were required for Billy to achieve that. Now it was barely forty-five minutes after the completion of the second game.

Was it possible, then, that Billy was sucking down a few pops in the tunnel behind the dugout during that second game? After the takeoff I summoned a flight attendant. If the gritty skipper was, as they say, already drunker than Sam Houston, I wanted to achieve a similar state of mind as quickly as possible. Shortly into the flight, a commotion in the front of the 727 interrupted the flow of refreshment supplies. Several of the players back in steerage where I was seated were standing up and gaping at some sideshow that was taking place in first class. Business as usual, I figured, somebody trying to get it on with the stewardess, as flight attendants were then called. Momentarily afterward, James Walker of the *Times-Herald* appeared from up front wearing a peculiar expression. Walker had replaced my friend David Fink as the baseball writer for the *Times-Herald.* Fink had gone to Pittsburgh to cover the Steelers. Walker spoke with a distinct Northeast Texas accent. Most outsiders believe that there is one prototypical Texas accent. Actually there are several. For instance, I can determine the difference between a West Fort Worth accent—"bin gittin' inny?"—from a North Fort Worth accent—*"no hablo Ingles."* Where James Walker came from, those Goodyear rubber products that people put on their trucks are known as "tars," and the most favored ethnic persuasion was "wyatt folks"—as in Earp.

"You won't believe what just happened," Walker told me. "Billy just punched out Burt Hawkins."

Walker was right. I didn't believe him. But my earlier suspicions that Billy's psyche had already advanced into the attack phase were all too correct. Billy was no longer a baseball manager but rather an aggressor nation eager to declare war on somebody. What happened was this: Martin had started shouting at Hawkins for the ridiculous reason that Burt's wife Janet had expressed an interest in forming some sort of Rangers Auxiliary. In other words, a Rangers players-wives club. Now Martin was demanding that Burt make Janet abandon the plan. "The goddamn wives," Martin said, "will poison a ball club if you let 'em . . . the last thing you need is gettin' 'em *organized!"*

Hawkins predictably suggested to Billy that he might go fuck himself, at which point Martin offered to heave Burt out of the airplane. "If you think you're big enough, Billy Boy, then give it a try," Burt responded. Thus challenged, Martin got up and smacked a sixty-five-year-old-man with a heart condition across the face.

Other than that episode, it was a quiet flight to Kansas City. Once at the airport, Billy marched about twenty paces ahead of the entourage and, once outside, hopped into what appeared to be a 1965 GTO with front-end body damage and sped away in a cloud of exhaust smoke. "Billy's gal needs a valve job," one of the players, Steve Hargan, noted as the rest of the Rangers climbed aboard the bus for the trip to the hotel.

As the bus pulled away, Burt Hawkins stood up in the front and made an unusual speech. The flight from D-FW airport to Kansas City probably doesn't take ninety minutes, but that's enough to get reasonably crocked on an empty stomach and the majority of the passengers on the bus had done just that, knowing that the hotel bar would already be closed by the time they arrived.

Hawkins wanted to talk to the players about what had happened on the airplane. His message included some colorful usage. "If that sorry little cocksucker doesn't apologize, then I am going to the ownership of the Rangers and tell 'em they can stick this job up their ass," Hawkins told the team. And he added that, until he had made up his mind he hoped that nothing would be mentioned about the airplane debacle right away in the newspapers. That presented no problems because, by now, everyone was safely past deadline.

During the course of the night and early morning hours, Ma Bell grew fatter as the phone lines buzzed from Kansas City to North Texas. News of Billy's behavior on the charter flight had somehow filtered back to the home office, and the ownership was appalled to the extent that an impromptu board meeting was apparently conducted to discuss what punitive measures should be imposed upon the problem child. Dr. Bobby Brown located Billy sometime around dawn and articulated his dissatisfaction.

WE CAN'T HAVE THIS SORT OF THING!

The phone in my room at the old Muhlbach Hotel was ring-
ing at the inhumane hour of eight-thirty A.M. It was Burt Hawkins and he wanted to see me. By the time I reached Hawkins'
suite the other two writers, James Walker and Randy Galloway,
were already there. Galloway was preparing his special Grand
Prairie Bloody Mary recipe, which consisted of two ounces of
Tabasco, nine ounces of cheap vodka and a teaspoon of tomato
juice.

Hawkins' mood was drastically altered from what we had seen
just hours earlier on the team bus. Now that the hostilities had
abated, he seemed actually jovial. He said that the Little Dago
himself had paid a visit to the suite and described Martin as a
living portrait of contrition. Old Burt was clearly amused by the
experience of the New Billy consumed with humility. "I suppose
Bobby Brown threatened to fire him," said Hawkins, "because
Billy was really kissing my ass. You all should have seen him."
Hawkins was laughing now. "According to Billy, nobody was to
blame. Booze was the real culprit."

Then Hawkins issued a special request. Now that Billy had
been sufficiently humbled, and his apology had been formally
accepted, wouldn't it be better for all parties to forget the whole
shabby episode? In other words, leave it out of the paper. This
whole affair, for sure, was like Galloway's Bloody Mary. It had an
unsavory taste to it. Janet Hawkins' club efforts had ignited Martin and publicity of the airplane event might restoke the fur-
nace. Furthermore, this was the lurid sort of media event that
presented the potential for one story eventually to become several stories. Before it was over, I could see myself interviewing
shrinks and social scientists to learn their views of the appropriate role of the baseball wife in contemporary culture. Burt then
added that, in my case, ignoring the incident might not be that
easy since the ceremonial publisher of my newspaper, Amon
Carter, Jr., was on the Rangers' board and knew about what had
taken place. Galloway and Walker then agreed that it would be
my decision, and mine alone, to determine whether the story
should run. My personal policy on matters like these was clear.

As long as nobody was killed or arrested, why bother the reading public with the sordid particulars? If Billy made headlines every time he "caused a scene" there wouldn't have been room in the paper for any Richard Nixon stories.

At mid-afternoon I called the *Star-Telegram*'s morning sports editor, Bob Lindley, at his private office that was located in the taproom of the Pecan Valley municipal golf course and outlined my predicament. Lindley was the kind of man who heartily endorsed laborsaving measures, and therefore, a great editor. "Do whatever you want," he told me. "I don't care."

So in the pressbox at Royals Stadium before the Saturday night game, I informed my writing colleagues that a decision had been reached. The airplane incident had never taken place. Burt Hawkins was now officially unslapped.

The Rangers beat Kansas City that night and again on Sunday to officially wrap up second place in the American League West. The flight to Minneapolis, where the season would end with two meaningless day games, was as festive as any I would experience with the ball club. The players could not have been more boisterous if they had won the World Series. In Minneapolis they staged a team party at Howard Wong's restaurant. The media was excluded and, later, Jim Fregosi told me that even with the Howard Wong discount, the liquor tab ran dangerously close to five figures.

Fergie Jenkins picked up his twenty-fifth win on the last game of the season at Metropolitan Stadium before an audience of probably less than 200. Since my labors for yet another regular season were now mercifully complete, I chose to remain in the north woods for a couple of days' worth of relaxation before returning to Fort Worth refreshed, rejuvenated and largely free from the anxiety-ridden day-to-day, night-to-night routine that accompanies the seemingly endless baseball season.

So imagine my surprise when I opened my Wednesday morning *Star-Telegram*, turned to the sports section and read an eight-column headline across the top of the lead page: "MARTIN APOLOGIZES AFTER AIRPLANE ALTERCATION." All of the nasty details of the flight to Kansas City were outlined in detail in a story beneath Harold McKinney's byline. Hastily, I phoned McKinney to inquire as to what, in the name of God, was going on here, and was informed that James Walker of the *Times-Herald*—upon returning to Dallas—had "spilled the beans" (Harold McKinney's words) to his editor, the esteemed Blackie Sherrod. Let me say here that I sympathized with James Walker's thinking at this point. Walker found himself stuck in a dilemma where it was necessary to "spill one's beans to "cover one's ass."

Without a doubt, Blackie Sherrod was and still is the best-known sportswriter in the history of Texas journalism, and with the possible exception of Jim Murray in Los Angeles and Mike Royko in Chicago, he enjoys the largest regional following of any newspaper writer in the United States. Blackie, I think, actually attended high school with H.L. Mencken and naturally is a product of "the old school" of journalism, as opposed to "the new school" that Mencken apparently found revolting. Consequently, James Walker's heartbreaking confession generated shock waves in the *Times-Herald* newsroom.

So the Martin-Hawkins conflict would see print after all—one week after the fact—and the *Morning News* and *Star-Telegram* would follow suit the next day. "This," I told Harold McKinney, "makes me look like a total idiot."

"Screw that," said McKinney. "I'm the one who had to come in on my day off and write the goddamn story. And don't sweat it. The whole thing has already blown over."

Right, Harold. That weekend, when I arrived in Los Angeles to cover the 1974 World Series between the Dodgers and the A's, an east-coast sportswriting contingent was eager to talk to me when I entered the pressroom at the downtown Los Angeles Biltmore Hotel. Dick Young, the noted syndicated columnist for the *Daily News* of New York, led the charge. In person, Dick Young was far too presentable ever to be mistaken for a sportswriter. Had he wished, Young could have gotten laid every night of his life simply by hanging out at El Morocco and posing as

Adolphe Menjou. But at the core, I think Dick Young was too much of a Seamhead to ever embark on anything so imaginative.

"Boy . . . Billy really has you guys by the balls, doesn't he?" Young demanded. I presumed he was talking to me. Dick was a man who tended to be in love with the sound of his own opinion and it would have been futile to attempt to explain that blowing off that story had absolutely nothing to do with protecting the dignity of the Little Dago.

Another of the New York guys, Jack Lang, joined the chorus. "What were you fuckers smoking?" he wanted to know. I suggested to Jack that his own little corner of the planet might be a more rewarding place if he sampled some of what he presumed we were smoking.

And one week after that, I was pleased to discover myself as front-page news in none other than the Washington Journalism Review, which serves as the official trade journal—I would hesitate to use the word "Bible" since journalism is involved—for ink-stained wretches throughout North America. This was the same publication that had just ranked the *Star-Telegram* as one of the ten worst major newspapers in the country. Walker, Galloway and I were castigated as irresponsible, incompetent, delusional, probably on the take and clearly not the sort of men that the New York *World* would send out to find Dr. Livingston. The article said that "Shropshire, for his part, at least cleared the coverup through his office . . ." I liked that part and am sure that the editorial offices at the *Star-Telegram* did as well.

Life is so full of irony. Here I'd signed onto this simple job because of free trips to Cleveland and complimentary cocktails. Now, thanks to Jimmy Piersall and Billy Martin, I was becoming a celebrity. Of sorts.

CHAPTER

21

IN PREPARATION FOR my third visit to Rangers spring training I had convinced the paper to rent me a new station wagon, which I would drive 1,400 miles to Pompano Beach. Now I had packed my inventory of supplies: seven cases of Lone Star beer, several new Lone Star caps, T-shirts and belt buckles to offer vacationing Canucks—they adored all that Texas paraphernalia crap—two bottles of sunscreen lotion, a typewriter, a 3-M telecopier, a tennis racquet, a box of E-Z Wider cigarette papers, a new pair of huaraches (Mexican sandals), a box of 8-track cassettes that included the recent works of artists such as Jerry Jeff Walker, David Allen Coe and Commander Cody and his Lost Planet Airmen, a cooler full of ice, and about $2,000 worth of traveler's checks. I was ready to roll.

For the first time, North Texas seemed alive with an abundant supply of genuine public enthusiasm for the soon-to-arrive baseball season. Jeff Burroughs was back as the American League MVP. Billy Martin had been Manager of the Year. Mike Hargrove had been Rookie of the Year. Catfish Hunter had edged out the Rangers' twenty-five-game winner Fergie Jenkins for the Cy Young Award but Jenkins had at least been named Comeback Player of the Year. Now Baseball Digest was already in print with an issue predicting that the 1975 Rangers would replace Oakland as the American League pennant winner.

About one-and-a-half blocks out of my driveway, as I was heading east toward Florida, a black cat sprinted in front of the station wagon. Had I only known of the events that awaited me in the coming weeks and months, I would have floor-boarded the car and run over that goddamn cat and, to this day, I will make sharp U-turns in heavy traffic to avoid crossing the path of those little beasts.

After two days of endurance driving through a compressed twenty-seven-hour tour of the Neo-Confederate Redneck-o-Rama and Great American Cream Gravy Belt, via Shreveport, Jackson, Hattiesburg, Mobile, Tallahassee and, at long last, a straight shot down the Florida Turnpike, my second home, the Surf Rider Resort, came into view, barely visible through the bug stains on the windshield of the station wagon. Fergie Jenkins, who had chosen to drive all the way from Texas in his new Continental, had beaten me to the registration desk by about fifteen minutes.

Jenkins, traveling alone, said that he had become drowsy in the red clay nothingness of northeast Louisiana and had picked up a hitchhiker so that the passenger might drive the night shift while he slept. "The guy told me that he'd been living in a fox hole . . . a small cave, actually," Jenkins said. "Then, when he couldn't figure out how to get the cruise control to work on the Lincoln, the guy looked at me and said, 'Ya know . . . I wouldn't have this piece of shit.' Some people are hard to please."

The first three days of what had been scheduled as a three-week assignment at spring training—Harold McKinney would take the last three when I went home to allow my liver to recover in time for the regular season—proceeded routinely. Wayne Carmichael, the entertainer who seemed dead-set on gaining entry into the *Guinness Book of Records* in the category of having sung "Tie A Yellow Ribbon" more times than any other human on the planet, was back at the Banyan Lounge.

So, too, was a whole new supply of carefree, vacationing Canucks. In a general sense, most Canadians are wrongly characterized as being tediously conservative in their approach to almost every facet of life. Once again, the Surf Rider version of the Canuck carried a looseness of spirit and attitude that belied almost any trace of inhibition, and if nothing else, seemed well-tuned for the tone of the Seventies.

Now back for Rangers Camp III, I had established some seniority. In the previous two years I had been stuck across on the wrong side of Highway 1, between a canal and a shedlike structure that housed the Wednesday meetings of the Pompano Beach Volunteer Fire Department (I used to wander in there and bum some beers). Now I had secured a room at the Surf Rider from which I could step out a glass door, walk seven-and-one-half feet and sit down at the poolside bar. Charlie Pride, the country music singer who now was a regular at Rangers spring training, was living immediately next door.

The other next-door neighbor was the Rangers' new centerfielder, Willie Davis, the famous ex-Dodger who had been picked up in an off-season trade with Montreal. Davis, who had come directly to spring training from a Los Angeles jail where he had been confined for a few days because of alleged non-payment of spousal support, was now rooming with Dartagnon, a Doberman pinscher with fangs like Cujo. Each night I would drift off to sleep to the dulcet sounds of Willie Davis, now a confirmed yoga advocate, chanting his mantra—*"aaahhhmmmm . . . aaaahhhmmm."* Davis at least looked the part of a yogi. His body-fat content registered zero. There was an absolute absence of muscle mass as well. In the lockerroom Davis was all skin and veins, the stylishly anorexic look that is so admired in the spiritual nudist retreats of northern California. Davis' physique presented a sort of extraterrestrial quality. He was quickly dubbed the Strange Ranger.

MY FIRST ACTUAL workday of 1975 involved writing an in-depth feature about Jeff Burroughs, fresh from his 118 RBI season, and the interview was conducted at poolside. My operational plan for the spring was concentrated around avoidance of conventional baseball jive and allowing my readers to become acquainted with their new Ranger heroes on a more personal basis. So I decided to ask Burroughs questions that might be a little out of the ordinary, such as:

"Jeff, there was an article in the paper this morning that contained some comments from a professor at Nova College over in Fort Lauderdale. This professor predicted that, because of world hunger and the world energy crisis, a hundred years from now, through the miracle of genetic engineering, the average American male will be fourteen inches tall. How do you feel about that?"

Burroughs didn't hesitate. "Huh. I guess they'll have to shorten the foul lines and bring in the fences," he said.

THE RANGERS CAMP officially opened with the highest degree of optimism. All of the key players had arrived, under contract and healthy, in Pompano Beach and most had even come down early. There was one exception: David Clyde.

Another Clyde, veteran lefthander Clyde Wright, had been added to the staff, and now David Clyde was a long shot to even make the twenty-five-man roster. Clyde was somewhere back in Texas, recuperating after having his tonsils removed, and there was some doubt that he would show up in Pompano Beach at all.

After the second workout, Martin sat in his office down by the rightfield fence. He was smoking a new pipe, one of those with the curved stem that Sherlock Holmes favored, and wearing a half-smile of contentment that told the baseball world "that everything is completely under control." In Willie Davis, Martin said that he now had a centerfielder who "didn't need to wear a whistle." Pepi Tovar was relegated to utility status and replaced in centerfield by a swami.

And in Clyde Wright, Billy figured that he had secured the lefthander for his starting rotation who could throw his break-

ing pitches for strikes whenever he wanted to and was mature
enough to withstand the psychological rigors of the long, long
season.

Martin also had a promising lefthanded candidate for his
bullpen, something the Rangers had done without in '74. The
pitcher was Mike Kekich, the man who had provoked all the
headlines two years earlier with the Yankees when he and teammate Fritz Peterson announced that they were trading wives.
Kekich might have been proficient as a pitcher but he was a flop
as a general manager. In the biggest trade of his career, one of
the "players" involved—Peterson's wife—refused to report to
her new team. "So I came up shorthanded," Kekich told me.
"And since the Yankees sized up Peterson and me after the
'trade' and quickly determined that I was the lesser of the two
talents, I wound up pitching the 1974 season in Japan."

Martin's assessment: "I don't care if he married a koala bear.
As long as Kekich can still handle lefthanded batters he's got a
spot in my bullpen." With these pieces now glued into place, all
that remained was the process of completing the formalities of a
162 season and an American League pennant would fly in Arlington above the otherwise humble baseball facility on the prairie.

Fortified with assurances like those from The Man Himself, I
began making plans to spend less time at the yard at Pompano
Beach and devote more of my daytime hours to the more elegant competitions at Gulfstream Park. But the Black Cat Syn-
drome was close at hand and any illusions that this spring training visit would be a some-work-mostly-play agenda evaporated
about six P.M. on Day Four, right after I had finished telecopying
my stories to the paper.

Harold McKinney called me from Fort Worth. "I've got good
news and bad news," he said. "My divorce is final and I've got
cancer." McKinney was astonishingly upbeat as he described
some dire findings from a biopsy. "Anyway, I'm starting these
treatments, so tell all the Canucks I won't be down there this
year." Three minutes later the phone rang again. This time it

was Bob Lindley, the *Star-Telegram* sports editor, calling to inform me of the news that Harold McKinney himself had just delivered. "Who," I asked Lindley, "will you send down to replace Harold?"

"Actually, since you're already there and know the territory, it's been decided that you'll do the whole tour," Lindley said— meaning, naturally, that in the finest American business tradition, one man would now be doing the work of what had previously been the responsibility of two. That night, I contacted a physician acquaintance and described the symptoms that McKinney had reported. "He won't last the summer," the doctor said. So, it was now confirmed that I was about to lose my partner in crime and I realized at once that for the long haul, I would not be able to hack it as a solo practitioner.

Two days after that, I awakened to discover that I couldn't quite stand up. My left leg felt paralyzed. One of the Rangers team doctors checked me out and said something about a herniated disc. He also suggested hospitalization. Isn't it funny how, when the mind is troubled, the body tends to follow? I'd always figured that a couple of my wires were crossed. Now it seemed like the whole damn transformer had blown. So I did what Harold McKinney would have wanted me to do. I drove back to the Surf Rider, iced down two six-packs of Lone Star and then drove directly to Gulfstream. Let me declare here that if you want hot numbers at the track, befriend an assistant golf pro. Because of such an acquaintance in Fort Lauderdale, I won eighty dollars on the fourth race at Gulfstream and used those proceeds to buy some prescription painkillers for my back. Now I knew what my then First Lady, Betty Ford, must have been going through.

That night in the Banyan, I experienced for the first time the little quirks that happen to the thought processes when pain pills are combined with scotch whiskey. On the plus side, Wayne Carmichael suddenly sounded sensational. But most of the Canucks seemed alarmed—disgusted might be a better word— that I was attempting to communicate with them in fluent Latvian. My pathetic efforts to charm these people seemed entirely consistent with the little notations in the *Daily Racing Form* that accompanied the recent outings of my favored horses: left in the gate; faded in the stretch; lost whip; never a factor; broke down.

In this condition a man might accidentally stumble into the wrong hotel room and come face-to-face with Willie Davis' dog. In extreme physical agony, it was now evident that either the pills or the scotch would have to go. So I threw away the pills. But . . . if this was some kind of borderline or even full-blown psychiatric event, it was entirely consistent with some of the events that were beginning to take shape with the baseball team.

The first new celebrity to emerge at Pompano Stadium was not a baseball player but rather a skinny sixteen-year-old kid from Grand Prairie who had decided to quit school and run away from home and—faced with nothing that qualified as a reasonable destination—decided to hitchhike to Rangers spring training. Equipment manager Joe Macko discovered the kid and gave him a job scraping mud from cleats and shining shoes and allowed him to sleep on a cot in the clubhouse. The kid became known as Midnight (from the title song of the movie *Midnight Cowboy*, which contains lyrics relating to his attire) and soon was a personality worthy of media attention. Midnight's living quarters were upgraded to the Surf Rider, he was welcomed at Billy Martin's table at the Banyan Lounge, seen giving autographs to Canucks and reportedly was about to sell his life story to Warner Brothers.

Like many baseball rookie sensations in spring training, Midnight's flash was quick to hit the pan. When Surf Rider management dispatched Midnight's bar tab over to Joe Macko, an emergency fund was established to pay the tab and purchase a bus ticket for him back to Grand Prairie. As Midnight was leaving camp, David Clyde was just arriving, long enough to say hello. Clyde was considerably underweight after having the tonsils removed. His bank account was emaciated as well. The kid pitcher's storybook marriage had ended in a quick divorce.

"There was a lot of pressure and some problems came up that I initiated," Clyde conceded. "I don't want to say anything bad about marriage. But it's just not for me."

Clyde clearly didn't want to talk at length to sportswriters about the divorce. "Ever since I came to the Rangers, everyone has written about how well I handled all that pressure," Clyde told me. "But the truth is that in important areas, I didn't handle things very well at all. When I signed that pro contract I was the all-American boy. Now I'm controversial, trying to prove that I can become the pitcher that I once was, and I'm not even twenty years old yet." The next day, David Clyde left for the Rangers' instructional league camp across the state in Plant City, where, it was now evident, he should have been dispatched out of high school.

David Clyde's departure received scant media attention, though. Billy Martin's Rangers juggernaut was now beginning exhibition play and everyone was eager to see the activation of this new machine that the Texas media was christening The Good Ship Conquest. Billy's pre-season sales pitch was universally embraced and I had bought into the hype just as blindly as the rest.

The Rangers were drawing double their customary crowds for the games at Pompano Beach. The Expos came down from their camp at Daytona Beach and one of their coaches, the ex-Dodger centerfielder Duke Snider, marveled at the throng. "This is even a bigger crowd than the game we had yesterday against a team of Japanese all-stars," said Snider, who was talking enthusiastically to Billy Martin. "And boy, you shoulda heard the recording of the Japanese 'Star-Spangled Banner' they played before the game. Bugles blaring and drums pounding. You could almost see the fighter planes zooming in over Pearl Harbor," added Duke, who touched his thumbs together so that his two hands formed into a dive-bomber.

Montreal beat the Rangers and Jim Bibby 9–0 that afternoon. Afterward, Martin offered the customary spring explanation that Bibby was experimenting with a couple of new pitches and his performance was to be expected. For two seasons, Bibby had gotten by all too well with one pitch, the heater, and he was hardly the type to suddenly introduce finesse into his repertoire. I was beginning to have some reservations about this team, although I wasn't expressing them yet in print.

The first actual problem surfaced when my next-door neighbor at the Surf Rider, along with his dog, disappeared. Willie Davis failed to show up for an exhibition game against the Orioles and was AWOL again the next day when the Rangers played the Dodgers. None of Davis' new teammates had the slightest notion about the centerfielder's whereabouts. Neither did Martin, although he denied being irked or in any way concerned.

Finally, Davis showed up, and he and Martin met, at which time Davis said he had earlier asked for and received two days off . . . and Martin had forgotten about that arrangement. "Yeah, yeah. Everything is fine," Billy assured us. So Willie was right and Billy was wrong. That was a managerial first and last in Martin's career. "Man . . . I'm happy here," Willie Davis told me. "Everything is fine and when it's not, I'll let you know."

I was phoning daily reports of the spring craziness back to Harold McKinney. These frequent communications were intended to serve as mutual catharsis. The conversations, sadly, were etched with self-pity. Mine, not McKinney's. "Here I am about to die and all you can do is piss and moan about your goddamn sore back," he finally said. "Jesus H. Christ."

Harold McKinney had a point, though my back still hurt. In order to travel to exhibition games the rented station wagon had been converted into a customized ambulance. Since I couldn't sit upright I would lie in the back with my feet propped on a beer cooler. Galloway was the driver. At a filling station on the outskirts of Vero Beach where the Dodgers trained, an old guy (anybody in Florida who isn't very old or very young does not fit in) who checked the oil peered inside the wagon. Then I heard the filling station guy ask my ambulance driver Randy Galloway, "What's with *him?*"

"Took too much dope in Vietnam," Galloway said. "Now he

keeps running off from the psych ward at the VA and I'm hauling him back again." Said the filling station guy: "And he seems
so young." Galloway couldn't stop cackling for two weeks. In
case you haven't figured it out by now, people from Grand Prairie maintain a low amusement quotient.

WILL ROGERS CLAIMED that he never met a man he didn't like.
During my baseball travels, I never met a man who didn't know
Billy Martin.

Billy must have been on a first-name basis with probably
10,000 notable Americans. Sen. Eugene McCarthy, the presiden-
tial peace candidate who had become chums with Billy when he
managed the Twins, came to Pompano Beach and stayed a
week. So too did entire squadrons of automobile dealers, tavern
owners . . . backslappers and hucksters and hustlers, all wanting to say hello to the Little Dago. A district judge from New
Orleans who had known Martin from God could only guess
where arrived at Billy's springtime cavalcade of thrills, claiming
he was in town "looking for a little keister for Easter."

The year before, the Rangers had witnessed what had
amounted to a pseudo Little Dago who, privately uncertain and
concerned about the nature of the Rangers' talent-base he had
inherited, was on the stage but underplaying his role. But Billy
thought he saw some face cards in his hand for this season's
game and now his customary demeanor surfaced, marked by a
territory bounded by cocky on one side and contentious on the
other. If an actor were to be reasonably selected to play the role
of Billy Martin in his prime years as a baseball manager, it sure
as hell wouldn't be Kevin Costner. Jimmy Cagney probably came
closest to the portrayal in *Public Enemy*.

With little more than a week left in what had dragged on and
on as a marathon spring, Martin would refuse to let camp close
without at least one skirmish. His opportunity arose in paragraph form, buried in a meaningless and obscure spring-training feature article about Yankee outfielder Elliot Maddox that

had run in the Fort Lauderdale paper. Maddox, the ex-Ranger, had not figured prominently in Martin's plans at the conclusion of spring training, 1974. He dealt Maddox to the Yankees in a minor transaction and Maddox had surprised both teams with a strong season. Now, in the Fort Lauderdale paper, Maddox said that Billy might have written him off prematurely as a Ranger and was quoted as saying, "Martin has a habit of lying to his players." Billy Martin is probably the only manager in the history of big-league ball who would choose not to ignore a remark like that in a recreational environment like spring training, particularly in a publication that was not exactly distributed worldwide. Martin regarded the article as a call to arms.

Martin's pressure valve was teetering over into the danger zone when I sat briefly across from him in a booth in the Banyan. "Elliot fucking Maddox." Billy spat out the words. "I was doing him a favor when I traded him to the Yankees. He wanted to go to New York. Isn't that something? I should have sent him to Spokane. Maddox has one good season and now he's running off at the mouth," Billy said, his voice rising with every syllable. "There's a lesson there. Give a skunk a break and he'll piss in your face every time."

Naturally, the Rangers had a game scheduled against the Yankees at Fort Lauderdale the next afternoon. Elliot Maddox would probably lead off for the Yankees. Surely . . . Billy wouldn't insist that his pitcher Jim Bibby dust off somebody's skull in an exhibition game? But . . . as I reclined on the press-box roof at Fort Lauderdale, I gazed down and . . . was that a mirage or did Bibby hit Maddox on the shoulder on the first pitch?

Another Rangers pitcher, Stan Thomas, threw in the direction of Maddox's head and missed on his next at-bat. So in the next inning the Yankee's Mike Wallace plunked the Rangers' Dave Nelson, and then both teams were out on the field. Burroughs was wrestling with the Yankee manager Bill Virdon. Meanwhile, Martin was attempting to fight his way around the familiar figure of Number 32, Yankee catcher Elston Howard, in an apparent effort to attach his hands to Maddox's throat. Afterward, Jim Fregosi told me that "this had to be a spring training first. The games don't count, but I guess the tempers are real."

Billy Martin remained in peak form as he changed clothes at the end of the game. "I saw Maddox and told him he was gutless," Martin said, describing the acrimonious folkdance that had happened earlier. "I called him gutless," Billy repeated, "and he didn't say anything back. Why? Because he's gutless. That's why. He's a disgrace to that uniform. He sets the Yankees back a hundred years. What would guys like DiMaggio think?"

About two dozen New York-based print and on-the-air reporters were there to record Billy's sentiments. That afternoon's whole spring training urban street scene, plus Billy's erstwhile post-game oratory, had been concocted entirely for their benefit and possible amusement. It occurred to me then and there that Billy Martin was not protecting the honor of his good name. He was auditioning for a job. The Yankees had failed to win a pennant for the previous eleven years. And Bill Virdon, the incumbent manager, maintained all the charm and charisma of an old man's nut sack. Martin knew too well that somewhere, George Steinbrenner was watching and listening.

The Rangers staged a huge going-away party at the Surf Rider pool on the last day of spring training. My back was still killing me and I was going to fly to Texas, having paid one of Joe Macko's clubhouse boys a hundred dollars to drive back in my rented station wagon. That was exactly the sum that Martin had paid some girl to streak naked through the going-away party. Given what was soon to come, that stood out as one of the more dignified events of the season.

CHAPTER

22

THE BEST PLACE in the world to watch baseball is Wrigley Field in Chicago. That opinion prevails not only throughout the Midwest but the entire country. True, most who contend that they love Wrigley have never actually been inside the place, but they've heard about it and read about it and seen it on TV. A fortune awaits the visionary who produces a Broadway musical set entirely in Wrigley Field and starring Julie Andrews.

Undeniably, the folksy and idiosyncratic Wrigley Field radiates a cultural magnetism that feels real to the traditionalist. What is puzzling is why Comiskey Park, at the other end of Chicago, remains vilified in the public eye. In terms of age, heritage and design, the ballparks were earmarked by all kinds of similar traits. But when the demolition ball went to work on Comiskey Park in 1992, the civic attitude was "good riddance." Meanwhile, Wrigley Field remains a shrine. It calls to mind the parable of the lovely twin sisters, identical in every way except that one chronically experienced acute attacks of flatulence.

Comiskey got a bum rap. With its Brit-like ivy walls, Wrigley was and is a mecca for closet quiche freaks. But Cosmiskey had a guileless and unfeigned brass knuckles feel to it. This was where the exploding scoreboard was born and the visitor would get the impression that here was a place where Frank Nitti and Eliot

Ness might have cast their differences aside on certain after-noons to go out and watch the White Sox play the St. Louis Browns. The place could be breathtakingly spooky on rainy nights and even in bright daylight seemed to transmit a vaguely sinister quality. There was a strange something about baseball at Comiskey Park that made the spectator feel as if he were watch-ing the game in 3-D.

That was viscerally evident when the Texas Rangers came to Comiskey Park for opening day, 1975, and the great man him-self, Mayor Richard Daley, was at the stadium to toss out the ceremonial first ball. From the pressbox before the game, through borrowed binoculars, I watched the last regent of the great urban boss breed take his front row in a box between the plate and the first-base dugout. Daley looked like a bullfrog wearing a trench coat. On impulse, I went down to see if I might get some opening day quotes from Daley or, failing that, get him to autograph my scorecard.

Ordinarily, autographs were not a large personal priority. I had exactly two—Linda Lovelace's and Lyndon Johnson's—and Daley's would make an outstanding addition to that collection. Some men near the mayor's box made it instantly clear that there would be no quotes and no autographs. Daley's plain-clothes security force seemed composed of men who might have been removed from the operational ranks of the KGB because they were too insensitive to the human condition. Their faces were like blue steel. I got the hell away from Daley's box as quickly as I could.

The start of the baseball game was the official signal for the fans to begin a strange opening-day Comiskey ritual. (I was in-formed by a man who covered the White Sox that this was, in-deed, sort of a rite of spring when the fans of South Chicago came to the park and unleashed months of latent hostilities that had been stored up from the cold and bitter winter.) Random fistfights broke out throughout the grandstand. This mayhem was marginally in step with the crowd patterns of the Beer Night Riot in Cleveland, but none of the antisocial behavior was di-

rected toward anything happening on the field. This was hand-
to-hand combat, fan vs. fan, then row vs. row, and occasionally,
in the outfield seats, one section would attack another. In the
fifth inning, directly beneath the pressbox, one fan clutched
another by the throat and attempted to pitch him off the upper
deck before a couple of cops and some fans formed an ad-lib
peacekeeping force. That display provided the initiative for the
boys in uniform to take charge. After a few thumps and whacks
the unruly segment of the fan population was quickly subdued.

If Daley was not mesmerized by the pageant of brutality, the
exhibition had certainly won over Billy Martin. After the game
he didn't seem too interested in talking about how his Rangers
had won a game in hostile territory. It was the crowd scene that
wowed him. "Man! Did you see those Chicago cops in action? I
had a great view from the dugout steps. I wish we had some
players in our lineup who could use the bat like those guys."

Law enforcement in Chicago had no more enthusiastic advocate than Billy Martin. But that was the last time, I think, that I
saw Billy smiling in a Rangers uniform. The Rangers did go on
to sweep the Sox in Comiskey, but in a much promoted early-
season series back in Arlington Stadium the rival Oakland A's
played a part scripted for the Chicago cops while the Rangers
found themselves cast in the role of the shoplifter getting
caught in the act. The first month of the season ended with the
Rangers slightly under .500. This was way too early to write the
Rangers off entirely as legitimate contenders, but ominous in-
dicators were lurking everywhere. Jim Bibby's fastball was no
longer feared like a death ray by American League batters.
Fergie Jenkins was yielding homeruns at twice the rate of the
previous season.

Most distressing of all was the performance of the Strange
Ranger, Willie Davis. At the plate, Davis was all but hopeless and
seemed every bit as off-stride and clueless as another National
League transplant, B-e-e-g Boy Rico Carty, had been two seasons
previous. In the field, Davis could still run like Seabiscuit but
was also not quite reaching some fly balls driven in the left and

right centerfield gaps and failing sometimes by a fraction of an inch to make the catch that would determine the outcome of the game.

The Rangers and, more unfortunately from my aspect, the media were being exposed to a version of Billy Martin that was not as affable as the one who was so effervescent in 1974. His tactic for the 1975 Rangers, a team that he was now convinced needed a hard kick in the ass for purposes of motivation, was one of "creative tension." That is a corporate term for a management technique that was perfected by Josef Stalin in which constructive criticism is employed in the form of a firing squad. In theory, it keeps everyone on his or her toes and enhances productivity.

Additionally, with a growing estrangement between Billy and his players, the manager decided to activate another formula that he favored from time to time—the "us against them" approach. "Us" being Billy and his players and coaches and "them" being the sportswriters and team management. As scapegoats, Martin first selected James Walker of the *Times-Herald* (better him than me) and Danny O'Brien, hired by the Rangers as general manager two weeks before Whitey Herzog had been canned by Bob Short. Martin was now fuming at O'Brien because he had failed to make a trade that would have brought one of Martin's favorites, veteran catcher Tom Egan, to the Rangers. "Egan is exactly the kind of guy this team needs right now," Billy declared in the newspapers. "He's a funny guy to have around in the clubhouse and he's tough in a fight."

"If that's what Billy thinks this team needs, then why doesn't he bring in Bob Hope and Mohammad Ali," muttered Burt Hawkins, the traveling secretary. The apologies from the previous year's airplane episode were all a papier-mâché facade. Hawkins despised Billy.

One trade Martin and Danny O'Brien had engineered was a big one. The Rangers had sent Jim Bibby and Jackie Gene Brown to Cleveland. In exchange they got Gaylord Perry. "Sure, I got one pitcher for the price of two," Martin conceded to me in the bar at Arlington Stadium. "But look what I've got now, with Perry and Jenkins . . . two future Hall of Famers, maybe, on the same staff. But also"—and now Billy's voice took on a whispery inflection that was half-devious, half-conspiratorial—"I don't think those two like each other very much and this personal rivalry will develop between them that'll make them both even more effective. It's a jealousy thing and it'll work in our favor."

Martin was correct on two points. Both Jenkins and Perry would be elected to the Baseball Hall of Fame. And they could hardly be described as inseparable companions while they played for the Rangers. But the additive ingredient of the rivalry thing never did take hold. Both pitchers had mediocre seasons in 1975 and of course the Rangers were now structured so that if that happened, the whole team would follow the example of the two star pitchers.

On another battlefront, the doctor who told me that Harold McKinney wouldn't last the summer was wrong. Harold didn't even survive the spring.

McKinney came out to cover some of the home games for about a month. He shaved his head and wore one of those little Chairman Mao caps. But his illness was too advanced. Every time I went into the Rangers' clubhouse for the post-game interview stuff, the first thing I heard from Martin and the players was "How's Harold?" In the fourteen years I actually covered sports, I never met anybody who was as universally well-liked by other media people *and* the jocks as Harold.

When I asked the sports editor who would take Harold's place for the regular season, he pursed his thin, cruel lips and said that since the paper so loveth my work, the whole Rangers beat—at least the road portion of it—was henceforth wholly and entirely in my lap. Except that now I didn't have a lap. The day after McKinney died, my herniated disc problem had been exacerbated by savage muscle spasms. Now it looked like somebody had screwed the top half of my body off and then screwed it back on backward. A man's torso would have to be composed entirely of silly putty to accomplish such a pose. I looked like a sculpture in a wax museum after a bad fire, although I have seen some surreal Picasso pencil sketches that depicted that posture as well. Only a newspaper would send something as pathetic as that out to represent the publication in the mainstream world.

Life on the road seemed to have degenerated from sometimes-sophisticated comedy to fifth-rate burlesque.

On a Saturday night in California, somewhere between Anaheim and LA, I found myself in a car with Randy Galloway, the sportswriter, who had borrowed the car from Jim Merritt, who lived in Fullerton. Galloway was desperate to locate a drinking establishment that somehow reminded him of home, that being Grand Prairie, Texas, where the theme song is "Chrome On The Range."

"Look, there's a place," he finally called out. "See? Nothing but Harley-Davidsons and pickup trucks in the parking lot. Go in there," he demanded, "and check it out."

So, with my gimpy back forcing me to sort of lurch along in a lateral direction like a bad special effect in a Grade-B horror movie, I hobbled into the place and discovered some go-go dancers performing on a stage—male go-go dancers wearing nothing but motorcycle boots and jockstraps. That single moment stands out as the singular example that typified—for me—the whole season.

IF NORMAN VINCENT Peale were looking for a new disciple, I was a bad candidate and so was Billy Martin. Gaylord Perry had lost his first two starts as a Ranger. Now, for PR reasons more than the standings, Martin needed Gaylord to turn things around. On his third start, at Anaheim Stadium, the Rangers gave Gaylord what he needed: a six-run lead (courtesy of future New York Met manager Mike Cubbage, whose first major-league hit happened to be a grand-slam homer) in the top of the first. But Perry was off-course again. The Angels hit everything Perry threw toward the plate. Martin wanted Perry to last at least five innings to officially get the win. But he waited too long and the Angels tied the game. To make the issue even more agonizing, the Rangers scored three runs in the top of the twelfth only to see the Angels match that and then top it with one more to win in the bottom half of the inning. California got the winner when Willie Davis ran underneath a fly ball to the centerfield fence with the bases loaded and then watched as the ball bounced off the heel of his glove.

The Friday night debacle was followed by a day game on Saturday. Less than an hour before the Saturday game I was leaving the Grand Hotel (most of which had been taken over for the weekend by a convention of square dancers) for the ballpark when I heard somebody—a solitary figure—going *"pssst . . . pssst"* from inside the bar. It was Martin. "What are you doing in here?" I asked him. Stupid question. He was having a pre-game pop, obviously. "I'm standing in here having a drink with all my friends," Billy said. Then he proceeded to blame the previous night's loss on Frank Lucchesi, his third-base coach. "Frank held up a runner (Toby Harrah) who would have scored easily in the second inning," Billy insisted. "Then we wind up not knocking him in. If Toby scores, no extra innings. Simple as that. And then I get a call from some asshole in Las Vegas at three A.M. claiming he lost two hundred grand because of the Rangers and he was raising hell with me . . . claiming I'd blown the game by keeping Perry in too long. I told the fucker that if he wanted to bitch at somebody, bitch at Frank Lucchesi."

BACK IN ARLINGTON, the fans were still streaming into the park in numbers that satisfied Brad Corbett and the rest of the ownership. Corbett hadn't completely outgrown his "fan" stage and a parade of celebrated figures who arrived at the park for various purposes was a source of real fun for him. It has often been said that the two happiest days in a boat-owner's life are the day he

buys it and the day he sells it. Thus it would also be with Brad
Corbett and his baseball team. But in the early stages of Big
Brad's Rangers ownership it was frequently noted that when
Corbett decided to buy a toy, he sure loved to play with it. After
just over one season, Corbett had been photographed with
enough sports stars, past and present, to open his own Italian
restaurant.

One of these was Don Newcombe, Dodger pitching great and
nemesis of the Yankee Fortress that had included Billy Martin as
the second baseman in the Fifties. Newcombe was not in Arlington, however, to help Corbett sample the newest case of Pinot
Noir or single malt scotch or whatever it was that Brad sipped
from his own private stock in the press lounge. Newcombe was
traveling the majors from team to team, warning players of the
hazards that lurked within the bottles that surrounded him in
the press lounge. I forget who was funding Newcombe on his
speaking tour, but his message was near-revolutionary for its
time. This was 1975 and the first big leaguer to publicly enter
alkie rehab, another Dodger pitcher, Bob Welch, didn't do that
until 1980. Newcombe, known around the country as Big Newk
in his prime, had a simple point—booze is bad. Booze, he told
me, was the singular reason his prime years had ended prematurely.

"My real downfall came when the Dodgers moved from
Brooklyn to Los Angeles," Newcombe said. "I had a deathly
fear of air travel. When the Dodgers were in Brooklyn we still
rode the trains a lot, but after heading to California it was nothing but airplanes and I was petrified. It was a phobia and the
only way I thought I could last out the flight was to drink and
drink some more. Before long I had developed a real drinking
habit. And that impacted my ability to pitch. So, for all intents
and purposes, I drank myself out of the game.

"And I'm not the only one. There have been hundreds of
players just like me. Maybe it wasn't fear of flying that made
them drink to extreme," Newcombe continued. "I don't guess
you can count the reasons that make people drink but I think

that fear of failure is a big cause with professional ballplayers. Big-league baseball is a great lifestyle, but with a lot of these guys, they know that they won't be experiencing that lifestyle for very long if they don't maintain their performance level and so that's a big source of anxiety. They don't realize how drinking can actually hasten their departure from the big leagues."

I wondered how many Rangers ballplayers had listened to what Newcombe was talking about when he had met with several of them earlier that afternoon. "And then . . . to make the problem much worse . . . after some of these players realize that they have drunk themselves out of the game, then they proceed to drink themselves to death," Newcombe said. "I can pick up a newspaper sports section any week of the year and see some one-paragraph item where ex-major leaguer so-and-so has died at some age like fifty-eight. They might list the official cause of death as heart failure or stroke or something, but when I see where a guy dies at a relatively young age like that, I often wonder if excessive drinking wasn't the real cause. For a lot of players, life really doesn't seem to have that much to offer them after they're through with the game. So hitting the bottle becomes a form of passive suicide."

ABOUT TWO WEEKS after Newcombe's visit to Arlington, the press lounge was jammed with photo opportunities for Brad Corbett. The Rangers had staged an Old-Timers Game promotion and plenty of regal names had participated. Joe DiMaggio was there. Willie Mays. Ralph Kiner. Bob Feller.

After the regular game was finished—Catfish Hunter, now pitching for the Yankees in the dawn of the free-agent era in baseball, had pitched a shutout—I hammered out my story and joined the party in the press lounge. Now I was heeding Don Newcombe's clearly prophetic forecast of doom . . . at my own pace, naturally. I had formed my own twelve-step program. Instead of twelve drinks a night, I would stop at eleven, and so on, until I got down to zero. Obviously, no timetable had been yet arranged, although the year 2000 seemed reasonable. But the fact was that I was growing weary of the taste of scotch.

Finally, much of the crowd from the Old-Timers bash had left, but Billy and Mickey Mantle were still at the bar, where I stopped to order Number Eleven before heading on to the Cave. When I mentioned my alcohol-reduction plans to Billy, he was not impressed. In fact, he referred to me in a well-known euphemism for the human reproductive system that does not appear in the male of the species.

Mantle overheard. "How old are you?" Mantle asked me. I told him that I was thirty-three. "Well," said the Mick, "cuttin' back is a mighty big decision for any man and I don't think you're mature enough to make that one yet."

CHAPTER

23

FORT WORTH, WHERE there is one chance in three that the man driving the gravel truck who just ran you off the road is named Duane, is equipped with an official city motto. It reads: If you can't get your job done before noon, then it's too big for you. Later, the motto was actually enacted into an ordinance stating that anybody who left for lunch and then made the mistake of returning to work would be charged with a Class-A misdemeanor. As a result, initiatives such as reserving a tee-time in the early afternoon hours must be arranged months in advance. Bowling alleys are jammed. And the taverns . . . my God.

The Quick Draw Lounge of Camp Bowie was the primary hideaway. Right after "As the World Turns" signed off, I would head straight for the Quick Draw and remain there until time to drive to the ballpark. Inquiring minds from various disciplines and occupations always met at the Quick Draw to trade ideas, creating a collective mind-force that confirmed the theoretic laws concerning the substance of synergism.

An air force major, in uniform, who headed a B-52 flight crew at the nearby SAC ("Peace Is Our Profession") installation called Carswell—at the time, the largest tactical bomber base in the world—once appeared at an adjoining stool at the Quick Draw and was talking about the missiles and gravity weapons that he carried on his aircraft. Gravity weapon? I didn't know what he was talking about. The major grinned. "Well, lemme put it this way . . . if all the gravity weapons on my plane were employed simultaneously, then there probably wouldn't be any more gravity. But the Soviets know we have the capacity to blow up the planet . . . so whenever they feel the urge to start something, then they look up the inventory of goodies I've got on my B-52 and say, 'Not today, comrade. Not today.' " Followed by a deep pull on his drink and a hearty guffaw. The fellow put me in mind of Stanley Kubrick's Dr. Strangelove.

That won the blue ribbon as the best conversational snippet I heard at the Quick Draw. First runner-up honors involved a chat with a staff psychiatrist at the John Peter Smith County Hospital. I don't think the doctor believed me when I said I traveled around the country with the Texas Rangers baseball team. "Boy," he said, "I'll bet you encounter a lot of [P-word here] on a gig like that."

"More than you could shake an inflatable penile implant at," I said. At this point, I was not being truthful, but why split hairs and spoil a good conversation?

"In that case, for your benefit, I'd like to point out some extreme danger signs in women that might prove helpful in your travels," the shrink said. "If you run across any of these, then steer clear, because they're crazy." Then he rattled off his list. "Nurses, stewardesses, owners of more than two pets, anybody with huge tits, excessive makeup, earrings larger than a fifty-cent piece, abdominal scar, painted toenails, poetry writer, prematurely dead father, Jesus freak, dyed or streaked hair."

These were the women of the Seventies the psychiatrist was talking about, and not the men of the Nineties. "That's been clinically and scientifically proven, time and again," the psychiatrist stated. "And from personal findings, I think you can add Scorpios and anybody whose name starts with L to that list."

Marvelous, isn't it, how a characteristically sex-crazed and sociopathic species can discourse at length on the unstable aspects of the opposite gender? In that regard, during the sum-

mer months of 1975 any competent mental-health professional
could have enjoyed several intriguing case studies on aberrant
behavior within the Texas Rangers traveling party. While Willie
Davis was apparently having out-of-body experiences in
centerfield, the Little Dago seemed to be in training for a mid-
dleweight title bout. It seemed the Rangers' manager had been
scheduling sparring sessions at least once a week, when he
would play his rendition of the "Moonlight Sonata" on the
nearest available face. Somebody suggested that Billy might be
on a cash retainer from the American Dental Association. I told
Billy that he might consider changing his name to Sugar Ray.
"Kinda has a nice ring to it at that," he conceded.

One bout took place during a weekend of turmoil in
Anaheim. In a restaurant the mixologist refused to pour another cocktail for one of Billy's coaching staff, claiming that the
gentleman already appeared over-served. Billy took umbrage.
While Martin and the bartender were engaged in a loud and
intense disagreement over (I'll swear to God) an American's
constitutional right to get as plastered as he wants to, another
customer entered the room.

After several minutes the customer—not realizing that he had
stumbled into some distinguished company—yelled at the bartender, "As soon as you get through arguing with these
shitheads, would you mind getting me a gin and tonic?" In seconds Billy had rendered the customer horizontal. The bartender called the cops. Given the notoriety of the winner of the
first-round KO, no arrests were made but the gendarmes did
confiscate the keys to Billy's rental car.

In mid-June, following another loss in Kansas City, I was
seated in the lounge at Royals Stadium sharing a beer and polite
conversation with Burt Hawkins, who the night before had summoned me to his hotel room to meet his old friend David Eisenhower, son-in-law of the recently ex president. I was now telling
Hawkins how Eisenhower, unlike his photographs, didn't look
anything like Howdy Doody in person, when somebody barged
into the pressbox and announced that down in the Rangers'

clubhouse Billy Martin and Willie Davis were beating the crap out of each other. Hawkins smiled, then said, "Hmm. Hard to figure out who to root for in that one."

The winner in the long run, probably, was Willie Davis. Not twenty minutes after the hostilities he was traded to the St. Louis Cardinals, who, unlike the Rangers, were involved in a pennant race. "I am gone like a cool breeze," Willie told me.

BACK IN TEXAS, according to a Rangers pitcher who claimed to be an eyewitness, Billy's winning streak turned down a dead-end street. At the County Line Bar in Grand Prairie, on the night before the team would leave on an extended road trip, Billy allegedly sucker-punched an off-duty ironworker. "Billy nailed him with his best shot . . . and the fucker didn't even blink," the pitcher said. "Then the guy grabbed Billy by the shirt and I saw something I thought I'd never see. He apologized to the guy. And then the big son of a bitch spat a mouthful of blood on the floor, looked at Billy and said, 'Lissen . . . 'pologies ain't enough.' And then Billy said, 'Look . . . I'm drunk and I didn't know what I was doing,' and the big guy said, 'Then I'll catch you when you're sober.' So Billy jumped in that big Lincoln and got his ass out of there."

Toward the end of the road trip, in the horseshoe-shaped bar at the Executive House Hotel in Chicago, Billy appeared to have selected a sportswriter as an opponent in his next bout. From his side of the horseshoe Martin began shouting over to our side of it. James Walker of the Dallas *Times Herald* was now the object of Martin's displeasure. "Walker . . . you are a [and here Billy used the same word that he used to describe me when I told him that I was considering moderating my drinking habits]. You are a double [same politically incorrect word of the Nineties]! Galloway! Don't you think he's a [I've heard men refer to their ex-wives using this word after they have passed through the denial phase of a divorce settlement]."

Galloway responded with what, for Galloway, was rare eloquence. "No!" he shouted at Billy, who, I thought, was now poised to wind up and throw a glass in our direction. The entire team was there to witness the exchange. I missed whatever happened next because I needed to return to my room upstairs. A particularly stimulating round-table discussion was scheduled on "The American Catholic Hour." Also, if Billy punched James Walker, I didn't want to be around to see that happen because then I would probably have to write a story about it. The next day Galloway told me that the mood around the horseshoe bar had remained turbulent but bloodless for the next two hours. "What it boiled down to was that I had to stand around and explain the theory of journalism to twenty-five drunk jocks," he said.

BEFORE THE FINAL game of the Chicago series I saw another interesting side to Billy Martin. He called two of his veteran players into his office when he overheard them reading aloud from what might be described as pornographic literature in the presence of a couple of batboys. "Don't ever do stuff like that around kids," he said. "To those kids you're supposed to be big leaguers. So try to act like it."

Fergie Jenkins had a bad outing that day and the Rangers lost to the Sox, completing a disastrous road swing. On the flight back to Dallas, Billy's mood had become contagious. Cesar Tovar and Joe Lovitto exchanged punches in the aisle of the airplane. Martin himself raced back and broke up the fight. Then Billy made a speech: "You fuckers all make me sick," he declared. "You're a bunch of losers and you're a bunch of quitters and what makes it worse is that it doesn't bother you one goddamn bit.

"As soon as this plane lands you'll all go home to your wives or your girlfriends or whoever and you'll get laid. But I'm not going home because I'm ashamed. I'm ashamed of myself for being associated with you fuckers."

End of speech. In the seat immediately behind mine I heard

Clyde Wright say, "The reason Billy ain't going home is because he's afraid that badass who pushed him around at the County Line Bar will be waiting for him on his front porch."

A ONE-FOR-ALL AND all-for-one spirit was not manifesting itself on this baseball team. What the Rangers needed was a good Ten-Cent Beer Night Riot to unify the troops. Unfortunately, happenings like that are somewhat rare in baseball. Billy Martin had clearly embarked on a pattern of activity that could be viewed only as self-destructive from a managerial standpoint. By now I suspected that Billy was attempting to get the hell out of this Texas deal. He was bored with Arlington, the convenient stepping-stone that would position him nicely for the ultimate step in his grand scheme. Billy Martin was a very shrewd man. A post-game interview with about five players after a game at Arlington Stadium proved enlightening. The interview was so prolonged—we were talking about the fact that I was actually being stalked by some woman who worked the front desk in the Sheraton Royal Hotel in Kansas City who was now following me all over the United States—that we found ourselves locked in the clubhouse. There was nothing else to do but drain the keg of Coors beer that was on hand for post-game use. When the keg was empty around sun-up we stacked some boxes, and climbed up and out of a window. But during the process of killing the keg, the players expressed their dissatisfaction with Billy Martin's behavior. "When we win, Billy talks about how 'I did this' and 'I did that' and when we lose, it's always 'You guys fucked it up.' It's starting to get old," one of them said.

THE NEXT ROAD trip began in Minneapolis, where I finally located some relief for my disabled back. Instead of lying on the floor with a heating pad and a bottle of muscle relaxants and pain pills, I took a proactive measure that entailed venturing across the street from the Leamington Hotel to receive therapy at the

Geisha Spa massage parlor. In less than a half-hour two Viet-
namese girls accomplished what the leading orthopedic special-
ists in Texas could not. The pain went away and I could stand
up straight again.

Now I was actually in shape to employ a can't-miss tactic for
alluring women that I had learned from baseball players. "It
works every time," I had been assured. "You draw a picture
puzzle on a bar napkin and ask the woman to solve it." The
picture puzzle involved drawing an angel, a fish, a glistening
gem, two eyes peering through glasses and finally a small rabbit
standing on the back of a huge cat. The punch line: "Holy
mackerel, Sapphire! Look at the hare on that pussy!"

In four tries, the puzzle hadn't worked yet, but when the team
traveled on to New York and then Boston, I was still fresh and
alert—once again the sharp-eyed newsman with keen instincts
for the hot-breaking news item. Actually, for the first time in my
entire career I stumbled across what might qualify as a scoop. In
the pressbox bar at Fenway Park, I bumped into Brad Corbett,
the fellow who owned the Rangers. "Come up to my suite for
breakfast with Gunnie and me in the morning," Brad said casually, "and I'll give you a good story."

"Such as?" I said.

"I'm going to fire Billy," Brad said. Or, at least that is what I
thought he said. So, under the circumstances, I thought it best
to show up, as invited, for the breakfast gathering. Unlike the
rest of the riffraff billeted at the Sheraton, Corbett's digs were
over at the Ritz-Carlton. I put on my best outfit, that being a
white Mexican wedding shirt with fancy stitched embroidery on
the cuffs and collar that I'd bought at Nieman Marcus, and wondered what kind of breakfast wine I should order. Brad was a
true epicurean and I was worried about revealing myself to be
the consummate hick. Gallo Hearty Burgundy would probably go
well with the mango crêpes, I figured, having seen an ad in
which Ernest and Julio said that the screw-top products of their
vineyard went well with damn near anything, from Malt-O-Meal
to Hormel chili.

Corbett met me at the door of his suite wearing boxer shorts. Again, the man could have been John Goodman's double. Only he was married to Ingrid Bergman instead of Roseanne. After the breakfast that took about an hour and a half to finish (Scott Fitzgerald was right . . . the rich *are* different from us), Brad got down to business.

"Like I told you last night, I'm going to fire Bowie [Kuhn, the commissioner of baseball]." The owners would shortly vote on whether to renew Kuhn's contract. Corbett said he had the swing vote and thought that baseball needed a new commissioner.

"Bowie?" I said. "I thought you said you were going to fire Billy."

"Why would I want to fire Billy?" Corbett said.

"I dunno. Maybe you should talk to some of your players about that."

IN THE GLORIOUS Saturday sunlight at a packed Fenway Park, where I would watch probably the best World Series of modern baseball in about ten more weeks, rookie outfielders Jim Rice and Fred Lynn swatted homeruns with men on base off Gaylord Perry, and Luis Tiant got the complete-game win for the Red Sox. Afterward Burt Hawkins approached me in the pressbox. "What did you tell Corbett this morning?" he said.

"I didn't tell him nuthin'. Why?"

"Well, *he* said you had some interesting things to say and now he wants me to go to dinner with him tonight, along with four of the players—Hargrove, Harrah, Sundburg and somebody else—to talk about Billy."

The next afternoon at Fenway Park, I asked Burt if anything eventful had taken place at the dinner session. "I was really proud of those players," Hawkins said. "They were uneasy at first. But then Corbett got 'em good and drunk and they unloaded on Billy pretty good.

"I believe," Hawkins said, "that Brad might actually get rid of him." Great. I didn't care who managed the Rangers, although, given a preference, it would have been nice to have had Whitey Herzog back. But that same week Herzog had been hired to manage the Kansas City Royals, a job at which he functioned very nicely.

After the Red Sox won again, I blew off the Rangers charter flight and stayed an extra night in Boston. It was at Logan Airport the next morning that I literally bumped into Ted Kennedy. He was standing there looking bored while Sargent Shriver was transacting business at the ticket counter. What followed was (to me) a memorable interchange.

"Good morning, Senator," I said.

"How ya' doin'?" he said.

On the plane later, I mused that Ted Kennedy thought he was simply talking to some jerk wearing a Mexican wedding shirt. Had Kennedy realized he was talking to somebody who would be blamed in some circles for getting Jimmy Piersall and Billy Martin fired, he might have asked for *my* autograph.

BACK IN ARLINGTON, the Rangers won two straight over the Orioles. After Fergie Jenkins had shut out Baltimore for the second win, shortstop Toby Harrah expressed a peculiar reaction. "Goddamn it," he said, "now we'll probably start winning and save his fucking job."

Toby was wrong. Corbett, unsuccessful in his effort to fire Bowie, fired Billy instead. Billy's crew of loyal "lieutenants"— pitching coach Art Fowler, first-base coach Merrill Combs and bullpen coach Charlie Silvera—all left town along with Billy. Frank Lucchesi, the third-base coach, was hired as the manager on a permanent basis. Billy congratulated Frank, then cussed him as a traitor every day for the rest of his life.

On the night that the firing was announced Billy sat with a group of sportswriters in his office and, I'm told, wept. I am glad that I missed that scene. There is a term that describes

Billy's emotional state at that point. Crocodile tears, I believe they call it.

The next time I laid eyes on Billy Martin was in the Pontchartrain Hotel in Detroit. Billy was on television, appearing on the game of the week. He was wearing his proud Number 1 on the back of a uniform that had pinstripes. Not two weeks after his operatic farewell scene in Arlington, George Steinbrenner had ditched Bill Virdon for Billy Martin. The new field manager of the New York Yankees looked real happy.

Like I said, say what you want about Billy Martin, he was smart.

CHAPTER

24

THE FORT WORTH *Star-Telegram* and I parted company in May 1976. That made sense because I had moved out of Fort Worth two months earlier. According to some recent court documents I had become qualified to appear on somebody's "Ten Most Eligible Bachelors" list and a town like Dallas is a better place to seek such an honor. Besides, my apartment in Fort Worth was next door to a drive-in theatre that showed Spanish-speaking movies. Around midnight the projector or the film would always break, people would begin honking their horns in angry protest and it was impossible to get any sleep.

My departure was the only feature of my four-year involvement with the paper that *did* make sense. During the final year I was probably actually inside the building a total of about fifteen minutes.

Some rumors were circulating that I had covered spring training from the Bahamas, just as there had been similar well-circulated fables that I had covered the 1973 World Series between the Mets and the A's from a hotel room in Chicago. While it was technologically possible to accomplish that, I never actually did. I also never bothered to deny the slander because stories like that bestowed an element of panache to my otherwise bland persona.

Most of the management people at the paper had been extraordinarily tolerant of my occasional outlandish behavior, which was unusual even in the context of the Seventies. They were genuinely worried that I might be a threat, as the old saying goes, to myself or society as a whole and if I ever did anything genocidal—I could just see the headlines: "Neighbors Describe Baseball Writer As Brooding Loner"—the *Star-Telegram* goddamn sure didn't want it to happen on company time.

I felt relieved when it was over, though probably not nearly as relieved as the paper. Even so, a reconcilation had been arranged with the paper's new publisher, Jim Hale, a week after I was gone. But I never followed through with my part of negotiating a new "understanding." Now the time had come for me to move forward with my new career as a scriptwriter for a commercial video company that some friends had just taken over in Dallas. They assured me that vast riches loomed smiling on the nearest hillside. Here, I would promptly learn that the ability to write a story about a baseball game did not necessarily translate into the skill of generating a TV spot that would satisfy the client. For instance, the people at a local bank simply couldn't see the potential of an ad in which an actor wearing an Uncle Sam costume tells the viewer: "Strapped for cash? Then do what the government does . . . go borrow some!" The bank people were even less impressed with a vignette that included the line "Who *was* that masked man?" Another tip for anybody writing the narrative for a fund-raising film: The mental health and retardation people take a dim view of comedy as a promotional vehicle. A side venture, my "Don't Blame Me . . . I Voted for George Wallace" bumper sticker, was not encountering universal acceptance, either. Fortunately, the company folded before anybody could find out the true depths of my ineptitude. Judging from client reaction to my work, instead of getting rich I was fortunate not to have gotten arrested.

While all this was going on, people were asking me if I missed covering the Rangers. These were the same people who would ask a U.S. Marine if he missed Guadalcanal. What I did miss was spring training, the sun and the sand and not the baseball, and I arranged future ceremonial pilgrimages to the Surf Rider.

I spent a month there in 1977 in order to prepare a page-and-a-half magazine article. My companion at the poolside bar one afternoon was the familiar figure of David Clyde, back in an abortive final bid for a spot on the Rangers' pitching staff. A newly arrived Canuck sized us up and said, "You two are from Texas. I can tell by your accents, eh? Are you associated with the baseball team by any chance?"

"Not for long," I said. "He's a washed-up pitcher and I'm a washed-up sportswriter." The Canadian guy couldn't figure out why David Clyde and I thought that was so funny.

The visit also served to confirm that life with the Rangers franchise would never be normal. Frank Lucchesi, who normally resided at the opposite end of the spectrum from Billy Martin when it came to the controversy department, was still managing the team. Now even Frank, toward the end of the spring, was involved in a flap with a player. Lenny Randle had been bemoaning the fact that Lucchesi wanted to hand his second-base job to a promising rookie, Bump Wills, whose primary credential at the time was being the son of Maury Wills.

Frank didn't like Lenny's attitude. "I'm tired of all these $90,000 a year punks complaining all the time. That's a quote. Print that," Lucchesi told some sportswriters. Frank apparently did not realize that the term "punk" had taken on a new context, a sexual one, in certain quarters. Randy Galloway told Lucchesi that calling Randle a "punk" might not be a prudent idea. Frank didn't get it. "Just like I said before—a $90,000 a year punk. That's what he is."

A punk was what Lenny Randle was not. Randle—introspective, soft-spoken, intensely bright, a martial-arts expert who never touched alcohol—took extreme offense at Lucchesi's comments. So, about an hour before an exhibition game against the Twins at Orlando, Lenny approached Lucchesi, who was still in street clothes, and in less than ten seconds literally beat his manager senseless, then nonchalantly jogged to the outfield and began running wind sprints.

I arrived at the park about a dozen minutes after the assault and discovered Lucchesi in a tunnel behind the dugout. His bloody head was in trainer Bill Ziegler's lap. Frank looked like he had been run over by a beer truck. The Rangers immediately suspended Lenny Randle and then sold him to the Mets.

The following day, before an exhibition game against a new team, the Toronto Blue Jays, one of the Toronto sportswriters was heard to comment: "Jeez. I guess that's how Americans settle everything these days. With violence, eh?" To which, Bob Lindley, of the *Star-Telegram,* replied. "Yeah. If Randle had hit him with a hockey stick he'd only have gotten a five-minute penalty."

Lucchesi filed a civil lawsuit against Randle and won, but the jury only awarded $25,000. Poor Frank. A warm, outgoing and caring person, it was not his fault that he looked and talked like one of the bad guys in *The Godfather* and did not come across to the jurors as a sympathetic figure.

At mid-season Brad Corbett rewarded Lucchesi for his pain and suffering by firing him. Eddie Stanky, fiery and aggressive when he had managed the White Sox over a decade earlier, was lured from professional retirement to replace Frank. Stanky proved to be the most prudent of all the Rangers' managers. After three days he quit. At seven A.M., following a night game at Minneapolis, he called three players (Harrah, Hargrove and Sundberg) from a pay phone at the Minneapolis airport to inform them that he had stared into the abyss of life in Rangersland and not liked what he had seen. Why, somebody wondered, would Stanky just call those three players? Randy Galloway had a theory: "Maybe he ran out of quarters."

ANOTHER HIGHLIGHT FOR the Rangers' Cuckoo's Nest happened before a game in 1978. Roger Moret, a pitcher, seemingly the victim of an evil spell, fell into a deep trance and stood rigid, motionless and buck-naked for over an hour with one arm extended straight in front of him gripping a shower shoe in his hand. Manager Billy Hunter was summoned from his office to view the weird scene. Hunter, a man of compassion, stared at Moret in bewilderment, then intoned, "What I need is a good lefthanded starter, not some damn statue." Moret was led off to a hospital and never again pitched in the big leagues. Once again, the fact was underscored that the Texas Rangers were not really a baseball franchise but rather a Kurt Vonnegut novel.

MY FINAL VISIT to Rangers spring training happened in 1982. Now writing features for the Dallas *Morning News,* I had traveled to Florida to write a heartwarming article about a sportswriter for the Clearwater *Sun* who as a senior at the University of Texas had strangled his date after a Christmas party and received a life sentence but was sprung after eight years. Jim Hale, my would-be benefactor back in Fort Worth, had been running the Clearwater paper at the time and hired the guy straight out of the joint. "He told me he was a first offender," Hale said, "but he didn't say what he had done." Later, the sportswriter's mother threatened to commit suicide if my article ran. It was a hell of a mess and probably the only time I ever wished I was covering the Rangers again.

By now, Brad Corbett had sold the team to yet another Fort Worth character, Eddie Chiles, who was famous, among other things, for the advertising slogan of his energy-supply business: "If you don't have an oil well, git one!"

It now seemed apparent that whenever I was around spring training, something strange was about to happen. In this case, the Rangers lost thirteen straight games early in the season and went downhill from there. The 1982 Rangers desperately lacked hitting and pitching. So Eddie Chiles, being a baseball man, brought in a motivational speaker and rumor had it that a hypnotist was on his way. When Don Zimmer, the then manager, raised some objections, Eddie fired him. Then Chiles asked

Zimmer if he might not mind sticking around for a couple of weeks until he could locate a replacement. This 1982 crew would fail to lose as many as 105 games like my all-time favorites, the 1973 Rangers, but they gave it their best shot.

THE PASSAGE OF years has seen the franchise struggle toward respectability. Nolan Ryan's heroics were of benefit in that regard and now the team is housed in a real honest-to-God major-league baseball stadium. What used to be Arlington Stadium is now a parking lot. Amazing, isn't it, how so many memories can be so quickly and efficiently bulldozed into oblivion in the name of profits and progress.

When the Seattle Mariners won the American League West in 1995, the Rangers would stand out as the only existing big-league franchise that had never, not once, participated in post-season play.

That new ballpark in Arlington was the site of the 1995 major-league all-star game. Will the place ever see a World Series? During the wild and nutty spring of 1975 I asked a female British psychic who also tended the poolside bar at the Surf Rider if the Rangers might win the pennant that year . . . and if not 1975, then when? This woman predicted that Billy Martin would someday get killed in a car wreck, along with some other off-the-wall visions that were coming true at the time. She knew her stuff. Madelyn peered into the future but at the exact instant that the World Series issue was coming into focus in her mind's eye, my friend Curly Dick (yes, that was his real name), an older guy who sold cars in Canada, played the guitar and knew how to yodel, leaned too far backward on his barstool and fell into the swimming pool while his banana daiquiri set sail and landed in inverted form atop Madelyn's lovely old head.

That caused Madelyn to lose her concentration. So as far as the question of the Rangers and the World Series goes, I guess we'll never know.

INDEX

DATE DUE
